D1066291

ENTERPRISE PROGRAMME MANAGEMENT

ENTERPRISE PROGRAMME MANAGEMENT

Enterprise Programme Management

Delivering Value

David Williams and Tim Parr

© David Williams and Tim Parr 2004

All rights reserved. No reproduction, copy or transmission of this publication may be made without written permission.

No paragraph of this publication may be reproduced, copied or transmitted save with written permission or in accordance with the provisions of the Copyright, Designs and Patents Act 1988, or under the terms of any licence permitting limited copying issued by the Copyright Licensing Agency, 90 Tottenham Court Road, London W1T 4LP.

Any person who does any unauthorised act in relation to this publication may be liable to criminal prosecution and civil claims for damages.

The authors have asserted their rights to be identified as the authors of this work in accordance with the Copyright, Designs and Patents Act 1988.

First published 2004 by
PALGRAVE MACMILLAN
Houndmills, Basingstoke, Hampshire RG21 6XS and
175 Fifth Avenue, New York, N.Y. 10010
Companies and representatives throughout the world

PALGRAVE MACMILLAN is the global academic imprint of the Palgrave Macmillan division of St. Martin's Press, LLC and of Palgrave Macmillan Ltd. Macmillan® is a registered trademark in the United States, United Kingdom and other countries. Palgrave is a registered trademark in the European Union and other countries.

ISBN 1–4039–1700–0

This book is printed on paper suitable for recycling and made from fully managed and sustained forest sources.

A catalogue record for this book is available from the British Library.

A catalog record for this book is available from the Library of Congress.

Editing and origination by
Curran Publishing Services, Norwich

10 9 8 7 6 5 4 3 2
13 12 11 10 09 08 07 06 05 04

Printed and bound in Great Britain by
Creative Print & Design (Wales) Ebbw Vale

Contents

Contents

List of figures

List of figures

List of tables

List of tables

Acknowledgements

In writing a book it is inevitable that a large number of people will be involved to a greater or lesser extent in the endeavour and in this case the authors have relied on the efforts, enthusiasm and contribution of others to a large extent. In particular we would like to thank the following for their contributions to Part II:

Programme management systems	Malcolm Wilkinson
Managing programme risk	Paul Mansell, Matt Litchfield
Benefits management	Amisha Lakhani, Nick Culver
Managing suppliers	Paramjit Uppal
Building a communications capability	Lyndal Petre
The enterprise programme management office	Philip Coleman

We would also like to acknowledge the following whose contributions ranged from encouragement to proceed with the writing, to proofreading to sharing some of their experiences and thoughts with us. As ever it is impossible to single out individuals, or to try and make judgements over individual worth, so in simple alphabetical order we would like to thank Neil Ashman, Richard Barton, Steve Brandon, John Connolly, Nick Griffin, Melissa Insley, Alethea Leong, Chris Loughran, John Ormerod, David Owen, Nick Owen, Eric Northcote, Ed Parry, David Turver, Tim Pitts, Jamie Turner and Ashley Unwin.

The ideas in the book are supported by a number of case studies, and we would like to thank the organisations that have allowed us to share their experiences with the readers through the case studies.

T-Mobile UK
Compaq Computer Corporation
Primavera Systems Inc.
Benchmarking Partners
Transport for London
MyTravel plc
TUI UK
ABN-AMRO

Finally we would like to thank Digby Jones of the Confederation of British Industry for writing the foreword, Joel Koppelmann of Primavera Systems for reviewing some chapters and encouraging us in our endeavours, and the partners and staff of Deloitte from whom our ideas and experience have come to fruition.

David Williams
Tim Parr

Foreword

One of the keys to the future of wealth creation in Britain and indeed the world is the productivity of 'UK plc', that inter-related network of private and public enterprise and endeavour that ultimately takes care of each of us in the country and many overseas. This is equally as true of private enterprise, which generates the wealth, as it is of the public sector, which has a duty to utilise that wealth as efficiently as possible. Productivity is probably today a more worrying issue for the UK public sector than its private sector brother. At the CBI we are, however, only concerned with giving British business a voice, so I will confine my comments to the private sector of the UK economy.

Productivity improvement is the result of a number of factors ranging from investments in capital equipment and technology to training, education and enlightened employment practices for the workforce. However, simply investing is not enough to realise the maximum productivity increase – the process of bringing about change also needs to be as efficient and effective as possible. It is this latter process, bringing about change in an organisation, ranging from moving a factory, office, or warehouse site, implementing a new computer system or way of working to a new organisational structure or cultural change, that this book addresses.

The economic drivers pressing organisations into major change initiatives in order to generate productivity improvements have never been greater. Fierce competition, changing business models, new technology, deregulation, cost pressures and globalisation are creating the need for organisations to undertake more and more initiatives of unprecedented complexity and with unprecedented speed. However, despite the increasing levels of investment being made by organisations in projects and programmes, a startling number of initiatives either fail to deliver the expected value, never get implemented, take substantially longer or cost substantially more than planned. So many are currently in the too difficult box – so many are presented badly to the point of self destruction.

The amount of wasted money, time and effort represents a huge opportunity for organisations that are able to utilise effective programme management techniques to maximise the likelihood of successful change. In addition, there is an opportunity to be exploited by organisations that can develop the agility to implement change more efficiently and effectively than their competition.

This book describes an approach to programme management that outlines the skills and capabilities that organisations need to develop in order to manage large change programmes effectively. It addresses key questions often asked by leaders of large organisations:

- What is programme management and how does it help in the translation of an organisation's strategy into a coordinated portfolio of initiatives?
- How can organisations address the challenges that occur in balancing the needs of operational management of core business activities with the needs of leading and managing programmes?
- What specific skills and competencies are required in order to lead and deliver major initiatives?
- How can organisations begin to understand their general level of capability at programme management?
- How can organisations develop and improve their agility through the adoption of programme management?

There exist few published works on programme management, the typical appreciation of the latter often being a collection of high-level variants of project management techniques and methods. This book suggest that programme management is not just about these methods: it is about developing capabilities to address the spectrum of organisational issues, to act as various means of managing programmes, as well as to deliver large-scale, long-lasting and effective change.

This book provides the reader with a non-theoretical but practical framework to develop the competencies in programme management and utilise this skill-set to implement change in organisations. It is equally applicable to the public and private sectors, and I recommend everyone to look in the mirror and think 'this could be me'!

This book will be a useful and interesting addition to your office reference material.

Digby Jones
Director-General
CBI

1 Introduction

The economic drivers pressing organisations into major change initiatives have never been greater. Fierce competition, changing business models, new technology, deregulation, cost pressures and globalisation are creating the need for organisations to undertake more and more initiatives of unprecedented complexity and with unprecedented speed. However, despite the increasing levels of investment being made by organisations in projects and programmes, a startling number of initiatives fail to deliver the expected value, never get implemented, or cost substantially more and take substantially longer than planned.

Although traditional programme and project management approaches and techniques are being used by many organisations to manage and deliver change, we believe that they are becoming less effective as the nature and challenges of change become greater. There are three trends that are driving the need for new approaches to delivering change in organisations. First, changes in organisations are becoming increasingly complex and interdependent. Second, delivering real business benefits involves more cross-departmental or functional coordination of change, usually changes to processes, systems and structures, and quite often collaboration with third parties as either suppliers or partners. Finally, existing organisational structures, processes and systems do not support this type of working.

The proportion of an organisation's resources that is committed to programmes and projects is increasing, and the succession of projects and programmes is continuous. Senior executives now have to balance carefully the management of existing 'business as usual' activities, and the resource and focus on change activities. The impacts and conflicts of investments in programmes and projects with the current business operations must be understood and managed carefully.

Now more than ever, with pressure from shareholders and stakeholders on CEOs and public officials to deliver their strategies and policies, there is a need to focus investment on strategic objectives. This demands a much closer link between the strategy and policy development processes and the delivery mechanisms in organisations.

Traditional programme and project management methods and techniques, which are primarily borrowed and developed from their engineering and construction heritage, do not fully address these new dynamics of

1

delivering change in complex organisations. The current inefficiencies and failures, resulting in wasted money, time and effort, represent a huge opportunity for organisations that are able to develop effective ways to maximise the likelihood of successful change, and enhance the value created from strategic investments. In addition, there is an opportunity to be exploited by organisations that can develop the agility to implement change more efficiently and effectively than their competition. The ability to implement change effectively and more quickly than others can create a competitive advantage.

This book describes an approach to managing continuous change in organisations that outlines the skills and capabilities organisations need to develop in order to deliver value successfully when faced with these new challenges. We call this approach enterprise programme management.

The ideas introduced in this book are based on the practical experience of the authors as leaders of major change programmes in business and the public sector, and their consulting experience with many clients over the last ten years. We introduce an enterprise programme management framework, which of course builds on the good practices and approaches to programme and project management we have seen in many organisations.

We define enterprise programme management as the capability to lead and manage resources, knowledge and skills in the effective deployment of multiple projects designed collectively to deliver enhanced value. This sounds quite simple, and not very different from other definitions of programme and project management. However the approach discussed in this book has some key elements that address the challenges of delivering changes in our complex organisations:

- Enterprise programme management is an integrated approach to delivering business changes, creating a means for continuous delivery. It is not just a method or technique for controlling individual initiatives.
- The approach we advocate in this book is about building a core organisational capability which enables organisations to be agile in response to their environment or markets.
- Building this organisational capability requires development and implementation of new processes, structures and systems, as well as the skills and abilities of key people.
- The approach addresses the need for a dynamic link between the strategy process and the selection, prioritisation, sequencing and management of initiatives, and therefore effective decision-making is critical to the approach.
- The approach recognises that change initiatives do not take place in isolation, and that the integration of mechanisms for delivering programmes and projects with the operational structures, processes and systems is key.

2

- We also recognise that managing people through change is often the key determinate of whether benefits are delivered and the approach integrates people change activities at all levels.

The book is structured around three main sections. In Part I, 'The enterprise programme management framework', we discuss further the new challenges in delivering organisational changes and value, and introduce the integrated approach of enterprise programme management. Chapters 3 to 7 describe each of the key elements of the integrated and organisation-wide approach. While we recognise that current methods and techniques are important within the framework, we do not go into detail about such approaches, as there is an extensive body of knowledge available in many of these areas.

The practical application of enterprise programme management is illustrated by reference to T-Mobile UK, which is reviewed in Chapter 8. This also acts as a summary of the ideas and approach outlined in subsequent chapters, set in a real-life case.

In Part II, 'Enterprise programme management essentials', we have selected a number of topics for further discussion. The subjects we have chosen for inclusion in this section are either key capabilities that are fundamental to developing an enterprise programme management approach, such as risk management, benefits management, resourcing strategies, and supplier management and communications, or areas of new interest and increasing importance in supporting an enterprise programme management approach, such as programme management systems and the enterprise programme management office. These chapters are supported by case studies illustrating practical applications of the ideas introduced. The cases include Compaq Computer Corporation, MyTravel plc, ABN-AMRO, Transport for London and TUI UK.

In Part III, 'Getting started', we have focused on practical ways of assessing your current organisational capabilities and situation. This will hopefully enable you to start developing your own organisation's plans for developing enterprise programme management. We have also included a chapter outlining a number of practical tips for programme managers in this section.

Part I

The enterprise programme management framework

2   Why an enterprise approach is required

WHY COMPANIES FAIL TO REALISE THEIR STRATEGIES

As business and consumer markets are becoming increasingly competitive and complex, the pressure on CEOs to create and maintain a competitive edge for their businesses is greater than ever. Equally, in the provision of public services, politicians and the public are becoming increasingly demanding of the quality and efficiency of the services delivered. In the private and the public sectors, senior executives and officials are under pressure to deliver change.

Significant time and effort is invested in formulating the 'right' strategies or policies, which will deliver value to stakeholders and consumers. However, development of the right strategy is not enough. At its most fundamental level, achieving strategic objectives means making organisations change. Executives need to be able to lead their organisations to deliver change and embed it throughout the business. Unfortunately, internal pressures often restrict the organisation's ability to do just that. Many executives often find themselves in the position whereby external forces are demanding change, but internal forces are impeding these very changes. The key result is that the organisation may fail to deliver its objectives and meet its stakeholders' expectations.

THE NATURE OF CHANGE IN TODAY'S ORGANISATION

It is becoming increasingly apparent that traditional methods of responding to and managing organisational change are no longer delivering the same returns, and may in some instances inadvertently create additional problems of their own. We believe this is for two key reasons:

The first is **independent versus interdependent change**. In the past, the requirements for (and impacts of) change were often containable to a specific function or business problem. Increasingly, we see that there are often strong systemic relationships between key change initiatives within the organisation. No issue exists in isolation, and 'point solutions' can often have opportunity costs and side-effects that extend beyond the scope of any one problem. Not only do changes increasingly span the people, process, technological, departmental and geographical boundaries of an organisation, they also increasingly

External forces

Internal forces

- The structure and shape of markets are changing – competition is taking many forms, competitors are more difficult to identify.
- Stakeholders are demanding delivery of value or improved quality of services.
- Customer needs continue to fluctuate and sophistication is increasing – how do you give customers what they want, when they want it?
- Technological advancements continue to change the way we do business and provide opportunities for step changes in the value chain.
- The costs of failure are greater than ever (annihilation) but the rewards are tempting (market dominance).
- Overall, the pace and scale of change is increasing, requiring faster response times.

Demanding change

Impeding change

- Complexity within organisations is increasing – often evidenced by a number of concurrent initiatives with divergent paths and competing priorities.
- Current organisational structures, responsibilities and capabilities support business as usual, rather than unique initiatives.
- The lack of common focus often means that scarce resources are allocated incorrectly – wasting time and money and ultimately failing to deliver the required change.
- Board members find it increasingly difficult to link current initiatives to strategic priorities, and do not have a holistic view of all initiatives.
- Employees are becoming change weary and are harder to bring onboard with each successive initiative.
- Some ideas don't get off the ground due to historical problems around financing, planning and delivery.

Figure 2.1 External and internal forces

cross organisational boundaries to impact suppliers, customers, strategic partners and other third parties.

Second is **core business concerns versus change initiatives**. In the past, executives were focused primarily upon managing their businesses. Any projects or initiatives were often seen as being of secondary priority, and hence managed as and when time allowed. In markets where stability was relatively high, executives directed most of their effort towards operational needs. However in dynamic and competitive markets like today's, the size, scope and profile of change initiatives have increased. This means that the proportion of the business effort that these initiatives represent has increased significantly. Unfortunately existing organisational structures are usually geared towards operating business as usual, rather than on delivering unique change initiatives. Strategic change initiatives can no longer be managed by upscaling existing project management efforts – a new approach is needed.

These issues are faced in an environment where time constraints on change (impatience among stakeholders including investors, leading institutions, employees, the government and the public) mean that the performance of executives is assessed over a shorter and shorter time horizon. In turn, this means that any changes undertaken have to be shown to be working and delivering results in shorter timeframes. Regular delivery of benefits is the modern way of business change.

If the need to undertake complex, multi-phase change is becoming the norm, how do companies position themselves to meet this need? What sort of organisation gets it right?

8

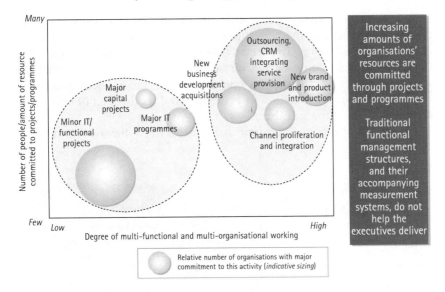

Figure 2.2 The project landscape is changing

AGILE ORGANISATIONS ARE MORE ADEPT AT CHANGING

Based on our experience, we have identified that those organisations that can be characterised as 'agile' are more able to identify and respond to changes in their environment and within their own organisation.

What is organisational agility? Agility can manifest itself in many ways (such as through flexible organisational design structures and fluid decision-making systems). However, at the most fundamental level we believe it describes an organisation that is able to direct effort and capability where and when they are most needed in order to deliver change. This means that an agile organisation is one that can quickly identify when change is required, articulate what that change should look like, construct the change programme as needed, and deliver that change in a timely manner.

How does an organisation become more agile? The key is in understanding what capabilities are required, and when to deploy them. When thinking of capabilities, agile organisations categorise them as either:

1. **Core business capabilities:** those capabilities that describe what the organisation fundamentally does. Examples include printing, content management, retailing, distribution and customer management; or
2. **Change capabilities:** capabilities that help create and deploy specific change initiatives. Examples include investment decision-making and prioritisation, programme management, leadership, human resource management and change enablement.

Agile organisations endeavour to strike the optimal balance between operational management of the core business, and creation and deployment of critical change initiatives. Importantly, there is no 'right balance' – the relative effort placed upon each will vary depending on business context, and will change over time. However, one thing is certain: as the number and complexity of change initiatives increase, so too does the level of effort and capability directed towards them.

Figure 2.3 shows the dynamic balance between the two groups of capabilities.

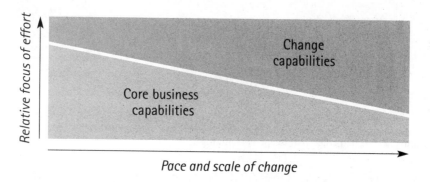

Figure 2.3 The balance between core business capabilities and change capabilities

As the pace and scale of change increases, many organisations find themselves devoting increasing effort towards change initiatives. Executives must learn to balance operational and project needs in order to deliver strategic objectives. Underpinning this is the need to build and deploy both core business and change capabilities.

For the purposes of this book, we focus on helping businesses create agility through understanding, building and deploying change capabilities.

CREATING AGILITY THROUGH ENTERPRISE PROGRAMME MANAGEMENT

An agile organisation is able to identify the need for change, articulate the requirements, and deliver the desired change in a timely and efficient manner. We believe that agility can be developed and deployed through effective enterprise programme management, a capability that captures a number of key change competencies, such as translating strategy or policy into actionable changes, leadership of change programmes, cross-organisational decision-making, communications and working, programme and project management, flexible resourcing, risk identification and management.

How do we define enterprise programme management? Across industry literature, the term 'programme management' is both loosely and poorly defined. It is often used interchangeably with 'project management' to describe the specific delivery of large projects. It is also defined, in many sources, as the management of a portfolio of projects, which while more correct still does not give much insight into how programme management processes, techniques and structures are distinct from other management disciplines.

We define enterprise programme management as the capability to lead and manage resources, knowledge and skills in the effective deployment of multiple projects designed collectively to deliver enhanced value.

At a high level, we consider enterprise programme management as the mechanism for translating strategic priorities into coordinated practical initiatives, and then managing the resultant programmes and projects to achieve those strategic priorities, and adapting to changing imperatives. Enterprise programme management can be understood more specifically as comprising three core management processes:

- strategic portfolio management
- programme delivery management
- project management

and two management disciplines:

- programme architecture
- change architecture.

It is the integration of these elements in to an organisation-wide approach that provides the capability effectively and continuously to deliver change in organisations.

Figure 2.4 illustrates these five elements and their relationship with the realisation of organisational objectives. Strategic portfolio management, programme delivery management and project management represent distinct levels within a hierarchical breakdown of the organisation's strategy into discrete and achievable units of work (projects). The two disciplines address management considerations that apply across the whole strategy through to implementation lifecycle, and are critical to and supportive of the delivery and change process.

The following sections summarise the five elements of the enterprise programme management framework.

Strategic portfolio management

The key purpose of strategic portfolio management is to ensure that a strong link is maintained between the initiatives being executed within an

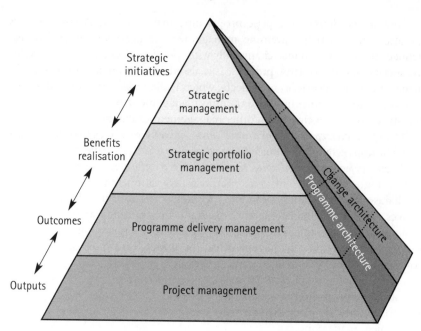

Figure 2.4 The enterprise programme management framework

organisation, and the strategic relevance and rationale for them. Strategic portfolio management is a senior executive driven process, and is the mechanism by which executives direct and control the organisation's investments to deliver future value.

It is critical at this level that decision-making is made with an understanding of strategic priorities, current initiatives, the impact on 'business as usual' activities, and the organisational risks of change programmes.

Strategic portfolio management is a continual process of creating, managing and evaluating a portfolio of strategic initiatives (investments) focused on delivering an organisation's strategic objectives. The approach is a cycle of four phases:

- **Strategy translation.** Before the portfolio of projects is developed, the business strategy needs to be understood and then translated into guidelines for the portfolio composition. These guidelines outline the desired portfolio mix of programmes and projects, agree the level of portfolio risk the business is prepared to undertake, set business targets, budgets, and agree business key performance indicators (KPIs) for monitoring and reviewing purposes.
- **Portfolio planning.** Following the set-up of the guidelines, suitable programmes and projects are identified to populate the portfolio. The

number of suggested programmes and projects is usually too great for a business to implement, especially within the constraints of budgets, time and resources. Hence these initiatives must go through a filter process that assesses the justification for undertaking the initiative, on both an individual and comparative basis, with those that pass through the process to make up the portfolio plan.

- **Portfolio management.** Once the right programme and projects are in place in the portfolio, the next step is to manage and track their progress and performance. The portfolio plan is executed and refined, required capabilities are developed, risks and issues are tracked and managed, dependencies coordinated and progress and outputs monitored. The prime focus of these activities is to ensure that organisational risks are managed, and that results and benefits are being realised as and when expected. The portfolio status is reported on a regular basis to higher management, and reviewed in the next phase.

- **Strategy and portfolio re-evaluation.** This phase provides a 'checkpoint' at which the portfolio progress and performance are reviewed – in terms of the benefits and results of the programmes and projects – to understand their impact on the realisation of the business strategy. Typical questions that management needs to address when performing the review include 'Are the initiatives delivering the intended benefits?', 'Have strategic objectives changed, and do they require a change to the portfolio mix?', 'Are these initiatives still relevant?', and 'Do the guidelines around the selection and sequencing of projects need to be re-examined in line with the risk strategy?'. The overall goal of the re-evaluation exercise is to ensure that the portfolio of initiatives, as well as the portfolio management process, continues to drive the achievement of strategic objectives. Adjustments to the initiatives, portfolio guidelines or even strategy will input into the strategy translation phase, and start the strategic portfolio management cycle again.

Programme delivery management

Programme delivery is the management and consistent application of specific processes, tools and methods in order to enable the coordinated delivery of projects within the programme, in a consistent and efficient way.

Developing a coordinated approach to delivery enables groups of projects that impact similar areas of the business, have critical dependencies, or are focused on developing a specific capability, to be coordinated and managed in an integrated way. Often the focus of a programme will be to deliver a specific element of an organisation's strategy. Examples of such programmes are all initiatives relating to new business development, a programme to develop integrated customer services, and a programme to improve back office efficiency. All these programmes will be made up of a number of related projects with a common purpose and objective.

A key element of programme delivery management is therefore the coordination and management of interdependencies between projects within the programme. Key processes include:

- **Planning.** The definition of the top-down programme plan, indicating the logical sequence of projects, and maintenance of a bottom-up consolidated plan highlighting the critical interdependencies.
- **Executing.** Implementing the programme-level infrastructure, and initiating and closing projects through execution of the programme plan.
- **Controlling.** Tracking, managing and reporting on programme risks, issues, changes, costs and benefits to meet expectations regarding the provision of information and data in order to evaluate the progress of executing the strategic plan.

Project management

Project management is concerned with the definition and delivery of a specific project. When deployed within a wider programme management approach, the project is framed within the context of the broader programme objectives and management mechanisms. The project management discipline is defined comprehensively in the standard text from the Project Management Institute (PMI), the *Project Management Body of Knowledge* (*PMBOK Guide*). Key processes include:

- **Initiating:** committing the organisation to a new project or a new phase of a programme.
- **Planning:** creating a series of documents that facilitates shared understanding amongst project stakeholders and guides the execution and control of the project.
- **Executing:** delivering the product of the project through execution of the project plan.
- **Controlling:** tracking, managing and reporting on project risks, issues, changes and performance.
- **Closing:** formal closure of a project and related contracts.

Programme architecture

As noted earlier, the above three processes are supported by programme architecture. Programme architecture is the establishment of leadership structures, team dynamics, behaviours and support mechanisms that enable the delivery of programmes and projects. It also establishes the support structures and mechanisms to allow effective programme leadership and provide the programme team with the environment, skills, tools and support it needs in order to work effectively.

There are five groups of activities within programme architecture:

- Establishing appropriate leadership, governance and decision-making structures for the programme.
- Team building and development in order to ensure that the necessary skill-set, culture and motivation are established to drive the programme delivery.
- Communication within the programme and project teams in order to maintain a common vision, focus and sense of programme community.
- Resource management in order to identify and source the skills required to deliver the programme.
- Ensuring that the basic programme infrastructure is in place, including suitable office space, access to technology, and appropriate administrative support.

The architecture described above must integrate to support the delivery hierarchy of strategic portfolio management, programme delivery management and project management.

Change architecture

As with programme architecture, change architecture is a discipline focused on the people aspects of the programme. However unlike programme architecture, change architecture is concerned with the human considerations of those in the organisation who will be impacted by programmes and projects *beyond the delivery teams.* For example, does the 'customer' organisation have a clear and shared vision of the solution? What structures do we need to establish within the organisation in order to embed the solution? Does the proposed change fit with the current culture of the business?

Therefore, change architecture can be defined as the approach to the planning and coordination of the human elements of change within the wider organisation. It is the process of understanding the overall strategic objectives, context and capability to change, developing the approach that will drive the required changes within the organisation, and then planning and delivering the required people and change (P&C) activities to ensure that the initiative is embedded within the business.

As a result, it is not just key at the start of a programme or project. It is an ongoing process to review and evolve activities and infrastructures to ensure the change is successfully realised and sustainable beyond the initiative's lifecycle.

There are three key phases in the change architecture discipline:

1. **Developing the change strategy.** The change architecture process begins by understanding the context and issues of the programme and

15

business, including an assessment of the organisation's readiness for change. Based on this, the appropriate people interventions are then selected to create the optimal solution given the available resources, money and time.

The interventions will fall into two categories: support infrastructures and people interventions. Support infrastructures are underlying support networks to enable people to make the change (such as communications, stakeholder management, and training and development). Support infrastructures are usually only in place for the programme duration.

On the other hand, people interventions are specific solutions that are designed and implemented for longer-term use. Examples include performance management systems, reward strategies and organisational designs. They exist beyond the programme and become part of the 'business as usual', future state.

2. **Planning the change journey.** Once the appropriate interventions have been identified, change architecture then focuses on planning these at a high level. This is called the change journey. The change journey outlines the key milestones and phases for each of the interventions. It provides a high-level view of what change activities must happen at what point in the programme in order to deliver the expected outcomes. A change journey will include both supporting infrastructures and people interventions.

    Undertaking this high-level planning prompts careful consideration of the synergies and interdependencies between different change activities. Mapping out activities in this way facilitates testing and manipulation of the plan, ultimately resulting in an effective plan that is closely aligned to the needs of the overall programme.

    Once in place, the high-level plan will inform the subsequent detailed planning, design and implementation activities which will be undertaken by other change resources.

3. **Embedding and reviewing the change.** A key outcome of the change architecture process is to ensure that the change is embedded within the organisation. It is critical that the organisation is able to sustain the change beyond the programme or project. There are two areas of focus here. The first is to identify and leverage opportunities to build individual capabilities and share learnings from the programme. The second is to identify and track 'indicators' of change throughout the programme, in order to ascertain whether or not the intended changes are taking place. The results of this review will allow adjustments to be made to the change architecture to ensure it is aligned to the desired programme outcomes.

These phases are repeated continuously as new programmes and projects are considered and initiated, executed and deliver changes.

In summary, the key to developing an enterprise programme management capability to deliver effective and continuous strategic change is the integration in your organisation of the five elements of the framework introduced in this chapter. The exact nature, design and approach required will be very specific to your own organisation, its culture, its processes, how it is organised, how decision-making takes place and the nature of your 'business as usual' activities.

Chapters 3 to 7 in this section describe each of the five elements of the framework. We have focused more on strategic portfolio management, programme architecture and change architecture, as these are the areas where readers will be less familiar with the approach described.

The T-Mobile UK case study in Chapter 8 describes how this organisation developed its own specific approach to enterprise programme management, which suits its business challenges and context. This also illustrates the practical and integrated application of the ideas described in the preceding chapters, and acts as a practical summary of the ideas contained in the first part of this book.

3 Strategic portfolio management

INTRODUCTION

'How does each of your programmes and projects support your strategic objectives?' Not many executives can answer that question. Large organisations may recognise the importance of the top and tail of the enterprise programme management framework – defining the business strategy, and running projects, respectively – and have no qualms investing substantial time, money and effort in these activities. However, a common failing is to ignore the value of creating strong alignment between the two. Enabling strong links between the strategy and the web of projects will allow optimal value to be realised from the projects, and create a business focus on the delivery of the strategy. Most organisations have some fragments of the interface already in place, but more often than not the links are weakest where strategy meets the management of projects as a whole. Strategic portfolio management is the first step in creating the alignment of strategy to programmes and projects.

Gone are the days where organisations operated simple business models and undertook few and manageable projects. Recent years have seen the number and magnitude of strategic initiatives grow to such an extent that even keeping track becomes almost impossible. The nature of these initiatives has also evolved, from those that are function-specific to those that transcend functional lines, which can lead to increased risks of conflicts and failures as a result of the cross-function complexities.

Typical symptoms of an organisation that lacks this capability are:

- No single clear and complete picture of all significant current and planned initiatives in the organisation.
- Lack of congruency between the strategic aims and purposes of the initiatives carried out in the organisation.
- Complex interdependencies between initiatives are not recognised, identified or monitored.
- Time, money and efforts are deemed wasted on the wrong initiatives in hindsight.
- Initiatives not relevant to the core business are implemented, and end up bringing little value to the firm.

The consequences of non-alignment of the business strategy and the programmes and projects are plenty, but the ultimate consequence is that the value and benefits derived from the programmes and projects will contribute little, if at all, to achieving the business strategy.

The challenge is clear: given that the initiatives (whether programmes or projects) create the future of the business, executives must ensure that the initiatives are well aligned with the strategy, and are managed in an integrated way to deliver the desired benefits.

WHAT IS STRATEGIC PORTFOLIO MANAGEMENT?

Strategic portfolio management is the continual process of creating, managing and evaluating a portfolio of strategic initiatives focused on delivering lasting results and benefits. Its overall objective is to manage the portfolio in tandem with the continual evolution of the strategy of the business, and to reap the maximum value from business investments.

The business's strategic aims and its portfolio of initiatives are very much interrelated, and drive one another. Defining the strategic intent of the organisation forms the foundation on which a portfolio of initiatives can be established. The results and benefits that arise from the portfolio serve to deliver the strategy, and make it possible to evaluate the effectiveness of the strategy and initiatives in delivering value for the business. We can illustrate this relationship as a cycle of four phases:

1. Strategy translation.
2. Portfolio planning.
3. Portfolio management.
4. Strategy and portfolio re-evaluation.

These activities, and their relationships to the wider enterprise programme management framework, are depicted in Figure 3.1.

Adopting a portfolio approach to the selection, coordination and review of projects, with continual reshaping and refinement of the business strategy, will enable an organisation to manage the conflicting demands between its initiatives, and maximise the aggregate value of the portfolio.

THE VALUE OF STRATEGIC PORTFOLIO MANAGEMENT

Often organisations underestimate the significance of maintaining a portfolio perspective of their change initiatives. Strategic portfolio management, applied well, will serve to:

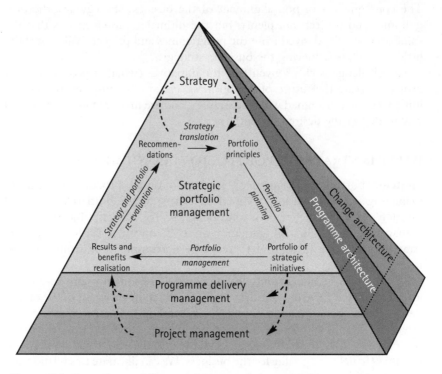

Figure 3.1 Strategic portfolio management and the enterprise programme management framework

- provide the essential link between the realisation of the business strategy and key strategic initiatives to ensure congruency
- perform a prioritisation of strategic initiatives that best achieve the targeted changes within budgetary and time constraints
- create a strong link between strategic development, investment decision-making, business planning and delivery activities
- provide a cross-organisational approach to managing the risks, capabilities and resourcing issues arising from the interdependencies of the initiatives
- give senior management the ability to direct and manage a portfolio of programmes, implementing the corporate objectives and strategy within a dynamic environment
- focus on strategic initiatives rather than project inputs, and use performance measures and reporting based on benefits realisation, rather than direct programme deliverables/metrics
- prevent poor return on investment on programmes and projects that do not support the overall strategy of the organisation.

THE STRATEGIC PORTFOLIO MANAGEMENT FRAMEWORK

As mentioned earlier, the strategic portfolio management approach can be represented as a continual cycle of four phases. This section gives an overview of each of the portfolio phases, which are illustrated in Figure 3.2.

Strategy translation

Before the portfolio of projects is put together, the business strategy needs to be understood and then translated into guidelines for the portfolio composition. These guidelines will, among other things, outline the desired portfolio mix of programmes and projects, agree the level of portfolio risk the business is prepared to undertake, set business targets, budgets, and agree business key performance indicators (KPIs) for monitoring and reviewing purposes.

Portfolio planning

Following the set-up of the guidelines, suitable programmes and projects are identified to populate the portfolio. There are usually too many programmes and projects suggested for a business to implement, especially within the constraints of budgets, time and resources. Hence these initiatives must go

Figure 3.2 The four phases of strategic portfolio management

through a filter process to assess the financial and strategic justifications for undertaking the initiative, on both an individual and a comparative basis, with those that pass through the process to make up the portfolio plan. Key considerations of the filter mechanism are:

- How much value would the initiative bring to the organisation?
- Is the organisation capable of delivering this initiative successfully?
- In the context of all other projects, when is the best time to deliver this project?

Portfolio management

Once the right programmes and projects are in place in the portfolio, the next step is to manage and track their progress and performance. The portfolio plan is executed and refined, required capabilities are developed, risks and issues tracked and managed, dependencies coordinated, and progress and outputs monitored. The prime focus of these activities is to ensure that organisational risks are managed, and that results and benefits are being realised as and when expected. The portfolio status is reported on a regular basis to senior executives, and reviewed in the next phase.

Strategy and portfolio re-evaluation

This phase provides a 'checkpoint' at which the portfolio progress and performance are reviewed – in terms of the benefits and results of the programmes and projects – to understand their impact on the realisation of the business strategy. Typical questions that management will need to address when performing the review include 'Are the initiatives delivering the intended benefits?', 'Have strategic objectives changed, and do they require a change to the portfolio mix?', 'Are these initiatives still relevant?' and 'Do the guidelines around the selection and sequencing of projects need to be re-examined in line with the risk strategy?' The overall goal of the re-evaluation exercise is to ensure that the portfolio of initiatives, as well as the portfolio management process, continue to drive the achievement of strategic objectives. Adjustments to the initiatives, portfolio guidelines or even strategy will input into the strategy translation phase, and start the strategic portfolio management cycle again.

APPROACH, TOOLS AND TECHNIQUES

Strategy translation

The first phase is all about setting up the framework on which the portfolio is to be created. This includes understanding the business strategy and strategic objectives, outlining the guidelines of creating the portfolio, desired project mix, and portfolio reporting structures.

- **Articulation of strategic requirements.** Before deciding on the appropriate programmes and projects to start, management needs to understand the high-level business drivers, organisational dynamics, and any external or market factors and changes. This will validate the organisation's strategy to achieve its vision and objectives, and shape the development of the portfolio.
- **Development of portfolio principles.** This activity spells out the principles of the key decision points, selection and sequencing, in the portfolio planning phase. It is an integral activity that determines the requirements an initiative must meet to qualify for the portfolio, and the desired portfolio mix and ranking criteria of programmes and projects that best represent the combined level of risk the business is prepared to undertake.

  Some questions to consider when developing these principles for selection include:

  Does the project enable other projects of greater value?

  Is there a minimum benefit-to-risk ratio requirement?

  Does the proposed initiative meet its agreed business case criteria?

  Are there strategic objectives that have a greater weighting than others when determining an initiative's strategic fit?

  What is the maximum percentage of high-risk, high-value projects that can be taken on in the portfolio?

  What are the exceptional circumstances in which a lower ranked project currently underway is given priority over a higher ranked new project?

  Is there a desired balance of people, process and technological projects?

- **Development of portfolio reporting framework.** This activity is to develop an ongoing reporting structure for results and outcomes of the initiatives to senior executives, including defining tolerance levels, reporting frequency, and exception reporting triggers.
- **Key performance indicator (KPI) development.** This activity is concerned with the identification of the milestones and indicators to be used to measure and track the portfolio's performance, in order to measure the strategic value it creates.

Portfolio planning

The portfolio planning phase is where the portfolio roadmap is developed, whereby programmes and projects that best support the strategic intent of the organisation are identified, scoped and scheduled into a plan. This phase can be divided into three stages, creation, selection and sequencing, and is illustrated in Figure 3.3.

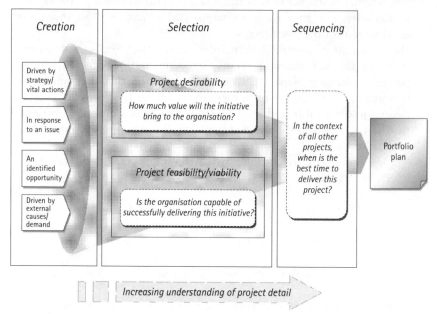

Figure 3.3 The portfolio planning phase

Creation stage

The first step to creating the portfolio plan is to identify the potential programmes and projects for it. Generating such ideas to improve the business and its operations will never be exhaustive, and they can surface from a multitude of sources. These ideas (that will become initiatives) can be categorised into four types:

- those that are driven by *strategy*
- those that arise in response to existing *issues*
- those identified as potential *opportunities*
- those that arise in response to *external causes and demand*.

Identifying initiatives may be seen as an ad hoc exercise, but there are useful tools that can assist in generating relevant and valuable initiatives, particularly at the strategic level. These include:

- **Gap analysis.** A gap analysis identifies the key changes required to achieve the new business and technical architecture, and translates and scopes these out into initiatives.
- **Performance audit of current programmes and projects.** It is very likely that organisations have a number of programmes and projects already underway when developing the portfolio. Performing an audit enables the organisation to review and validate the relevance of its current programmes and projects against the strategic initiatives, and allows it to identify any additional programmes and projects needed. This exercise has a dual purpose in that it also highlights programmes and projects that do not support the strategic initiatives outlined by the business, and questions their relevance and value they bring to the business.

Selection stage

Those ideas that are of most value to the organisation are translated into initiatives, and implemented through programmes and projects. The purpose of the selection stage is to weigh out the risk and rewards of carrying out each initiative identified in the earlier stage, based on whether it is ideal and pragmatic to do so.

This splits into two questions to address: 'Is the initiative desirable?' and 'Is the initiative feasible?' The initiative must meet both requirements before it moves on to the next phase, in which it is placed into the portfolio. Failure to meet either one will make the project a lost cause for investment. We discuss these two requirements, and the activities, tools and techniques that support their assessment, in greater detail below.

Desirability

How much value would an initiative deliver to the organisation? By ascertaining the expected rewards and the certainty of the outcomes of each initiative, the value of the proposed initiative can be understood. The objective of this first part is to assess the 'attractiveness' of the project to the business in terms of its strategic fit and proposed benefits, factoring in the likelihood of reaping those benefits. A combination of tools can be used:

- **Project brief.** In order to understand what the initiative is about, we need to draw up the project objectives and scope, and a proposed plan outlining key deliverables and milestones. This forms the basis of the other assessment tools and techniques.
- **Strategic fit.** This assessment identifies specifically the reasons and ways that the initiative aligns with the business strategy. A simple example of one approach is to use a rating scale of low – high of how the initiative meets each of the business's strategic requirements.

- **Business case modelling.** This is the quantitative or financial justification for the initiative, and outlines detailed cost–benefit analyses, including investment and cashflow requirements, payback schedules and back-fill costs of resources. A business case is the crux of any strategic investment decision, and requires a rigorous approach to quantify and chart its returns versus its outlays. Common financial modelling methods include net present values (NPV), investment rate of return (IRR), and payback period.
- **Benefits realisation plan.** This charts out the expected periodic returns and action plans associated with the initiatives, in order to help users understand the quantified value and the length of time in which the benefits are to be realised. This plan is reviewed and updated regularly in line with the progress of the project.
- **Change impact assessment.** This activity considers the roles, processes and systems impacted by the project or programme, to gauge the magnitude of the overall change that will be brought about by the project. More detail can be found in the change architecture chapter.
- **Portfolio impact assessment.** Where there are ongoing projects and programmes, an analysis has to be performed to identify whether the proposed project will affect or is dependent on the projects and programmes underway. This will identify any interdependencies between the proposed and current projects, and how the projects enable one another. The indirect returns and risk of a project can then be taken into account, together with the more obvious impacts to show the full impact of the investment to the business.

Feasibility

An initiative may be recognised as being highly desirable, but may not be worthwhile to undertake if it is not feasible to implement. This second part of the selection stage considers the ability of the business to undertake the proposed initiative, by identifying the likely complexity, challenges and constraints (the three Cs) the business will face in implementing the project. The objective of this is to assess the implementation risk of the initiative.

Identifying the three Cs includes assessing the following:

- **Capability assessment.** This evaluates whether the business has the necessary level of physical and human resources required for the project, as well as the capabilities and competencies that exist. Areas to consider include the physical infrastructure, finance, people, resource expertise and leadership capability. In the process, any additional capabilities that need to be developed internally or procured externally should also be identified.

- **Change readiness assessment.** This activity assesses the business and its willingness to change, and identifies the challenges and risks. This includes examining this organisation's history of change, and the readiness of the business to move to the desired changed state. This information can be used to plan change strategies to mitigate the risks if the project is implemented. More detail can be found later in the change architecture chapter.

The desirability and feasibility of each initiative should be reviewed by a board which uses the portfolio principles defined earlier in the strategy translation phase, and approves the project for inclusion into the organisation's portfolio. Following approval of each initiative, planning and risk management may commence and owners are assigned.

Sequencing stage

A portfolio incorporating these initiatives is created once the initiatives have been approved. Existing projects also have to be compared with the new ones, to assess their priority relative to one another.

The goal of the prioritisation exercise is to create the optimal mix of programmes and projects, within a designated timeline, that will provide the greatest contribution to the business goals while minimising any conflicting demands on resources and maximising the use of the latter. The criteria applied in this stage are based on the portfolio mix principles defined earlier in the strategy translation phase.

As decisions are made on a comparative basis, the projects are initially compared and ranked to produce a prioritised list. Using this prioritised list together with the principles around the desired portfolio mix, we can then formulate the portfolio and put together the schedule. Note that this prioritisation exercise is not an exact science, and there may well be a few possible portfolios drawn up to be deliberated on by the board, which will choose one of them.

Aside from the portfolio mix principles, we can apply some of the following tools to assist in the portfolio scheduling:

- **Comparative risk and reward analysis.** Each project needs to be scored, using the results of the project's desirability and feasibility from the portfolio planning phase to represent reward and risk respectively, and then ranked. A two-by-two bubble chart, with axes representing the levels of risk and reward, is a useful diagrammatic technique to plot and group the programmes and projects based on their level of risk and reward type.
- **Portfolio plan.** Also known informally as a road map, the key deliverable of the portfolio planning phase, this establishes the framework, high-level budgets and communication plans to roll out the next programme delivery and project management chapters. The plan serves as a tool to gain a holistic

view of the individual and collective contribution of the initiatives to the strategic objectives, as well as to identify and monitor the key interdependencies. The portfolio plan should ideally span a few years to provide management with a long-term view, but it is advisable to refrain from charting periods longer than five years, as the further into the future the timeline is extended, the more difficult and less reliable those estimates will be.

- **Portfolio risk assessment and containment strategy.** Subsequent management of the portfolio will need a plan to manage the portfolio risks, that is, those arising from interdependencies between projects in the portfolio. This activity allows us to evaluate the organisational risks as a result of the interdependencies that exist within the portfolio, and establish risk strategies and control processes.

Portfolio management

Once the portfolio has been developed, (EPMO) enterprise-wide mechanisms to monitor and control it need to be in place, to ensure the ongoing performance and progress of the projects and the portfolio. The activities in this phase are usually carried out by a portfolio management or enterprise programme management office, the equivalent of a programme management office, but at a portfolio level. This has the responsibility of maintaining the plan, and tracking and reporting the portfolio's progress and performance against targets, and risks against portfolio tolerance levels. Most of the activities here are similar to those performed at the programme or project management level (see programme delivery and project management chapters), but on a portfolio scale instead. Key tools that are worth mentioning here are:

- **Progress and performance monitor.** To track and assess the progress and performance of the programmes and projects at a portfolio level against high-level budgets, milestones, KPIs and so on. This also captures reporting issues, based on the reporting framework developed earlier, to provide input into the next re-evaluation phase.
- **Risk and issue management and control.** To track and manage inter-programme risks and issues based on the portfolio risk assessment and containment strategy developed.
- **Quality assurance review.** To maintain quality assurance documentation and processes. This is to ensure that standards in monitoring and controlling are not compromised, and to preserve the effectiveness of the portfolio management process.

Re-evaluation of the strategy and portfolio

With new initiatives in the pipeline, current projects not delivering to expectations and constant market changes, the portfolio plan needs to be reviewed and adjusted continually to reflect projects undertaken that maximise utilisation of resources, best support a company's strategy, and reflect the business's response to changing market conditions. The key activities that support this are:

- **Review of the portfolio plan.** This review is concerned with ensuring that interactions and dependencies between projects in the current portfolio generate the most value to the business.
- **Review of the strategy and portfolio principles.** This looks at whether the portfolio policies that were used to shape the portfolio need to be adjusted or refined in response to changes to the business strategy, or the view of the level of acceptable risk.

These reviews ought to take place on a regular basis to ensure that significant deviations in the portfolio plan can be corrected in a timely manner, and that the projects embarked on are in line with any changing market conditions or events. The outputs of the reviews feed back into the strategy translation and portfolio management phases, and are used to refine the strategy, portfolio principles and portfolio plan where necessary.

Sample reporting mechanisms typically used for the reviews are outlined below:

- **Project exception reports.** These could be generated on a needs basis, and brings to the attention of the review board projects that run into significant issues and risks in performance or progress. These exception reports should be used for those problems that cannot be resolved at project management or programme delivery levels, or those that are particularly material in terms of their size, or impact on other projects in the portfolio.
- **Executive dashboard.** The dashboard represents the status report of the portfolio, and presents an overview of the performance of the organisation, going beyond simple measures of financial performance, to be used as input into the re-evaluation process. It usually comprises a series of KPIs that look beyond financial performance alone and can address a very wide range of issues. An example of one is shown in Figure 3.4.
- **Action log.** As the name suggests, this is simply a checklist that minutes the key tasks and amendments the board has agreed to action.

SUMMARY

A strategic portfolio management system can be designed using the approach, activities and tools described in the chapter. However, the robustness of a strategic portfolio management system also depends on other factors:

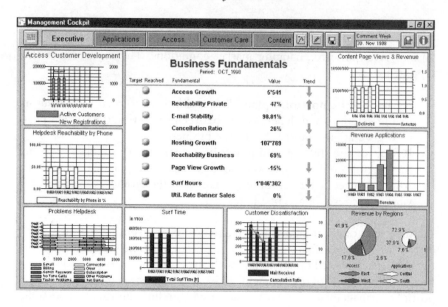

Figure 3.4 A sample executive dashboard

- The portfolio should encompass all significant programmes and projects within the organisation, whether cross-function or function-specific, in order to realise the organisational values of the projects.
- There need to be high visibility, clear communication and transparency of the value of the discipline and its processes. This is to generate buy-in of the processes from the organisation, and ensure they are utilised effectively, and not seen to be just more bureaucratic red tape and hence bypassed.
- Executive managers need to recognise the business need for the discipline and to act as internal champions to endorse it to their staff.
- To be effective, strategic portfolio management processes need to be linked strongly to the programme delivery and project management processes, and underpinned by supporting mechanisms in programme architecture and change architecture. Without these elements working together, the effectiveness of the discipline will be watered down.

In conclusion, strategic portfolio management provides a 'big picture' view of all programmes and projects within an organisation, and enables a system of collective benefits tracking and realisation. It is the critical first step to maintaining a line of sight between an organisation's business strategy and its programmes and projects.

The next chapters will explore how this strategic focus can be cascaded down to the programmes and projects in the four other disciplines and processes of enterprise programme management.

4 Programme delivery management

INTRODUCTION

If strategic portfolio management is largely about 'what' organisations should do to deliver strategy and policy through investments, then programme delivery management is about 'how' to deliver. The focus of programme delivery management is therefore on delivering maximum business benefits from the investments made through multiple projects.

So what are programmes? The process of translating strategic objectives into initiatives will often identify large-scale investments. The organisational capabilities required, which can only be developed and implemented through a series of interrelated projects, are also programmes, and need to be managed in a joined-up way. They are often quite long term and usually complex, impacting multiple parts of the organisation.

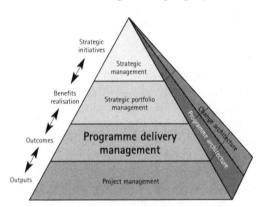

Figure 4.1 The enterprise programme management framework

Examples of programmes are the rebranding exercise at T-Mobile UK which is mentioned in the case study in Chapter 8, and the MyTravel e-commerce business development discussed in Chapter 13 in relation to supplier management. Another example is implementing an enterprise resource planning system such as SAP or Peoplesoft, as this ultimately impacts most areas of the business and has to be implemented in multiple planned phases.

Programmes are characterised by having multiple elements to be implemented, which need to be managed separately, but the sequencing of implementation and the management of critical dependencies between them require a level of management coordination over and above that at the individual project level.

What is programme delivery management?

Programme delivery management is the consistent application of specific processes, tools and methods, to enable the coordination and delivery of the projects within the programme to maximise business benefits.

Programme delivery is about proactively planning to ensure that projects are executed in an effective and coordinated way. Programme delivery management is also concerned with implementing the business changes required to deliver the benefits, and not just project deliverables and outcomes.

The core of programme management therefore includes activities such as integrated planning of multiple projects, identification and understanding of dependencies, managing risks relating to complex interdependencies, maintaining a focus on the overall business benefits of the programme, and coordinating large and often dispersed project teams.

Because programmes often entail large investments, impact multiple organisational stakeholders and are key to delivering strategy, they are usually highly visible and of high profile within organisations. Managing decision-making and organisational politics is often critical to their success.

This chapter outlines the value of programme management, introduces a high-level lifecycle model of programme delivery, and provides an overview of the basic tools and techniques available for programme management. However, effective programme management requires the integration and support in an organisation of all elements of the enterprise programme management framework.

Investment approval, decision-making and continuous leadership support are required at the strategic portfolio level. The right programme architecture must be adopted to support effective governance, management coordination, and team working. Resourcing processes must be adequate to provide the right levels of skilled resources throughout the programme. As business change is almost certain to impact people, the right change architecture and change management initiatives should be incorporated into the programme. Critically the success of the overall programme will only be as good as the quality and effectiveness of project management at the individual project level.

Part II of this book discusses in more detail areas such as supplier management, benefits management, communications, programme management systems, risk management and the role of programme management offices. All of these are critical for effective programme management, but they are not covered in depth in this chapter, which provides only a framework for a programme management process.

Common symptoms indicating the lack of a programme delivery infrastructure are:

- 'Not enough time spent planning or understanding what we were trying to achieve – we went straight into solutions.'
- 'Over-optimistic or unrealistic estimates (cost, benefits, time).'
- 'Budget cuts halfway through – couldn't complete the project.'
- 'The timescales moved – we needed to complete it yesterday and that was impossible.'
- 'Activities were not integrated and coordinated effectively, causing delays.'
- 'Unexpected issues and problems have caused overruns.'
- 'Projects deliver solutions or deliverables but no or limited business benefits.'

The value of programme delivery management

Programme delivery focuses on the continuous guidance needed to support the delivery of a business capability through multiple projects and phases. Appropriate approaches, techniques and tools are used to plan and organise the work, and to manage the incremental delivery of the new business capability. The benefits of effective programme delivery management include:

- effective control and execution of major business investment in projects
- improved delivery of benefits in agreed timescales by understanding key dependencies, effective sequencing of projects and managing critical interfaces
- effective deployment of the organisation's resources on projects with the right skills with clear accountabilities
- reduced potential for overrun in time and cost, and for negative impact on current operations, by identifying and managing major risks
- effective decision-making concerning the conflict between scope/output quality, time and resources, made from a business perspective, by the right people
- increased value from supplier inputs by effective management of suppliers and contracts
- enhanced overall delivery capability through shared approaches and best practices
- increased realisation of benefits through integration of process, system, people and organisational changes.

The bottom line is that programmes are the mechanisms often used to manage the execution of some of the largest investments that organisations will ever make. Creating the programme management capability to maximise effectively the value created from these investments should be a top priority in our organisations today.

The programme delivery management framework

The rest of this chapter introduces a simple lifecycle framework for programme management delivery. This covers the core management processes required to plan, execute and control programmes effectively. As with all processes they require the right organisational structures, systems, people skills, and experience and supporting tools to be effective.

The programme delivery management framework can be broken into three process groups:

- planning
- executing
- controlling.

Throughout the three process groups, tools and techniques from nine control areas are deployed as shown by the programme delivery framework diagram (Figure 4.2). The three process groups can be described as follows.

Planning

This involves the creation of a series of documents that facilitate shared understanding among programme stakeholders, and guide the execution and

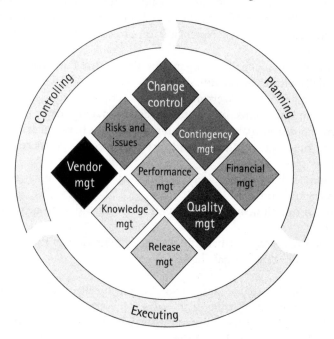

Figure 4.2 The programme delivery management framework

control of the programme. There are three distinct planning processes employed:

- **Top-down planning.** This process takes the goals, objectives and expectations that were defined in strategic portfolio management and develops a logical plan of how those goals, objectives and expectations will be delivered through a portfolio of interrelated projects.
- **Bottom-up planning.** This takes the output from the planning work done at the individual project level, and rolls up the project plans into a programme master plan. This allows for a focused and detailed analysis of interdependencies and risks to take place.
- **Infrastructure and policy planning.** This establishes a plan describing how the programme will be managed and executed, and detail protocols and policies from the nine control areas illustrated in Figure 4.2. (Standards set out by an organisation's enterprise programme management office are tailored and agreed for this programme.)

Executing

This is supporting the execution of the programme plan. It involves initiating new projects, closing out completed projects (or projects no longer relevant), and tracking the success of the portfolio in achieving the programme's goals and objectives.

Controlling

This involves identifying, managing and reporting on programme risks, issues, changes and costs, tracking deliverables and monitoring milestones. Outputs of this phase include formal feedback to the strategic owners of the programme in order for judgments to be made regarding the progress of the strategic plan.

Programme control areas (tools and techniques)

Change control approach

Change control is the orderly process of managing, investigating and authorising/rejecting a request for a change on a project or programme. Changes can be related to scope, schedule, resources or the agreed supporting management processes. Changes to a programme are referenced against an agreed scope, plans and budgets, collectively known as the baseline. (See Table 4.1.)

Table 4.1 The change control approach

Approach, tools and techniques	Rationale/benefits
Scope baseline	Ensures that all items subject to change are identified, organised, controlled, consistent, complete, correct, visible, traceable and verifiable.
Change control procedure	Provides a formal process for requesting, reviewing and authorising changes. Ensures that up-to-date records exist on what has been agreed thereby allowing control to be maintained on the scope of the programme. This will also mitigate risks as changes will be assessed before being implemented, reducing risk of unforeseen but dramatic impacts to other project areas.
Change control reporting	Provides a formal process for publishing changes, and aiding team understanding of related changes.

Contingency management approach

Contingency management involves the determination and subsequent allocation of the programme's contingency. This involves both budget contingency (that is, management reserves of unallocated workdays to accommodate budget overruns) and schedule contingency (the additional 'float' built into the programme's milestone dates to accommodate schedule overruns). (See Table 4.2.)

Financial management approach

Financial management involves the control and management of the programme's budget and other finances, as well as financial reporting for the

Table 4.2 The contingency management approach

Approach, tools and techniques	Rationale/benefits
Expected monetary value (EMV)	Enables risk exposure to be financially assessed for risks, enabling the response development process
Earned value analysis (EVA)	A tracking mechanism for both cost and schedule performance that can be used predictively to determine likely total overruns, hence contingency impacts

Table 4.3 The financial management approach

Approach, tools and techniques	Rationale/benefits
Programme budget allocation process technique	Lowers risk of maverick spending
Standard costing techniques (NPV, IRR etc)	Provides detailed data for business case
Budgeting	Provides cost baseline to measure progress against
Cash and accrual accounting	Lowers risk of unpredictable cashflow
Financial reporting	Lowers risk of business case not being realised due to lack of control or overspending
Earned value analysis	Provides mechanism to forecast project overruns, and enable early decisions on project lifespan

programme. It ensures that the programme's leadership has explicitly defined the financial controls and processes for the programme, including financial management and the programme's financial reporting. It thereby ensures that the cashflow requirements for a project or programme are understood, and provisions are made for expenditures as they are planned to occur. (See Table 4.3.)

Risk and issue management approach

Issue management involves the process for identification, analysis, resolution, reporting and escalation of the programme's issues, in other words, current programme problems. Risk management involves the systematic process of identifying, analysing and responding to project risk, that is, programme problems that may occur in the future. It includes maximising the probability and consequences of positive events, and minimising the probability and consequences of adverse events to project objectives. (See Table 4.4.)

Performance management approach

Performance reporting involves the documentation of the programme's performance against the plan. Performance reporting addresses a variety of audiences, both internal and external to the programme. (See Table 4.5.)

Table 4.4 Risk and issue management approach

Approach, tools and techniques	Rationale/benefits
Issues log	Provides a process for issues to be identified, communicated, assigned accountability, logged and tracked so that they are actively managed and escalated through to resolution. It also facilitates the resolution of issues that are not resolvable at project level and which require involvement from other participants within the programme.
Issue discussion/ resolution forum	Enables communication to those impacted by issues and creates a process for this communication.
Expected monetary value	Enables financial values to be attributed to risks, and can be used as a prioritisation tool to determine mitigating actions.
Decision tree analysis	Method of determining decisions to be made.
Critical path analysis	Aids identification of high-impact risks and issues to schedule.
Risk log	Allows potential problems and opportunities to be identified and managed proactively before they become critical issues to the project.
Risk response planning	Determination of whether a response to a risk is to accept, mitigate or avoid, and implement change controls to execute additional actions where required.

Table 4.5 Performance management approach

Approach, tools and techniques	Rationale/benefits
EVA (earned value analysis)	Provides visibility of project status and early warning of potential issues and risks.
Progress and expenditure reporting tools and templates	Provides visibility of project status and performance to allow appropriate interventions to be identified and actioned. Also provides early warning of potential issues and risks.
Milestone charts	Provides visibility of project status.
Tracking Gantt charts	Provides visibility of project status and performance against baseline.
Resource histograms	Snapshot view of amount of resources required versus resources available.
Cumulative cost curves	Provides visibility of project status.

Quality management approach

Quality management involves ensuring that the expectations and quality requirements of the programme are understood and actively managed. The quality management approach contains six components: expectation management, quality verification, process management, metrics, continuous improvement, and rewards and recognition. (See Table 4.6.)

Release management approach

In technology-related programmes, release management involves the coordination of activities that contribute to a release (that is, cross-project management) and the coordination of products that contribute to a release (architecture, integration and packaging). It is concerned with the management of a single release as opposed to cross-release management. (See Table 4.7.)

Vendor management approach

Vendor management involves selecting and managing resources from outside the organisation, both suppliers and contractors. This relates to products and services that will either be included as part of the business capability (such as software or physical assets) or used to create the business capability (such as office space or temporary workers). Vendor management supports resource management for resources procured from outside the organisation. (See Table 4.8.)

Table 4.6 Quality management approach

Approach, tools and techniques	Rationale/benefits
Cause and effect diagrams (Ishikawa and fishbone diagrams)	Provides a mechanism to identify the root cause of a particular problem. Helps ensure that the programme products meet the needs and expectations of the stakeholders.
Regular planned checkpoints and output reviews	Process to review plan and progress, reducing potential risks.
Implementation of standards and regulations	Provides a framework to aid resources meet the stakeholder expectations of programme products and service quality levels. Also will help prevent re-work.
Formal sign-off process	Ensures that the programme products meet the needs and expectations of the stakeholders.
Project audits	Mechanism to identify health status of project.

Table 4.7 Release management approach

Approach, tools and techniques	Rationale/benefits
Release plan	The release occurs in a structured way such that impacted parties understand what they need to do and when they need to do it.
Stepped validation procedures	Ensures that the release occurs in a structured way and that there is uninterrupted service to the business. Stops an implementation continuing when the signs are showing critical problems ahead.
Measurement process	Tool to identify issues before work is moved into the live environment, ensuring that live applications don't fail in the real business environment.
Crisis war-room	Defined approach to deal with release issues.

Table 4.8 Vendor management approach

Approach, tools and techniques	Rationale/benefits
Formal tender process	Process to help ensure that the appropriate mechanisms are in place to select third party products and services. Also ensures that the appropriate commercial arrangements are in place with third parties.
Criteria weighting model for vendor selection	Process to help ensure that the appropriate mechanisms are in place to select third party products and services.
Contract change control procedure	Enables cost and scope control. It is important to put in place a set of these policies, procedures and processes to manage change.
Billing and payments system	Mechanism to ensure timely payments, links into financial management
Output verification and sign-off process	Deliverables meet sponsor expectations. Checkpoint to ensure scope has been met and at the right level of quality.
Correspondence notebook	Record of correspondence.
Responsibility assignment matrix	Accountabilities and interfaces between different parties are clearly defined.

Knowledge management approach

Knowledge management involves ensuring that knowledge created on a programme is shared with the right people at the right time. It defines the strategy and principles behind the extent of knowledge sharing in addition to defining the processes by which knowledge will be shared. In this context, knowledge refers to existing and new information created as part of the programme. (See Table 4.9.)

SUMMARY

This chapter has described the rationale for managing initiatives that require multiple projects to deliver and build business capabilities as coordinated programmes. The sequencing of these related projects, and the management of their interdependencies and impact on the business to deliver benefits, require a level of management coordination over and above individual project management.

The basic management process of planning, executing and controlling programmes was described and a number of tools and techniques that can aid the process were outlined.

However programme delivery management is at the heart of the enterprise programme management approach, and its success in an organisation

Table 4.9 Knowledge management approach

Approach, tools and techniques	Rationale/benefits
Project library (physical location or virtual)	To capture knowledge capital created as a result of the project and/or programme as well as to utilise the knowledge capital stored from previous projects
Central document repository system (e.g. Quickplace)	Enables document version control, team communication and system central resource pool (in terms of documentation, process etc.)
Template library	Removes the 'reinvention of the wheel' risk, saving time and reducing possibility of missing actions
Lessons learnt workshops	Removes the 'reinvention of the wheel' risk, and improves process and knowledge for future work
Documentation, coding etc.	Removes conflicting methods and approaches standards
Sign-off register	Ensures that all documentation is approved and that the delivery meets previous expectations
Policies and procedures	Removes conflicting methods and approaches

depends upon the appropriate integration of the support provided by programme architecture (governance, structures, resourcing processes, team working), the supporting and enabling change architecture to provide effective business change management, and disciplined and effective project management.

Programmes by their nature are large business investments, and leadership and business ownership are critical; therefore the appropriate strategic portfolio management processes are key to supporting and leading programmes in organisations.

A number of critical competencies are required for effective programme delivery management, and these are described in detail in Part II of this book.

In conclusion, programmes are often the way organisations manage their key strategic investments. It is critical, if maximum value is to be created from these investments, that organisations develop programme management capabilities and invest in the appropriate infrastructure to support delivery of their programmes.

5 Project management

INTRODUCTION

The entire framework described so far exists for one purpose, which is to enable the right projects to deliver effectively within an organisation. Projects are the individual efforts that deliver specific measurable results. Strategic portfolio management and programme delivery management are concerned with ensuring organisations invest in the right initiatives to deliver strategic value, and that the delivery is coordinated and executed in a way that delivers the right results and contributes towards meeting strategic aims, while managing the organisational risks involved in business change. However, it is in the projects that the results are actually produced.

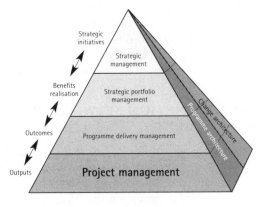

Figure 5.1 The enterprise programme management framework

In this chapter we briefly outline the characteristics of projects and a high-level project lifecycle management approach. The literature on project management as a management discipline and method is rich, and standardised methods such as PRINCE2 are fairly well known and widely used. We have therefore not repeated that body of knowledge in this book. The key to effective execution of project management techniques is the environment and organisation's capability to deliver change that is associated with the other elements of the enterprise programme management framework. Too often in organisations, executives believe that execution of an appropriate project management method is the key to successful delivery of business change.

Effective project management is a key building block for developing an enterprise programme management approach, but without the integration and link to strategy, the appropriate structures for governance and business ownership, the application of change management approaches

43

and a coordinated approach to interdependent changes, projects will fail to deliver value.

WHAT IS PROJECT MANAGEMENT?

A project is defined as a temporary endeavour that is undertaken to create a unique product or service (*PMBOK Guide*). Project management is further defined as the application of knowledge, skills, tools and techniques to project activities to meet project requirements (*PMBOK Guide*). The key elements to note in these definitions are as follows.

- **Temporary:** projects are distinct efforts. They end when specific objectives have been achieved. As such, projects are characterised by start and end dates and criteria. Note that while the projects themselves are temporary, the results or product of the projects may not be. For example, a project to build and erect a monument is temporary, but the monument is intended to become a permanent fixture.
- **Unique:** there is something unique about every project. Even projects where there is a lot of previous history of doing similar work are unique as the context, people and environment will be different.

THE DISTINCTION BETWEEN PROJECT AND PROGRAMME MANAGEMENT

There is a large volume of literature that attempts to define distinct differences between a project and a programme. In truth the distinction is blurred, and in many cases it becomes a judgement call. It is often more helpful to determine what management disciplines a particular change initiative requires, rather than to get hung up on definitions. Nevertheless, the following points offer some guidance as to whether an effort can best be considered a project or a programme.

- Programmes can be ongoing and do not end until they are judged complete or no longer relevant.
- Programmes evolve as more information is obtained. Progressive definition of desired results and plan elaboration is a common feature.
- Programmes tend to be more complex and deliver multiple distinct results, each of which has some value on its own, but which collectively have a value that is greater than the sum of the individual parts.

PROJECT MANAGEMENT APPROACH

Unsurprisingly, the project management approach is similar to, and overlaps with, the programme delivery approach. The programme delivery approach sets out standards for component projects to follow. From a project's per-spective, if programme standards exist, they are taken and used; if they do not exist, then the relevant structures are established for the project.

Figure 5.2 shows the five process groups (four phases) of project manage-ment and the nine knowledge areas as defined in the *PMBOK Guide*. Whereas programme delivery management follows three process groups, planning, executing and controlling, project management follows two addi-tional process groups, initiating and closing, reflecting the temporary, defined start and end characteristics of the project.

SUMMARY

Project management has only been outlined briefly in this chapter. Standards such as Project Management Body of Knowledge and PRINCE2 provide very comprehensive approaches and methods of project management.

Project Management capability is a critical element of the enterprise pro-gramme management framework, and developing a common approach, standards and professional project managers within an organisation is key to enhancing a delivery capability.

The application of project management methods should be done in the context of the type of project and change programmes an organisation is

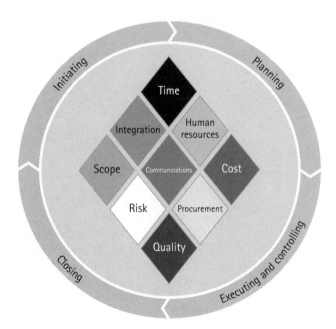

Figure 5.2 The five process groups and nine knowledge areas of project management

likely to undertake. Many organisations adapt and customise standard methods to suit their requirements. It is also likely that different levels of control and standardisation way be required for projects of a different scale and with different risk profiles. Flexibility in the use of project management standards, based on a clear understanding of the right level of control that is required, will limit the overhead to that which is absolutely necessary.

6 Programme architecture

INTRODUCTION

Since 1995, the Standish Group have regularly published and updated a report entitled *Chaos*, which studies the trends and factors that cause projects and programmes to either succeed or fail. The top three critical success factors that have repeatedly been identified are:

1. User/team involvement.
2. Executive support.
3. Clear statement of requirements.

The message is very clear. Getting team and leadership involvement right is of critical importance, ranked here as being more important even than having a clear statement of requirements! This reflects an obvious truth: no change, no matter how well defined or planned, can be achieved without clear accountability, commitment and support from both leadership and the people who need to make it happen within the organisation. Programme architecture is about implementing and using appropriate management and leadership skills and mechanisms, so that programmes can be resourced and managed effectively.

The design of the appropriate structures, roles, decision-making and resourcing processes, team building approaches, human resource policies and supporting infrastructure for programmes and projects in organisations is very contextual. The architecture must be integrated with the approaches to strategic portfolio management, programme delivery management and project management. The type of projects and programmes undertaken will influence the appropriate architecture, as will the need to integrate and dovetail with the 'business as usual' structures and accountabilities.

This chapter therefore provides an overview of the key considerations when designing programme architectures. It covers all the elements that need to be considered relating to accountabilities, decision-making, resourcing and managing people on projects and programmes. The specific approach and mechanisms adopted should be customised to your own organisation's situation.

WHAT IS PROGRAMME ARCHITECTURE?

Programme architecture is the establishment of support structures and mechanisms that allow effective programme leadership, and provide the programme team with the environment, skills, tools and support they need in order to operate effectively.

Unlike other programme activities, which tend to generate formal documentation, the outputs of programme architecture, although very tangible, are often subtle and invisible when things are working well. Characteristics that indicate the presence of an effective programme architecture include:

- a clearly articulated, and shared vision for the programme
- a stable and effective working environment with access to appropriate technology and other programme infrastructure
- identifiable and effective programme governance and decision-making bodies
- appropriate stakeholder and sponsor commitments, and clear business ownership for delivery of benefits
- an integrated programme culture representing the needs of different groups of team members from potentially different organisations
- appropriate skills and capabilities that exist or are being actively developed
- a clearly understood schedule of communication events and meetings to address the need for shared understanding and information sharing
- retention, appraisal and performance management and reward structures for programme and project resources.

THE VALUE OF PROGRAMME ARCHITECTURE

While putting effective resource and leadership structures in place may seem an obvious and intuitive thing to do, it proves time and time again to be difficult to achieve effectively. As mentioned above, programme architecture generally becomes most visible through problems indicating that it is either missing or inappropriate. Symptoms indicative of poor programme architecture are:

- 'People didn't really understand how their project fitted into the bigger picture.'
- 'Nobody involved in the project really wanted to be working on it. As a result they did not really commit to making it work.'
- 'Nobody could make a decision. By the time a decision was made it was too late.'

- 'When things went wrong, senior management started shooting, not supporting.'
- 'Some of the people working on the project did not have the necessary skills or knowledge. The team seemed to be made up of people who had some spare time rather than the people who were most appropriate.'
- 'Working on projects and programmes is seen as a bad career move.'

Figure 6.1 illustrates how some of these symptoms interact to create vicious cycles (failure paradigms), which lead to the establishment of 'blaming' cultures, fear of accountability and ultimately a reduction in capability to deliver change successfully.

There are also a number of environmental factors in organisations that, if left unmanaged, will conspire to jeopardise the effectiveness of programme leadership and programme teams. (See Table 6.1.) Programme architecture proactively establishes effective responses to these risks.

Programme architecture can further be understood as the establishment of five distinct programme support structures (see Figure 6.2):

- **Leadership and governance.** Ensuring that the programme has appropriate leadership and ownership within the organisation; identifiable and responsible authorities for decision-making and issue resolution; clear

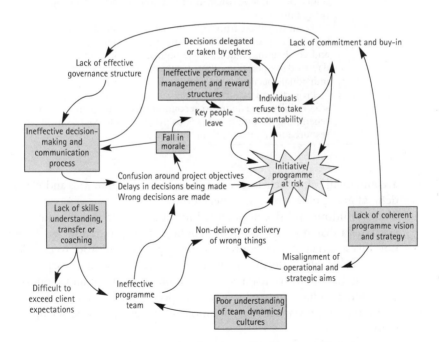

Figure 6.1 The interaction of symptoms of poor programme architecture

Table 6.1 Environmental factors in organisations

Leadership challenges	Senior executives in organisations are typically organised around functional roles and responsibilities focused on the management of ongoing operations, not the delivery of complex unique initiatives. The management and leadership style and skills appropriate for the management of operations can often be inappropriate in managing complex change initiatives. Accountability for the success and failure of initiatives is not placed at a level senior enough within an organisation. This leads to a mismatch between the accountability and authority required to make things happen. The lack of accountability can cause paralysis of initiatives when senior stakeholders disagree and try to exert influence over a programme, the success of which they have no accountability for.
Programme team challenges	Potential team members may be reluctant to leave established career structures and progression paths within line operations to take on project/programme roles where there is perceived to be greater personal risk and less career development opportunity. Where team members are shared with operational functions, the primary loyalty of individuals tends to reside with the established organisation. Functional managers are also typically reluctant to release their most valuable resources to projects and programmes. Team members from operational backgrounds often find working in project and programme environments uncomfortable and challenging, and miss the regular gratification that day-to-day operations provides them. This can lead to talented individuals becoming demotivated. Projects and programmes are often dependent on specific scarce skill-sets. Failure to recognise this in the planning and scheduling of initiatives leads to projects and programmes with resource needs that are impossible to fulfil.

accountabilities for the success or failure of the programme; and clearly defined goals, objectives and expectations.

- **Team building and development.** Ensuring that the programme team possesses a shared vision and understanding of the programme goals and objectives, and agrees appropriate working patterns in order to establish a sustainable and effective team culture. This area also focuses on ensuring that the whole team is suitably trained, equipped and supported to be able to fulfil members' roles and responsibilities. Additionally, suitable retention, reward and recognition processes should be set up and used.
- **Communication Infrastructure.** Establishes mechanisms for appropriate team communication. These include defining reporting

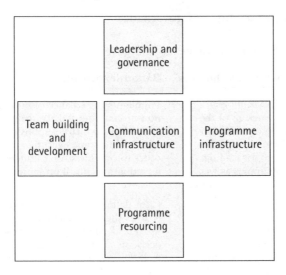

Figure 6.2 The programme architecture framework

requirements and frequencies, meeting calendars and attendance requirements, and key programme review points. Support for dispersed working teams may also need to be facilitated.

- **Programme infrastructure.** Ensuring that executing the programme is enabled by the provision of appropriate physical and technology infrastructure. This includes office space, access to information and technology, meeting rooms and so on.
- **Programme resourcing.** Policies, tools and structures for managing resources. This function is essential in balancing the availability and scheduling of resources across operational needs and different projects and programmes. Effective programme planning and control cannot occur without this support structure in place. Having effective human resource policies that address the needs of staff deployed onto project and programmes is also vital.

APPROACH, TOOLS AND TECHNIQUES

The following section examines the key activities, tools and techniques that are used in the provision of the five-programme architecture support structures described above. These tables should act as a guide and checklist to the key considerations when developing the appropriate programme architecture.

Programme leadership and governance

Table 6.2 Programme leadership and governance

Approach, tools and techniques	Rationale/benefits
Leadership organisation review Examines the structure of the leadership in the organisation and assesses how appropriate the structures are for leading successful programmes as well as managing ongoing operations.	Highlights the balance of programme versus non-programme activity against the balance of leadership's primary responsibility and focus. May lead to some executive restructuring in order to provide strong leadership and direction for critical programmes.
Leadership responsibility assignment matrix Identifies specific roles responsibilities and accountabilities for programme leadership activities.	Clear definition of roles and responsibilities enables the programme team to locate and call upon leadership support in order to expedite decisions or resolve issues.
Workshop with programme leadership and sponsorship group To develop and articulate programme goals, objectives and expectations.	A clear definition of stakeholder requirements facilitates a shared understanding within the team of what is expected and what success looks like.
Leadership development training Where appropriate, training can be given to leaders to enable them to understand the nature of the programme being undertaken, the risks involved and the type of issues and requirements that the programme team will have of them in the support of the delivery of the programme.	Helps to create a level of common understanding with leadership around the nature of the uncertainty and risks being managed and the nature of the information and issues likely to result from the programme. May also provide insights into areas where different management approaches from those of typical day-to-day management would be more effective.

Team building and development

Table 6.3 Team building and development

Approach, tools and techniques	Rationale/benefits
Smart-start kick-off meetings Workshops designed to introduce quickly and mobilise a team. Key items include working patterns, goals and objectives, context and background.	Provide team members with a memorable introduction to the programme, which sets a shared understanding of the context, approach, vision and objectives of the programme.

Table 6.3 continued

Approach, tools and techniques	Rationale/benefits
Team charter A document created with the programme team that sets out working patterns, principles for effective teamwork, and personnel policies and procedures. Often developed in a workshop format on or around the time of the smart-start kick-off workshop.	The development of a team charter with the team allows the team to develop a set of constructive principles and behaviours which together can form the cornerstone for a team culture where mutual respect, support, teamwork and delivery are enabled.
Team induction pack A suite of materials that allows new people joining a programme quickly to familiarise themselves with the scope, goals and objectives of the programme and the working practices that are being employed.	It is a well-known phenomenon that introducing new people to a project or programme at a critical time often slows progress up in the short term due to input of the established team in assisting in the learning curve. Effective induction materials enable new resources to be integrated and productive with much less distraction to critical effort than would otherwise be the case.
Team skills matrix A complete view of the programme team and the skills that the team possesses. Also includes team aspirations and training plans.	Allows programme management to match role requirements against skills of the team and determine where training or alternative resource procurement is required.
Team review meetings Ongoing scheduled events where the team can get together and review progress, analyse lessons learnt and keep up to date with what is happening on the programme.	Ensure that the team continues to maintain a big picture of the programme and members understand their own role in the context of the wider programme. Also reinforce team spirit, morale and culture.
Team appraisal A formal and recognised process for the team to set objectives and be measured formally on their performance on the programme in meeting those objectives.	Provides continuity of career management for individuals working on the programme team and a mechanism for reward and recognition to be equitably distributed.

Communication infrastructure

Table 6.4 Communication infrastructure

Approach, tools and techniques	Rationale/benefits
Meeting schedule A schedule of meetings that illustrates the frequency, purpose and audience for meetings.	Ensures that a disciplined routine of meetings is established and that the audience is appropriate to the needs of the meeting. Typically includes work stream review meetings, one-to-one reviews, steering group meetings and project communication meetings Also ensures that meeting conflicts between different projects with a programme are visible and managed.
Meeting output templates and follow-up procedures A format and process to ensure that decisions, issues and actions from meetings are recorded appropriately and then actioned.	Ensure that discussions are recorded and actions are taken and managed to completion.
Reporting templates A series of templates for the recording of project and sub-project status.	Provide a consistent format for the provision of data and status information from the projects within a programme.
Programme newsletters Provide an informative and light-hearted way of communicating with a large programme team.	Foster a sense of programme community which deepens sense of programme culture and belonging to the team.
E-mail/voicemail/web-based collaboration tools Use of technology for the exchange and dissemination of information.	Use of multiple channels for information exchange allows for different receptor styles to be accommodated and quick and fast distribution of information over a geographically distributed team.

Programme infrastructure

Table 6.5 Programme infrastructure

Approach, tools and techniques	Rationale/benefits
Office space Setting up of working office space (spaces) for the programme effort. The key consideration is location of teams; co-location is always desirable, however, not always possible.	Working environments contribute to productivity and morale. Poor or no working environments lead to poor or no performance. Sensitively balancing co-location issues with team members' personal circumstances and needs also can contribute to team morale and performance.

Table 6.5 continued

Approach, tools and techniques	Rationale/benefits
Technology infrastructure Provision of computers, access to telephones, servers and passwords, technology support and help, appropriate project software.	Most programmes today heavily utilise information rechnology. Provision of suitable access to team members allows their work to be completed. Barriers to access will be barriers to work being completed.
PMO administration resource This includes resources and processes in order to manage the project administration, including diaries, meeting schedules, room booking, travel arrangements, document production, timesheet administration, building access and regulations control, plan updating, risk, issues and change log maintenance, production of newsletters, presentations, etc.	Provision of suitable administration support to projects allows core team members to stay focused on the delivery of the project.

Programme resourcing

Table 6.6 Programme resourcing

Approach, tools and techniques	Rationale/benefits
Project scheduling A mechanism of scheduling people to specific projects within the programme portfolio. Utilises the team's skill profiles and project role definitions in order to balance needs with resources.	Projects within programmes routinely compete for resources; Similarly, programmes within organisations frequently compete for resources with other programmes and operations. A scheduling function enables the balancing of fulfilment of resource requirement with the business priorities and also identifies where additional training or skill sourcing may be required.
Recruitment A mechanism of obtaining skills from outside the programme or organisation. May involve relationships with contractor suppliers and consultancies.	Programmes need to be able to source resources and skills when required in order to proceed efficiently. A speedy mechanism for obtaining resources keeps the programme moving and prevents delays due to resource non-availability.
Performance appraisal This human resource tool includes setting objectives, developing a plan on which to assess the performance of an individual, and regular review.	Provides regular feedback on an individual's performance against targets and helps to manage and develop the personnel skill-sets in line with the business needs.

Table 6.6 continued

Approach, tools and techniques	Rationale/benefits
Roles and responsibilities Documentation describing the roles that need to be fulfilled and what responsibilities and accountabilities exist.	Ensures that the programme team has an agreed source of reference to keep, and agree roles and responsibilities for programme and project team members.

PROGRAMME LEADERSHIP MODELS

Leadership of programmes in organisations is central to developing successful enterprise programme management capability. The role of leaders is key, and as we have described, senior executives need to be involved actively in the process of developing and leading programmes of change. The structuring of executive responsibilities is critical to decision-making and governance. In this section we discuss a number of approaches to organising these executive responsibilities. We have simplified these in order to draw attention to the key considerations when developing leadership models.

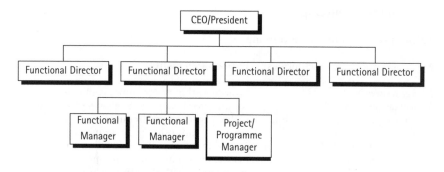

Figure 6.3 Typical organisation leadership structure

Typically organisations have leadership structures focused primarily on the management of ongoing business operations. (See Figure 6.3.) Project and programme leadership tends to come from within a function. This structure can be effective for management of small initiatives, where the scope and impact of the initiative falls under the remit of one particular function, but tends to be less effective when cross-functional needs have to be considered. Often with this structure, programme/project work is pushed to second place whenever operational crises (the day job) occur.

When a larger proportion of an organisation's activity is dedicated to change programmes, the programme leadership organisation can be changed to reflect the balance, and the need for leadership focus and support across both programmes and operations.

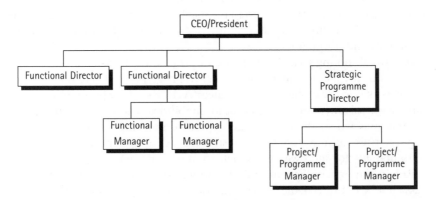

Figure 6.4 Organisation leadership structure incorporating project/programme management

In the structure shown in Figure 6.4, the delivery of programmes is recognised on a par with the management of the business, and has direct executive-level focus and clear programme delivery accountabilities defined. There may also be dedicated and skilled programme resources supporting a strategic programme division.

One problem not overcome by this model is the fact that programmes need to call on resources and expertise which typically reside within the operational functions. Having two separate executive organisations for programme delivery and functions can lead to power struggles and competition for critical resources. This is often referred to as a matrix environment, and is illustrated in Figure 6.5.

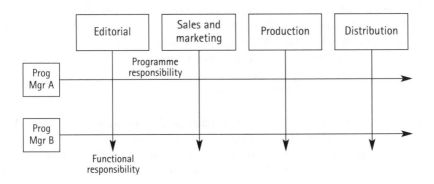

Figure 6.5 A matrix environment

Matrix environments vary across different organisations. in so far as the balance of power can vary between the programme managers and the functional managers. In all matrix environments, a key element of programme architecture is to identify and establish mechanisms by which resources can be utilised most efficiently according to the combined priorities of both operations and programmes.

It is worth noting that the structure of programme leadership can change throughout the lifecycle of a programme. In programmes where the majority of the work is in the design or development cycle, a separate programme structure with distinct programme accountabilities can be effective. For programmes where there is a large degree of implementation activity that impacts the business functions, a structure that incorporates functional accountability for successful implementation becomes more appropriate.

Resolution of conflict around the sourcing of resources is sometimes managed by having a dedicated organisation-wide scheduling function. More often, the process for sourcing programme resources resides within a programme management office (PMO).

PROGRAMME MANAGEMENT OFFICES

There are many different PMO models, and there is no correct model, as the role of the PMO is always best designed to fit the needs of the specific organisation or programme. However, there are a number of PMO types that commonly occur. In this section we describe these, and draw attention to the pros and cons. However this is a developing area in supporting programme and project delivery in organisations, and we have devoted a whole chapter in Part II to our view of a new model that supports the enterprise programme management approach described in the book.

Strategic portfolio management office

The primary objective of a strategic portfolio management office (SPMO) is to facilitate the strategic management of key programmes and projects within an organisation, such that the portfolio of initiatives reflects what is most critical to the organisation. An SPMO usually reports to a CEO or at an executive team level (see Figure 6.6).

Key functions of a SPMO are as follows:

- Works with the senior executive team in developing the design of the programme portfolio based on the strategic plan.
- Prioritises programmes and projects in terms of strategic value, using high-level financial and benefit assessments of alternatives.
- Initiates new programmes and projects.

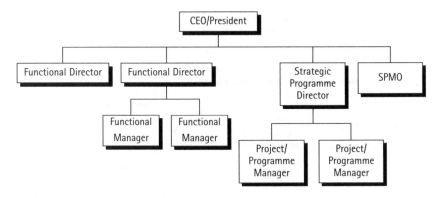

Figure 6.6 Organisation leadership structure incorporating strategic programme management

- Closes down or kills programmes and projects where the objectives have either been met or are no longer considered relevant or important.
- Tracks the realisation of benefits from programmes, and the progress against high-level plans.
- Creates 'programme charter' documentation that describes the programme and priority, and details the nature of the authority that is being given to the programme manager in order to take and deploy the organisation's resources.
- Ensures priorities are clearly understood by the organisation such that resource is deployed in the most appropriate way.

Programme management office (directive)

In this model (see Figure 6.7), the PMO leads and controls the projects and programmes. The PMO has the power to dictate standards and processes, and has the authority to resolve disputes across competing initiatives. Typically, the PMO has full-time staff, some of whom are deployed onto specific projects and programmes in order to establish and enforce the common standards and programme architecture requirements as set out by the PMO. This type of PMO typically manages the sourcing and scheduling of resources.

While involved in supporting strategic programme management activities, this type of PMO is primarily focused at establishing programme delivery mechanisms and controls.

Programme management office (supportive)

In this model (see Figure 6.8), the key activities of the PMO are similar to those of the directive PMO; however the power relationships are different.

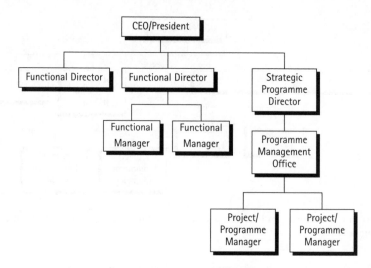

Figure 6.7 Organisation leadership structure incorporating a directive programme management office

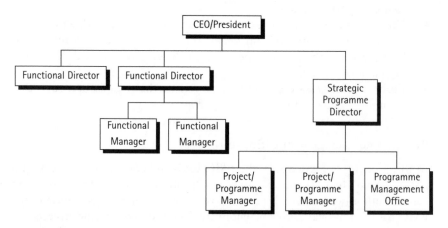

Figure 6.8 Organisation leadership structure incorporating a supportive programme management office

Also known as a programme support office (PSO), it exists to support and provide assistance to projects and programmes, often focusing on more administrative support. The programmes themselves, however, report to and are controlled and steered by leadership outside the PMO function. The risks of this model are that the PMO can become ignored and marginalised, and lose effectiveness if not profiled effectively by strategic programme leadership.

Typical functions of both the directive and supportive PMO are as follows:

- Sets the PMO function as a critical process embedded into the organisation's infrastructure, so that use of it cannot be bypassed. (Rules tend to be more stringent for the directive model.)
- Develops and maintains processes and procedures for gathering and reporting consolidated project data and schedules. Documents what deliverables are being produced and when.
- Highlights key programme interdependencies.
- Aligns implementation plans across interdependent initiatives.
- Monitors all key decision points, the dates by which a decision is required, and the impact of the decision, through maintenance of schedules.
- Performs regular project risk assessments by identifying future areas of major risk and providing advice on potential corrective actions to mitigate the risks.
- Manages the mechanism for early issue raising, issue communication and issue resolution.
- Highlights the key critical issues that may impinge on the successful delivery of the projects.
- Monitors changes in terms of their impact on scope, cost and delivery time frames against the target schedule.
- Enhances problem solving by proposing alternative high-level solutions and their associated implications.
- Assists in timely decision-making on the overall control of projects.
- Manages resource scheduling across the projects in a programme, and sources new resources where required.

STEERING GROUPS, DESIGN BOARDS AND CHANGE CONTROL BOARDS

Other common programme leadership mechanisms are the steering group, design board and change control board.

Steering group

This is a committee, usually composed of the programme or project sponsor and other executives who have a legitimate stake and interest in the programme or project. The role of the steering group is to monitor the progress of the initiatives, act as a decision-making body for the resolution of issues, take a strategic view of programme risk management and approve risk response strategies. Typically, the steering group is responsible for authorising changes to the programme or project budget and the use of contingency funds.

Criteria for successful steering groups include:

- a composition of people who have legitimate interest in the programme and have the authority to take decisions and make things happen

- ability to consider the programme in the context of the wider strategic issues
- accountable for the decisions that are taken.

Design board/design authority

On programmes where there is a strong technical aspect to the product, a design board can be used as a body responsible for the coherence and applicability of the product design. This group is responsible for ensuring that the design of the solution meets the needs and objectives of the organisation, and acts as a key quality assurance and control function.

Change control board

Where the nature of the project is complex, the total impact of a change request may not be fully apparent to the programme management or leadership. A change control board, (often, but not always the same composition as the design board) is composed of people who understand the technicalities of the products being produced, the methodologies and processes being employed, and the risks involved. The role of this group is to assess the impact in terms of cost, schedule and above all risk, of a request for change. To be effective, this board needs the authority to say 'yes' or 'no' to particular changes.

Typically, design and change control boards report alongside the programme manager to the steering group.

SUMMARY

Independent research and our experience have shown that effective leadership and team working are critical determinants of the success of programmes and projects in delivering value in organisations. However these areas are the least well developed in many organisations, and often little time and effort is given to supporting programmes effectively.

We have identified five key areas that should be considered and addressed in the design of the appropriate programme architecture to support development of enterprise programme management capability.

The roles of senior executives in leading and supporting decision-making need to be defined clearly and the appropriate governance bodies implemented. These may be different from existing organisational structures, and how they interrelate needs to be determined carefully. Senior executives may need support in developing change leadership roles.

The development of high-performing programme and project teams needs to be supported with the appropriate human resource policies addressing recruitment, training, performance management, reward structures and career development for those deployed onto projects and programmes.

Communication mechanisms need to support the sharing of knowledge, create an understanding of how programmes and projects are linked to business objectives, and support collaborative and often dispersed team working practices.

The appropriate infrastructure, whether working environment, technology or systems, needs to be provided for project teams.

A process of cross-organisational resourcing needs to be developed and visible to allow effective resourcing of critically skilled people onto projects and programmes.

All these elements need to be specific to the organisational environment and the nature of the programmes being delivered. This chapter has given an overview of some of the key considerations for developing an effective programme architecture to support enterprise programme management. The process of adapting and flexing programme architecture is likely to be continual, to support the evolution and development of the organisation.

7 Change architecture: managing the human side of change

Imagine you are in the midst of managing the biggest programme of your career. However, some of the board members don't support your plans – they now have very different views on what the end game should be. Employees are not making the changes you told them about. Is it because they do not want to or are not able to? The current team structures do not lend themselves to the new routines, so people are getting frustrated. You worry that you are about to lose some of your best performers.

This scenario is more common than it needs to be. In today's complex business world, we tend to forget some basic logic:

Delivering a programme means changing the organisation in some way.

We know that organisations are made up of people.

So delivering a programme means helping people to change.

Helping people to change is absolutely crucial to delivering a successful programme. An effective change management approach can help you to:

- ensure that everyone in your business has a clear and shared vision of the programme and its goals
- secure the commitment of top leadership and key stakeholders
- build organisational structures that will embed, rather than prevent, the change
- communicate to the wider organisation so that they know what is going on and when they need to take action
- maintain motivation in employees who might be weary of successive changes
- develop a culture that will support the required change
- build a change capability that helps drive organisational agility in the future.

The above is not a wish list – it is attainable, and for a successful programme it is a must. The objective of this chapter is to guide you through a simple framework to identify and manage the people challenges that will drive (or else hinder) the success of your programme. We call this 'change architecture'.

A FEW THOUGHTS ON CHANGE

Hundreds of books have been written on the theory of change management. We do not intend to replicate that work, but do encourage you to explore the theory further if you would like to build or improve your understanding. However, there are some fundamentals to keep in mind as you read this chapter.

First, all those impacted by (or involved with) change will go through their own process of accepting the change. This is a highly personal journey, although from experience we can identify some key phases:

- **Understanding:** being aware of the upcoming change and its basic rationale.
- **Positive perception:** starting to support (though perhaps not openly) the change.
- **Try-out:** willingness to experiment with the new work processes or behaviours, whilst essentially doing jobs as before.
- **Adoption:** following a positive try-out experience, implementing the changes on a day-to-day basis (although effort is still required to avoid slipping back into the 'old ways').
- **Internalisation:** accepting the changes and turning them into habits and routines. Sustaining and improving them moving forward.

Each phase brings diverse human reactions, and requires the use of a variety of change interventions, such as education, coaching, new team structures and cultural change. We will return to the idea of acceptance throughout this chapter, but be aware of the different phases as you build the change architecture for your own programme.

Figure 7.1 depicts the change acceptance process, as well as the risks of not managing the change.

Second, there is no 'one-size-fits-all' approach to meeting the needs of your programme. Change is situational. Both the magnitude of the change and the organisation's readiness for that change differ from company to company, from programme to programme. They probably differ in the following two ways:

- Magnitude of the intended change:
  - number of stakeholders involved
  - impact on core competencies
  - timeframe to implement the change
  - number of people impacted by the change
  - extent of behavioural change required
  - number of simultaneous changes to processes, technologies and skills.

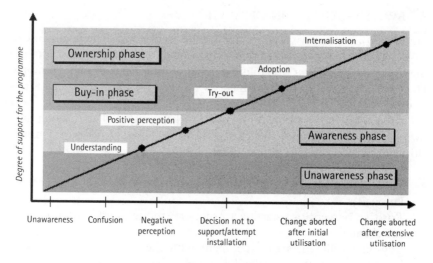

Organisational response to a lack of coordinated change management

Figure 7.1 The change acceptance process

- The organisation's readiness for the change:
  - support from key decision makers
  - degree of management consensus
  - understanding of the need for change by those impacted
  - past history (success/failure) of change
  - need for changes in the company culture
  - resources allocated to the change.

Third, change is systemic. Change cannot be viewed from a purely 'technology' perspective, nor for that matter from a purely 'people' perspective. Remember to see the bigger picture of change, from all angles (such as behavioural, procedural, technological and structural). Also be aware that what you do in one part of the business may impact other parts, and vice versa.

Fourth, the change process must be linked to business and performance goals in order to be both aligned and effective. Successful programmes articulate the impact of the programme on the business, and then set about developing and measuring indicators of success.

Above all, keep in mind that it takes time to change. For example, while a technology implementation can theoretically be done in a defined number of months, it takes significantly longer to gain user buy-in and to realise the intended benefits. Expect the change journey to be an ongoing commitment.

WHAT IS CHANGE ARCHITECTURE?

As with programme architecture (discussed in Chapter 6), change architecture is a management discipline that supports each programme level, from strategic portfolio management through to individual project delivery. But while programme architecture is concerned with what happens within the programme,

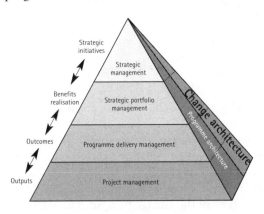

change architecture is clearly focused on the human impact of the change beyond the programme.

So what is change architecture? It is the process of crafting an overall change strategy and planning interventions to drive the change. It also involves overseeing the detailed design and implementation of the change interventions, and making appropriate adjustments to the strategy and plan. Change architecture is relevant to individual projects or programmes as well as a portfolio of programmes.

Figure 7.2 The enterprise programme management framework

Specifically, it involves three overall phases:

1. Developing the change strategy.
2. Planning the change journey.
3. Embedding and reviewing the change.

The emphasis of change architecture activities will typically change as the programme progresses. In the early stages of the programme, for example, the focus will be on understanding the specific needs of the business and developing the optimal change strategy. The focus will then shift to planning, at a high level, the appropriate interventions to enable the change, such as communication networks or organisational restructuring. As these interventions are put in place, the focus will shift to embedding and reviewing the change activities to ensure that the 'right' changes are actually taking place.

Each programme has specific needs; however the typical focus on change activities can be summarised, as shown in Figure 7.3.

Change architecture is not a linear process. The critical factor underpinning successful change architecture is to identify and meet programme needs, whatever the maturity stage of the programme at hand. For example, a portfolio of programmes may require a continuous, long-term cycle of checking

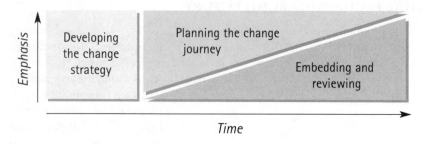

Figure 7.3 The phases of change architecture

the indicators of change against the portfolio's change strategy and plan, and making adjustments where necessary.

In summary, however, we believe that there is a huge advantage in taking the time to design the optimal change architecture, and then making strategic adjustments as the programme progresses. This is where change architecture differs from contemporary change management. The latter often jumps to the what, why and how of the change plan, such as a detailed organisation design or a new performance management system. In some cases, these detailed areas can become independent work streams of their own, with little strategic coordination. Change architecture avoids these pitfalls by first designing the overall solution at a high level, then overseeing design and implementation.

Why do we use the word 'architecture'? Consider the role of the design architects on a building development. They are responsible for interpreting the client's brief, developing a vision for what the building will look like, then creating the blueprints that will bring that vision to life. Once the blueprints are agreed, the architects then commission builders, plumbers, plasterers and electricians to bring the plan to life. The architects brief these tradespeople, but they leave the details to the experts in each area. As the building work proceeds, the architects closely monitor building progress, making adjustments where necessary to ensure that the work continues to reflect the overall vision.

THE VALUE OF CHANGE ARCHITECTURE

We discussed earlier the benefits of an effective change programme, including ensuring that everyone has a clear and shared vision of the programme, building organisational structures that will embed the change, and motivating employees who might be weary of past changes. When it is viewed as a key component of the strategic programme management framework, however, we can also see how change architecture contributes directly to the success of the overall programme. (See Table 7.1.)

Table 7.1 The contribution of change architecture

Programmes that are effective	Change architecture contributes by:
Shape the right programme strategy for the organisation	Ensuring that the programme strategy is aligned to the strategic direction of the business, is attainable, and is tailored to the business context and capability to change.
Deliver the programme objectives and realise the expected benefits	Scoping the activities needed to realise the benefits from a people perspective, assessing evidence of the actual organisational change against the planned change journey.
Flex in response to changing business needs	Revisiting the people activities and adjusting appropriately.
Achieve a successful organisational transition making the best use of scarce resources, money and time	Selecting and prioritising the optimal people interventions, e.g. performance management, cultural development, organisational design.
Have visible commitment from the programme's stakeholders	Defining the strategies for generating ownership of the change within the stakeholder group.
Mobilise employees to work effectively in new ways	Establishing the conditions in which employees understand and are enabled to change.
Create capability within the organisation to sustain the change	Working with the organisation to identify responsibility within the organisation to ensure knowledge and skills transfer.

In practice, the benefits of change architecture are specific to the programme and business under consideration. In later sections, we highlight the need to identify the benefits and expected contribution of the specific change activities being undertaken.

THE CHANGE ARCHITECTURE FRAMEWORK

Earlier on we identified the three phases on change architecture. What actually happens in each phase?

Developing the change strategy

The change architecture process begins by understanding the context and issues of the programme and business, including an assessment of the organisation's readiness for change. Based on this, the appropriate people interventions are then selected to create the optimal solution given the available resources, money and time.

The interventions fall into two categories: support infrastructures and people interventions. Support infrastructures are underlying support networks to enable people through the change (such as communications, stakeholder management, and training and development). Support infrastructures are usually only in place for the programme duration.

On the other hand, people interventions are specific solutions that are designed and implemented for longer-term use. Examples include performance management systems, reward strategies and organisational designs. They exist beyond the programme and become part of the business as usual, future state.

Planning the change journey

Once the appropriate interventions have been identified, change architecture then focuses on planning these at a high level. This is called the change journey. The change journey outlines the key milestones and phases for each of the interventions. It provides a high-level view of what change activities must happen at what point in the programme in order to deliver the expected outcomes. A change journey will include both supporting infrastructures and people interventions.

Undertaking this high-level planning prompts careful consideration of the synergies and interdependencies between different change activities. Mapping out activities in this way facilitates testing and manipulation of the plan, and ultimately results in an effective plan which is closely aligned to the needs of the overall programme.

Once in place, the high-level plan will inform the subsequent detailed planning, design and implementation activities which will be undertaken by other change resources.

Embedding and reviewing the change

A key outcome of the change architecture process is to ensure that the change is embedded within the organisation. It is critical that the organisation is able to sustain the change beyond the programme or project. There are two areas of focus here. The first is to identify and leverage opportunities to build individual capabilities and share learnings from the programme. The second is to identify and track 'indicators' of change throughout the programme, in order to ascertain whether or not the intended changes are taking place. The results of this review allow adjustments to be made to the change architecture to ensure it is aligned to the desired programme outcomes.

At the same time, change architecture must also be sensitive to changes to business and programme priorities. If these changes take place, then the change architecture must be reviewed and adjusted as necessary.

APPROACH, TOOLS AND TECHNIQUES

The objective of this chapter is to provide some practical guidance for identifying and managing the people and organisational challenges of your programme. Because change is so situational, there is no generic solution or methodology that can be plugged into your own programme. Instead, we can help you to ask the right questions that will enable you to create the change architecture that will work for your organisation.

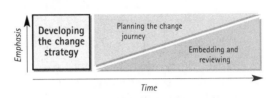

The following sections therefore tap into our experience to pose questions to consider and suggest outcomes of each stage.

Figure 7.4 Phase 1 of change architecture

Phase 1: Developing your change strategy

This first stage is critical. The aim is to work with key stakeholders from the organisation and the programme team to:

- understand the programme vision, strategy and goals
- create a comprehensive solution to meet your people challenges
- identify the links between the people work and the broader programme objectives.

Understand the business case for change

Before doing anything else, you need to understand the context of your business, the reasons for changing, and its ability to make the change. Ask yourself (and others):

What is our business strategy, our key goals?

Why is the organisation undertaking this programme? What are the business drivers?

Are there any related programmes planned or underway?

Is there evidence of the need for change? Can we describe why this is critical?

What is our experience of past changes?

Taking the time to find answers to these questions will provide a good context for identifying the real needs of the business. It will also help you understand (even if only at a general level) the company's inbuilt capability to change.

Question the scope and pace of the programme

At this point, you will want to understand the extent of the change to be undertaken:

What is the 'people' scope of this programme?

What will be the magnitude, pace and style of the change for key groups across our organisation (for example, employees, management, shareholders, suppliers)?

What change principles or assumptions should guide this programme?

After answering these general questions, you will need to understand exactly who will be impacted by the programme and how they should be involved.

Analyse the needs of stakeholders and audiences

There are two general groups of people you should be interested in: stakeholders (who have an influence on the programme) and audiences (who will be impacted by the programme). The buy-in of both groups is critical. A failure to understand this will jeopardise programme success. See Chapter 14 for advice on how to conduct an analysis of stakeholders and audiences.

Investigate current capabilities to make the change

Is your organisation ready and able to make the necessary changes? Questions to ask include:

Have stakeholders bought into the upcoming changes?

Are audience groups aware of what will happen?

Is there a shared vision of what the future will look like, after the programme?

Will the company's culture help or hinder the changes we need to make?

Do our leaders have the ability to lead this change?

Do we have an ability to communicate to the right audiences at the right time?

Does the current organisational structure support the future vision?

How robust are our People and HR processes? Will they support the change?

In some cases, programme resources and senior personnel will have the answers. In other cases, you may need to hold focus groups or conduct staff surveys to answer these questions.

The output for these steps should be a documented understanding of your company's context, the business case for change, and a preliminary assessment of your company's readiness to make the change. Based on the above, you can then begin to shape the change strategy for the business.

Select the most appropriate change interventions

Once a good understanding of the high-level people requirements is achieved, you can then choose the appropriate people interventions that will help deliver the change. Remember that there are two types of interventions: support infrastructures and people interventions.

Every programme and business will require a unique set of interventions. However these may include those listed in Table 7.2.

Table 7.2 Change interventions

Support infrastructures	People interventions
Creating a programme vision	Changing the culture
Managing stakeholders	Redesigning the organisation structure
Development of leadership abilities	Identify future competencies
Communication to audiences (internal and external)	Designing performance management and reward systems
Building employee skills	Updating human resource policies and processes

How do you know which interventions to include? Ask yourself the following:

What are the critical success factors from a 'people' perspective?

What interventions will be required to deliver this change?

Which interventions will deliver the optimal solution given the available resources, money and time?

These are hard questions which will take time to answer, and will also benefit from the experience of those who have been through similar exercises.

The output should be a list of agreed interventions within the constraints of resources, money and time.

Clarify the contribution of your planned change activities

The involvement and commitment of the organisation is a key driver of programme success. Ironically, the investment made in people and change activities is often the hardest to justify. You should identify the contribution of your change activities: this will be critical when explaining the work of your resources as well as focusing team efforts:

What benefits are we trying to achieve?

How do they link to the bottom line?

When will these be delivered?

How are we going to measure the success of the change initiatives?

Define the change strategy

Document your change strategy early on. While it is expected to be a living and breathing document, actually writing the strategy can help clarify the intended approach and identify possible gaps. It is also a useful document when describing the change activities to others.

The content of your change strategy is strictly situational. However you may want to use the following sections:

Executive summary

Introduction

The business case for change

Description of the future state

Programme requirements

Scope of the change activities

Guiding principles

Assumptions

Recommended interventions (and rationale)

Contribution management

Next steps

Phase 2: Planning the change journey

Following creation of the change strategy, this phase will focus on:

Time

Figure 7.5 Phase 2 of change architecture

- defining each intervention in further detail
- building an integrated high-level plan describing each intervention
- creating a one-page journey map to describe the overall change programme.

When we speak of the change journey, we mean the high-level activities and milestones that need to take place in order to realise the intended changes and benefits. It is a high-level plan of what needs to take place, and when.

In phase 1 you have identified the appropriate interventions. Before creating the high-level plan, these interventions will need to be explored in further detail. To do this, you may find it useful to complete Table 7.3 for each intervention.

Table 7.3 Analysis of change interventions

Intervention	E.g. Organisation design
1 Purpose:	
2 Objectives:	
3 Milestones and outputs:	
4 Requirements:	
5 Stakeholders impacted:	
6 Links to other work streams:	
7 Assumptions:	
8 Resource requirements (including numbers and skills/experience):	
9 Risks:	
10 Timeframes:	

This basic information will allow you to continue with your high-level planning, and is also a good way to identify your resourcing needs. Be as specific as possible when detailing your resource requirements: skills, experience and knowledge are critical when it comes to change management. Consider the best strategy to acquire these skills: internal (already exist; develop skills; recruit) and/or external (consultants, contractors). Once resources are assigned, be sure to involve these people in your planning from now on.

When creating the high-level change plan:

How will the people activities be integrated with the overall plan?

What are the inter-dependencies between the people interventions?

What are the key milestones and deliverables?

What do these look like over time?

The output should be a high-level change plan including key dependencies between the various areas of focus and with other parts of the programme. Most people choose to use Microsoft Excel or Project for this. Many companies also find it useful to create a one-page pictorial representation of the plan. It focuses the team on the key activities, and helps communicate them to others. An example is shown in Figure 7.6.

Remember that it will take some time to scope each intervention in sufficient detail. The need for and scope of each intervention will be specific to your programme. To give you a head start, however, we have explored some of the more common support infrastructures and people interventions below.

Every programme is unique: only some of the following are likely to be applicable to your needs.

Shape your approach to stakeholder management

Stakeholder management is the process of identifying and involving those who will have an influence over the success of your programme, both inside and outside the organisation. Your stakeholders might include the board, your shareholders, employees, customers, business partners, suppliers and the community.

Effective stakeholder management is vital for every programme. To define your stakeholder needs, ask the following questions:

Who are the stakeholders in this programme?

What roles do they play?

Can we influence them?

Is there visible sponsorship of the change?

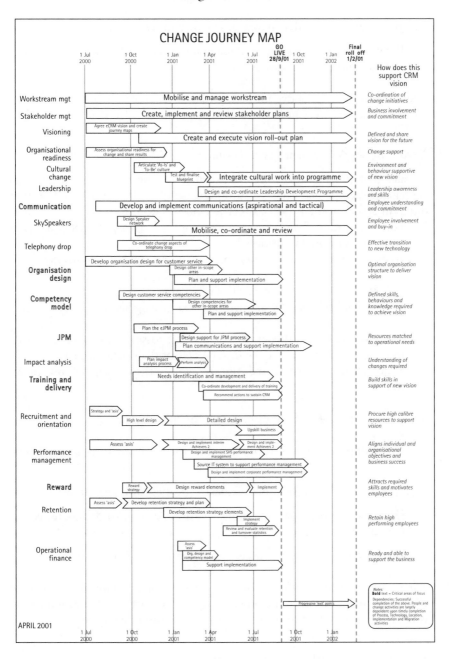

Figure 7.6 Example of a high-level change plan

Where are they in the change acceptance process?

What process do we require to maintain effective relationships with both internal and external stakeholders?

You can translate the above into a high-level stakeholder management plan, and mobilise resources to create and manage the detailed plan.

Shape your high-level strategy to manage individual transitions

We already know that those involved with your programme will go through the change acceptance process. Although people will probably start out at different stages of the process, every person will need to make a personal or individual transition from one stage to another. This personal journey is often called 'individual transitions'.

Why focus on individual (rather than organisational-wide) transitions?

- Individuals have unique capacities for change.
- During change, there is the need to acknowledge and address the 'me' issues.
- Change involves both personal gains and losses (and there are often more losses than gains at the lower levels of the organisation).
- Major change, implemented quickly, can tax the capacity of individuals to absorb it.

To craft an effective transitions plan, ask the following questions:

Do people themselves recognise that they will go through a change acceptance process?

What can we do to help people deal with their own change issues?

How can the other change infrastructures be used to deliver transition messages?

What are the transition messages that we need to get across?

The outcome of your work will be a high-level strategy to manage individual change through the use of the other change infrastructures. For example, use your training resources to deliver your key transition messages.

Shape your approach to communication

Effective programme communication is about communicating with the right people at the right time in order to secure their involvement and buy-in. It means understanding what is important to those who have an influence over the programme, and interacting with them in an engaging and effective way. Ask yourself the following questions:

Is there a need for immediate communication with and involvement of the wider organisation?

How can the initiative be positioned within the organisation in a compelling way?

What has worked/not worked before?

What are the key messages we need to get across?

Answering the above should give you an early view on the communications needs of your programme, enabling you to agree first principles and mobilise the appropriate resources to develop and execute the plan.

Communications – both internal and external – is a vital area of focus for any programme. For advice on how to build a programme communications capability, please refer to Chapter 14.

Shape your approach to a change agent network

Delivering on a programme vision often requires change (sometimes dramatic) at various levels in a business. Our work with clients shows that face-to-face communication, involvement and role modelling are vital in assisting people through change. In addition, most people tend to prefer face-to-face communication to more formal mechanisms.

But in large organisations today, it is not possible for leadership, or even the programme team, to reach everyone in this way. We also know that many people prefer communications to come from people they know, often those who work with them, rather than from a distant senior manager. So in some programmes, particularly those that are large scale, we need to create a local network of people to reach everyone and help them make the change. This is what we call a change agent network. The objectives and processes of these networks vary from company to company. Would your programme benefit from a change agent network? How would it work? Ask yourself the following questions:

Will the organisational transition require support from a change agent network?

Do infrastructures already exist in the organisation that can be utilised as a change agent network?

Are there other programmes and business initiatives that the change agent network should be integrated with?

Should the change agent network focus on those directly impacted by the organisational transition, or should it also include those indirectly impacted?

The outcome of this exercise will be an understanding of the need for a network, high-level principles for its operation, and potential resources. If you decide to go ahead with this network, then you will want to assign resources to its development.

Shape approach to training and leadership development

Training and development opportunities for both leaders and employees will play a crucial role in building the necessary capabilities for programme success. In our experience, every programme has required some form of training and development support

Training and development is often a time and resource-rich exercise. Before launching any training initiatives, think through the following:

Do the organisation's leaders require additional capability to support the organisation transition?

Will the organisation's transition best be supported by a formal training programme or utilising informal organisational learning?

What is the extent of training needed in terms of audiences impacted?

The key outputs here are areas of focus for capability building as well as an understanding of the extent of training and development required. You will want to mobilise resources as early as possible.

Shape approach to cultural change

Company culture is a key factor of programme and business success, but what do we mean by 'culture'? Basically, organisational culture describes 'the way things are done around here', including:

- the shared attitudes people have towards their work and the organisation
- the behaviours that are predominant and valued
- the quality of relationships (both internal and external)
- what constitutes success and how it is recognised.

Do the current behaviours and values of the organisation drive or hinder the changes you are trying to make? In our experience, every significant business change requires some form of behavioural or cultural change.

How would we describe a culture that would support the new vision and strategy?

What would this 'to be' culture look, feel and sound like?

How would we describe the 'as is' culture?

Are there any disjoints between the 'as is' and 'to be'?

Is cultural change needed? What interventions should we consider?

Cultural interventions can vary widely, but may include:

- articulating a new culture (including values and behaviours)
- delivering training to reinforce new behaviours
- updating performance management and reward systems to reward the new behaviours
- helping leadership to 'model' the new behaviours.

Key outputs include a high-level view of the gap between the 'as is' and 'to be' as well as opportunities to close that gap.

Shape approach to organisation design

Organisation design is a key method of implementing change. If departmental and team structures continue to reflect the 'old way' of working, then change is harder to embed. If employee role descriptions remain unchanged in the face of new processes, then change is again hard to secure. In practice, organisation design is a practical and tangible way of signalling and supporting change.

In general terms, organisation design is defined as:

- **Scope:** the processes and activities that each part of the business completes and is accountable for.
- **Structure:** the formal structures, boundaries, groupings and reporting relationships required across the business to deliver the above scope.
- **Roles and dependencies:** the resources required to deliver the scope and structure, including the purpose and dimensions of each role, and specific indicators of performance.

Before undertaking any detailed organisation design activities, consider the following:

What are the key structural implications of the change we are undertaking?

How are our competitors structured? Can we learn from them?

How are we currently structured?

Will our current structure meet our future needs?

If there is a need for organisation design, at what point in the programme must structures and roles be changed?

The outputs of this exercise include a view on what organisational design changes, if any, are required as well as the point at which they will be needed.

Shape approach to performance management and reward

Aligning the change process to performance management and reward is one of the fundamental principles of change architecture. If people are to change the way they work and behave, then these changes need to be aligned to the way they are measured and rewarded. This concept is relevant to all organisational levels, and can also be applied to external parties such as suppliers and partners.

Do people in our organisation understand what they are measured and rewarded on?

Are our current performance management and reward systems linked to key performance indicators?

If we could change the current systems, what would they look like?

What are the biggest hurdles we face with respect to performance management and reward?

The key outputs from this high-level analysis include an outline of the 'to be' performance and reward infrastructure, and an appreciation of the barriers faced.

Shape approach to human resource processes and policies

The human resource (HR) processes and policies will underpin the extent to which both the programme is successful and the proposed changes become 'business as usual' activities. HR processes and policies include resource planning, recruitment, induction, performance management and reward (as discussed above), retention and succession planning. Each of these processes must support achievement of the programme and business goals. Ask yourself:

What are the key HR processes and policies in our business?

How do these relate to business success?

To what extent do we think they are fulfilling their objectives?

Can we prioritise the redesign of those processes that will have the biggest impact?

The key outputs include a summary of the contribution of current HR processes and policies, and a view on which require redesign.

Phase 3: Embedding and reviewing the change

So far the focus has been on building and mobilising change activities that will support achievement of the programme goals. However, we also need to make sure that the change architecture continues to be aligned to the programme, and that these activities are actually having the right impact.

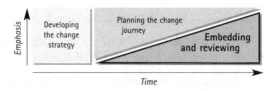

The focus for the 'embedding and reviewing the change' phase is therefore

Figure 7.7 Phase 3 of change architecture

to interpret evidence of the organisation's transition, and to ensure that the change initiatives planned are aligned with the changing state of the organisation. In addition, this phase concentrates on embedding changed behaviours, and transferring skills and knowledge to ensure long-term sustainable change.

Interpret indicators of organisational change

To establish if you on the right track, think through the following:

Is the organisation showing early signs of responsiveness to the change?

What evidence indicates that the organisation is changing in the desired direction?

Are people becoming more aware of the change and the reasons behind it?

Are people demonstrating new behaviours?

How is the value in the contribution model being realised?

Carefully examining these questions should result in:

* an understanding of the areas in your organisation in which people are successfully demonstrating new behaviours, and areas in which they are not

- an assessment of actual change against the planned change journey
- a sense of the actual pace of change at grassroots level
- An assessment of the contribution of your team.

This valuable information enables you to refine or redevelop aspects of your change architecture.

Review and evolve the focus of change resources

Re-examine the way you have allocated change resources. The programme itself will go through a number of changes through its lifecycle; your focus must reflect this. Ask yourself:

Where is most focus required now?

How do the change journey and focus need to be adjusted in response to indicators of organisational change?

As the organisation is evolving, what new change interventions are required to embed the change?

Are there any new change initiatives being undertaken which necessitate a change in our activities?

The outcome of this should be a continuously evolving change plan in response to changing programme and organisational needs. Remember that change is situational: changing your approach based on new circumstances can be a positive step, not a failure to deliver.

Build organisational capability to embed and sustain the changes

One of the objectives of this book is to help to build internal capabilities for use beyond the programme. This is essential not only to sustain the benefits of the current programme, but also to maximise returns from future initiatives. To build this capability, ask the following questions:

How do we ensure that capability required to realise the business benefits exists within the organisation?

What does successful handover look like?

Is the organisation in a position to sustain the newly designed processes and structures?

What requirements are there for ongoing change architecture support beyond the programme?

How do we build capability within the organisation to ensure future change initiatives benefit from the experience of this initiative?

The outputs should include:

- an agreed focus and approach to capability building
- agreed success factors for handover
- agreed handover plans and close-out documentation.

SUMMARY

Delivering a programme means changing your organisation in some way. We know that organisations are made up of people, so delivering a programme means helping people to change. However, helping people to change is not easy. Change is situational: no two programmes will have the same needs. No two people will respond to change in the same way.

The key to success is to take the time to develop and deliver the appropriate change architecture that will meet the specific needs of your programme:

1. **Develop the change strategy.** Understand the context and issues of your business and programme, including the organisation's readiness for change. Based on this assessment, select the appropriate people interventions.
2. **Plan the change journey.** Scope each intervention and develop a high-level view of what needs to happen, and when. Consider the interdependencies between the various interventions and with the overall programme plan.
3. **Embed and review the change.** Leverage opportunities to build capability and share programme learnings. Track indicators of change and make the appropriate adjustments to the change architecture to put the programme back on course. Be sensitive to changing programme priorities: ensure that the change architecture continues to be aligned.

In closing, change architecture is a simple process that guides you through the above activities, helping you to identify and manage your specific people challenges. This not only enables programme success in the short term, but also creates future organisational agility to deal with, and prosper in, changing circumstances.

8 Developing an enterprise-wide approach to programme and project management

The T-Mobile story in this chapter describes how the company has developed its own specific and successful approach to enterprise programme management, which suits its business challenges and environment. The case also illustrates the practical and integrated application of many of the ideas contained in Chapters 3 to 7, and acts as a real-life summary of the first section of this book.

T-MOBILE UK: CASE STUDY

Background

T-Mobile UK is part of one of the largest mobile communications companies in the world, and has more than 12 million mobile subscribers. It is the UK network of T-Mobile International, the mobile telecommunications subsidiary of Deutsche Telekom. Deutsche Telekom's subsidiaries and affiliated companies currently serve more than 86 million mobile customers worldwide. T-Mobile's UK network covers over 99 per cent of the UK population, and its customers make around 260 million calls every week.

T-Mobile UK's business has grown rapidly in a dynamic and evolving market over the last ten years. Over this period, the huge scale and pace of change and growth in the telecommunications market have demanded great agility from telecommunications operators. This has resulted in the need to deliver new business initiatives and products, serving new customers and building a strong business infrastructure to support this growth. Maintaining a strong focus on delivering value from strategic investments has been critical to achieving business success in the sector.

This case provides an insight into how T-Mobile UK has succeeded in building an enterprise-wide investment and programme management capability that is integral to the development of their business. The approach has enabled the organisation to maintain the critical focus and control required to create value from investments in a multinational business environment.

We initially describe the story of how T-Mobile UK evolved and developed this capability over the five years to 2003, and how it currently manages a portfolio of strategic investment projects through an enterprise-wide approach. We also highlight the relevant examples of good practice from T-Mobile UK to illustrate the practical application of the framework.

The T-Mobile UK Story

In 1998 One 2 One (as T-Mobile UK was then known) behaved as a start-up business, managing initiatives to develop the business with speed and agility but with very few formal controls. This approach served the business well in the early days when the market was developing so quickly that achieving rapid customer growth was the main goal. Most of the change initiatives arose from sales and marketing activities, creating as many problems as they solved because of the lack of structured implementation. Asher Rickayzen, T-Mobile's Director of Programme Development and Management, described it as 'an anarchic situation that we were trying to get on top of'.

T-Mobile UK's first step was to create a Commercial Planning function to start prioritising marketing initiatives into a programme, and to provide full visibility of the marketing plan to the rest of the business. A project review board was established to prioritise projects, using the strategic context and resourcing requirements. Projects were evaluated serially in a chronological, piecemeal fashion, with a limited amount of attention paid to the financial consequences of a proposal.

The next transition involved leadership changes at the top of the organisation following the purchase by Deutsche Telekom. The new leadership team recognised the need for better company-wide control of initiatives, broadening the scale of the Commercial Planning function to make it a business-wide role. The expanded scope involved prioritisation of initiatives from across the entire business, including those originating from Finance and Customer Services.

With greater visibility of the organisational impact of all current and proposed projects, it became clear to the leadership that T-Mobile UK was trying to carry out too many initiatives. In response to this, the leadership instigated two events that signalled its seriousness about managing strategic change and focusing resources: the head of the Commercial Planning function was appointed a director of T-Mobile UK, and the number of projects that were underway was radically reduced by 75 per cent through a two-day review by the top leadership.

Other factors also played a role in creating the momentum for the development of enterprise programme management. Among these was an organisation-wide enterprise resource planning (ERP) implementation which forced T-Mobile UK to examine closely its business processes for the management of funds, with the objective of increasing investment control. This indirectly gave rise to a process supported by systems to measure and track the allocation of funds.

External factors were also important. The collapse of the value of the telecommunications sector in 2001, brought about by the over-optimistic demand forecasts for wireless communications and the ensuing scarcity of capital, encouraged a more rigorous approach to understanding the value delivered from investments in programmes and projects. Through establishing a more formalised and consistent approach to financial business cases, a tighter link was developed between the financial investment process, and programme and project management activities.

Finally an internal business review, aimed at rationalising and streamlining the way T-Mobile UK's business was organised, resulted in all its project management and project office resources being consolidated into a single function called Programme Development and Management (PDM).

These various events and developments contributed to T-Mobile UK's current approach of supporting its business investment and development through an enterprise PDM function responsible for managing project management resources and key process experts, together with facilitating the investment decision-making process.

T-Mobile UK's journey towards developing an enterprise programme management capability evolved through a combination of needs and catalysts. The business requirement to focus and control strategic investments, the need to respond to a crisis in the market, and the implementation of operational and system improvements, all created the desire for better control and management of their initiatives. Strong leadership support from the Chief Executive Officer (CEO) and Chief Finance Officer (CFO), clear demonstration of leadership's determination through the discontinuation of non-priority projects and empowerment of the programme management function, by creating representation and leadership at director level, were the nurturing drivers that enabled the development of T-Mobile UK's enterprise programme management capability.

T-Mobile UK's approach to enterprise programme management

T-Mobile UK's approach is built around three fundamental principles, 'Choosing the right things', 'Doing them right' and 'Achieving the benefits', and these are supported by the appropriate organisational processes, systems and structures. Figure 8.1 illustrates the three elements and their relationship with one another.

The investment management process is focused on the decisions of senior executives to select projects that will create most value for T-Mobile UK: 'doing the right things'. The project management process is focused on developing and executing a consistent and effective approach to delivering projects, supporting all projects with professional project managers and utilising a consistent project management process: 'doing things right'. The third element of the approach is project ownership, which ensures clear business ownership for projects and the delivery of business benefits. This involves developing the necessary leadership skills and capabilities to own projects, and change management skills to deliver business changes: 'achieving the benefits'.

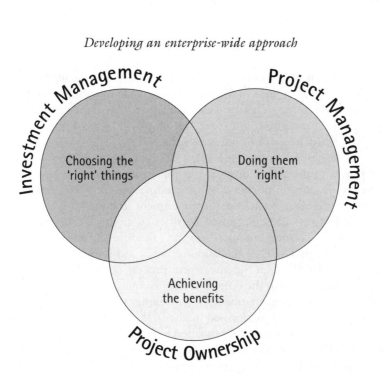

Figure 8.1 The three elements of T-Mobile UK's approach to enterprise programme management

Investment management process

The organisation has a central fund available for investments in new business initiatives. All project proposals require a business case that is presented in a standard format. The business case is developed by both the business owner and an independent specialised team of 'business case consultants' who sit within the finance function.

Business cases are clearly linked to the business strategy, as they have to demonstrate the way they will impact critical business key performance indicators (KPIs). These cases are reviewed and approved by a Senior Investment Board comprising key senior executives of the organisation. This includes the CEO, CFO, Chief Technology Officer, Commercial Director and PDM Director, thereby ensuring that the project will be assessed from a number of dimensions.

Beneath the Senior Investment Board are a number of sub-investment boards which review investments that are focused in one area of the business. For example, the Network Investment Board deals with initiatives related to their communications network. These boards have delegated power from the Senior Investment Board, and also function as filters for the more complex, cross-functional programmes or projects that need final approval from the highest level.

The board that approves the project business case will usually be the same board that reviews progress of the project, tracks the investments and reviews the benefits delivered. This provides consistency in decision-making and accountability throughout the lifecycle of the project, from investment through to the delivery of business benefits.

Another key aspect of the T-Mobile UK's investment process is its strong integration with the annual business planning process. Once a year, the business reviews its current portfolio of programmes and projects, and identifies additional initiatives, including the investment required to achieve their strategic objectives. These proposed activities are built into the yearly investment budget and resourcing plans, but their funding and resource allocation are not signed off. The final allocation of funds and resources to commence is only authorised through the investment process outlined above.

In order to ensure that the output of this planning is a selective set of initiatives focused on the organisation's strategy, rather than a 'wish list', up to 80 per cent of the process is performed by the PDM and Finance functions. It is also the responsibility of the PDM function to ensure that all these planned and budgeted initiatives are developed into project proposals and assessed by an investment board. Projects that are authorised for implementation are allocated project resources and a programme or project manager by the PDM function through joint consultation with line resource managers.

Where possible, T-Mobile UK schedules its project portfolio so that not all activities are happening at the same time. However, for extenuating reasons such as competitive pressures, there are occasions whereby the business has to execute more projects than is viably sensible. In these cases, T-Mobile UK attempts to mitigate the additional risks by strengthening management controls and increasing the focus on change management processes.

Corporate project process

At T-Mobile UK, the investment process is strongly linked to the corporate project process, as you can see from the first two steps through the development of the business case (Figure 8.2). Once the project has been approved and funds allocated, the project becomes part of the portfolio of projects that are reviewed and reported as part of the portfolio management process.

Progress, issues and risks for all projects in the portfolio are tracked by a Corporate Project Office. These are reported to the relevant investment boards, which meet fortnightly to review proposals and the status of investments. An overall portfolio report is produced to illustrate the progress of the projects, drawing attention to key issues, such as risks arising from interdependencies between projects.

A Programme Board also meets to review the management of the portfolio on a more regular basis than the investment boards. The Programme Board is made up of a cross-functional team of senior programme stakeholders,

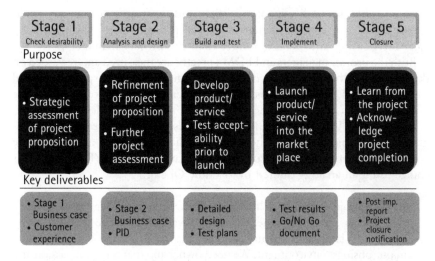

Figure 8.2 T-Mobile UK: the corporate project process

again of a diverse make-up, allowing the portfolio of projects to be reviewed from different perspectives.

Although the corporate project process has now been established in the organisation for some time, it is recognised that there is an ongoing need to challenge, strengthen and enhance control of project execution. These needs are met through a continuous improvement routine based on full documentation of procedures and standards, updating of documentation as the processes evolve, and proactive communication to all parties involved in project execution. Training courses have also been created to familiarise programme and project managers with the approach.

T-Mobile UK's current initiatives are mostly organised into projects, with programmes set up as and when the need arises to manage larger, more complex and interdependent projects. One major programme that T-Mobile UK recently undertook was its rebranding from One 2 One to T-Mobile in 2002. This was managed as a single programme of multiple, interrelated projects. The whole programme was reviewed and approved by the investment board but projects within the programme were still individually assessed as and when they occurred.

Leading and supporting delivery: creating clarity, defining roles and developing skills

Most of the key groups involved in the management of the portfolio (investment boards, Programme Board, Corporate Project Office) have been described above. Each project in T-Mobile UK also has its own governance, and is typically organised to have a project owner who is responsible for delivery of benefits, and a project manager who is responsible for the implementation of the project. The project owner's role starts earlier and persists longer than the project manager's.

Both the project managers and PDM Director are measured and rewarded on the basis of whether projects are delivered on time, within the expected cost and with the desired quality. It is the project owner's responsibility to deliver the business benefits from the business changes the projects have delivered.

In T-Mobile UK, there is a lot of emphasis placed on the role of a programme or project owner. Choosing to deliberately steer away from the common title of project sponsor, Asher Rickayzen explains T-Mobile UK's choice using an analogy quoted from Eddie Obeng:

> Being a project sponsor is like being the Queen: you turn up to launch a ship, smash the champagne, wave goodbye and welcome it back to port six months later. This attitude is totally inappropriate for leading projects in our business environment. We need ownership that is one of passion and continual involvement in order to drive maximum realisation of benefits out of the project.

T-Mobile UK therefore fills the role with a manager who is senior enough in the business to be effective in ensuring the delivery of the benefits, and to manage the integration of the project outputs into normal business operations.

The project manager is appointed from a central pool of trained project managers, and is responsible for the quality and timely delivery of the project within the budget. Project managers are all trained in a project management approach developed internally by T-Mobile UK, which draws some of the key concepts and best practice methods from PRINCE2.

A common risk for project managers is that they take on additional tasks, as a result of insufficient resources, which are actually line rather than project responsibility. Clarity of the roles of project managers, project owners and business managers is hence critical to the business. Training these project owners and managers with the skills to perform these roles is therefore key. Much of the training at T-Mobile UK focuses on leadership and 'softer' management skills such as stakeholder management, coaching skills, and influencing and negotiation skills.

T-Mobile UK has started to invest heavily in activities that enable those involved in managing change programmes and projects to be equipped with the necessary 'people' skills to support their project teams' delivery, as well as to overcome organisational resistance to change. During the large-scale ERP implementation, the importance of investing in the skills to support people through business change was vital to the organisation embracing the new system. Initially, T-Mobile UK relied on external professional support in this area. Since then, the business has set up a team of dedicated change management specialists within its Human Resource department, who have developed an approach and toolkit to support change management. These trained change agents are deployed onto projects where there are major change requirements or implications. They also train project managers in the change management skills.

The PDM function includes a resource pool of process experts. These experts in specific business process areas are also deployed onto projects to act as architects and catalysts to help improve core business processes.

Supporting systems

With the building blocks of its enterprise programme management capability in place, T-Mobile UK is now looking to improve the efficiency and quality of its project management processes by implementing a programme management system. It is its intention that basic project processes such as planning, scheduling, resourcing, issue and risk management are not only automated, but also tied into its ERP financial applications. The objective is to have a common platform of interaction between activity-level project control and financial information. The programme management system will enable company-wide portfolio reporting and management information, strengthening integration of the investment management and project process – one of the key objectives of the T-Mobile UK approach. Currently, the ERP system is the main tool for the financial management process of managing allocation and tracking project spending.

The future for T-Mobile UK's enterprise-wide programme management approach

T-Mobile UK has developed a robust programme management approach but still acknowledges that it has some way to go to develop its programme management capability to its full potential. The business will continue to invest in building the skills and capabilities of project and programme managers, and in its change management capabilities. There is still more work to be done in the area of benefits management, to create better visibility of the business benefits delivered. T-Mobile UK also believes that automation of the processes through the implementation of supporting systems will create a much clearer view of its capacity for future change in the business. Finally, the biggest challenge ahead for T-Mobile is to implement an effective enterprise programme management approach in its pan-European business environment, to promote the efficient use of funds and resources at both a national and international level. This will involve flexing the model that currently operates in its UK business; however, the principles of clear decision-making, control of resources and ensuring a return on investment will undoubtedly remain.

SUMMARY

Circumstances highlighted the organisation's need for an enterprise programme management approach, but identification of the issue was only the beginning of its journey. We have seen T-Mobile UK's model transform from what used to be an approach foisted on the business in its early days to being the de facto approach the business now embraces to initiate or manage business change. The business has seen and acknowledged these processes to be the easiest, most effective and objective way of approving and delivering change in the business.

What was and still is key to T-Mobile UK's success in implementing such an organisation-wide approach and obtaining buy-in is not strangling the business with bureaucracy and controls, but instead, providing support for processes that enable the delivery of business change more quickly and with greater benefit. This has been made possible through strong leadership understanding, and support for development of programme management capability as an effective means to control and focus investment and deliver business value.

T-Mobile UK has grasped an excellent understanding of the need to develop processes, structures, systems and personal skills to enhance its organisational ability to deliver change and value as the company grew into a multinational business. The challenge to improve and maintain its programme management capability still continues.

Asher Rickayzen sums up what T-Mobile UK is constantly trying to achieve:

> The objective of what we are trying to do is very, very simple. It is to create an environment where the whole organisation understands the change we are trying to implement, understands the value of that change, ensures that we have the capacity and ability to deliver the change, and understands (after the change has been implemented) that the expected benefits have materialised.

It is important to remember that the T-Mobile story is one of evolution and development of an approach specific to its own business requirements. The development of enterprise programme management in any organisation will take time, and will need to be contextual and sympathetic to the nature of the organisation and its environment.

Part II

Enterprise programme management essentials

9   Introduction

In this section, 'Enterprise programme management essentials', we have
selected a number of topics for further discussion. The subjects we have chosen
for inclusion in this section are either key capabilities that are fundamental to
developing an enterprise programme management approach, such as risk
management, benefits management, resourcing strategies, and supplier
management and communications, or areas of new interest and increasing
importance in supporting an enterprise programme management approach,
such as programme management systems and the enterprise programme
management office.

The topics covered in Chapters 10 to 15 are summarised here.

Chapter 10: Programme management systems

Systems to enable enterprise programme management go far beyond the
capability of typical desktop project management tools, and can add radically
more value to the organisation as a whole. (Payback on systems support for
programme management can be very rapid.) This chapter explores the specific functionality required to unlock that value in a variety of programme
management situations, and provides practical lessons in implementation. It
includes: a definition of programme management systems; the functionality
that programme management systems must provide to be effective; the business case for investment in programme management systems; systems
selection and implementation considerations; the interaction between programme management systems and programme architecture and processes;
and example application mappings for typical programme management situations. Compaq Computer Corporation's successful use of programme
management systems is described as a case study.

Chapter 11: Managing programme risk

This chapter looks at some of the key challenges faced when managing risk
across programmes, and identifies effective ways of rising to the challenge.
Through discussion of appropriate techniques for identifying, assessing,
communicating and managing risk, some developed from project disciplines,
some unique to programmes, you will see what approaches are suitable for

97

you. A case study provides a real example of what has worked for a successful organisation managing a successful programme. The experiences of delivering London's Congestion Charging provide a framework for dealing with large, complex, time-critical and highly political programmes that have interrelated social, economic, environmental, political, financial and technological constraints. If these risk factors had not been managed proactively and pragmatically, it is unlikely the programme would have been successful.

Chapter 12: Benefits management

Many business change programmes fail to deliver the benefits on which their business case and investment was originally justified. The Office of Government Commerce estimate that 30–40 per cent of projects to support business change deliver no benefits whatsoever. The ongoing costs and risks will usually be monitored, but the anticipated benefits are not so easy to define and quantify. Benefits management, within the enterprise programme management context, tries to ensure that business change achieves valuable results by translating business objectives into identifiable, measurable benefits and systematically tracking and communicating the results.

Benefits management is the activity of identifying, realising and tracking the expected benefits from business change to ensure that they are achieved, and of identifying and minimising the negative impact of change.

This chapter focuses on the continual process of planning, identifying, structuring, tracking and evaluating benefits.

Chapter 13: Managing suppliers

It is one thing delivering programmes involving multiple internal organisations, with the usual conflicting priorities, organisational boundaries, internal politics and previous histories. When it comes to working with external providers, particularly multiple external service providers, in a business change programme with tight commercial and delivery demands, there are a huge number of new challenges for the programme team to understand and manage. These challenges arise from differences in style, cultural, contractual and commercial pressures, as well as more familiar problems such as coordination and issue resolution.

In this chapter, we consider the practical approaches that programme leaders should adopt when delivering complex, integrated and technology-heavy programmes. We consider the pressures and approaches when working with multiple internal and external service providers working together to deliver an integrated IT solution within an overall programme that also includes new business processes, and organisation and commercial/legal arrangements to achieve a business imperative. We follow through a recently completed programme that involved many internal and external service providers to deliver a new online internet business for an existing global travel and leisure company, MyTravel plc.

Chapter 14: Building a communications capability

Effective programme communications are about communicating with the right people at the right time in order to secure their involvement and buy-in (whether they are employees being impacted or senior managers who will need to make key decisions). It means understanding what is important to those who have an influence over the programme, and interacting with them in an engaging and effective way. It means establishing communication mechanisms that are relevant to the programme, rather than just using 'business as usual' techniques (which are made for 'business as usual' situations, rather than complex cross-organisational changes).

Importantly, programme communications is not just about sending the right messages: it's also about tapping into ideas and expertise that exist outside the programme team, then using this feedback to improve the programme.

Overall, we believe that the ability to communicate with your organisation as you implement programmes is an essential capability in today's market. Developing and using this capability will not only help you achieve the goals of your programmes, but will also help you deliver long-lasting and sustainable change within your business. In addition, a communications capability is just one characteristic of high-performance programme teams – teams that can act as a competitive edge for your business, as discussed in earlier chapters. The objective of this chapter is to help you build this capability by laying the foundations for a robust communications strategy and plans.

The approach is illustrated by a case study on a major change initiative at TUI UK (formally Thompson Travel Group).

Chapter 15: The enterprise programme management office (EPMO)

This chapter integrates many of the ideas introduced in this book and examines the role, benefit and value of an enterprise-wide programme management office in providing, maintaining and developing an organisation's programme management capability and infrastructure. In using the term EPMO we are referring to an enterprise programme management function and capability. This deliberately goes beyond the traditionally accepted definition of a programme management office (PMO). The case study on ABN-AMRO, one of the world's largest banks, illustrates the new role of a more strategic and enterprise-wide programme management office.

10 Programme management systems

INTRODUCTION

Almost everything in a modern organisation is automated, yet the activities that can contribute most to an organisation's success, strategic programmes, are frequently run with little or no specific systems support. Organisations that embrace the need for enterprise programme management must implement the necessary systems to support and drive the development of that capability.

Programme management systems can provide assistance to:

- ensure alignment of activities across multiple projects
- optimise the use of resources
- communicate with and involve people, both within and outside the programme
- drive the achievement of strategic objectives, and the delivery of benefits.

Systems to enable enterprise programme management go far beyond the capability of typical desktop project management tools, and can add radically more value to the organisation as a whole. (Payback on systems support for programme management can be very rapid.) This chapter explores the specific functionality required to unlock that value in a variety of programme management situations, and practical lessons in implementation.

This chapter includes details relating to:

- a definition of programme management systems
- the functionality that programme management systems must provide to be effective
- the business case for investment in programme management systems
- systems selection and implementation considerations
- the interaction between programme management systems and programme architecture and processes
- example application mappings for typical programme management situations
- case studies to illustrate the successful use of programme management systems.

This chapter does not include a specific analysis of any of the currently-available software packages, beyond references to packages within the case studies. The software solutions for programme management are developing rapidly, and any specific analysis would likely be out of date before publication. In addition, any specific analysis would not address organisations' requirements in their own context, and thus could be misleading.

WHAT ARE PROGRAMME MANAGEMENT SYSTEMS?

Programme management systems are those applications that enable the delivery of interrelated projects with common goals. They:

- assist in the coordination of resources, timescales and scope across project teams
- facilitate the effective deployment and sharing of skills and knowledge across the programme
- track and manage issues, risks, delivery of benefits and alignment to programme objectives
- provide executive management with a 'dashboard' on programme progress
- provide programme management with the information and levers that they need to effectively manage programmes.

Programme management systems are often thought of as multi-user project management systems with enhanced resource management, and this is where many current solutions originated. However, to effectively deliver the above objectives within and across organisations, the scope of programme management systems must extend beyond this into areas such as workflow/collaboration, knowledge management and management reporting. In addition, to work effectively within an enterprise, programme management systems must be integrated with the other applications used to run the business.

WHAT DO PROGRAMME MANAGEMENT SYSTEMS DO?

Although programmes vary greatly in scale, complexity, cost and goals, the systems requirements of programmes are typically very similar (as with the processes and organisation structures to run effective programmes). The systems requirements of a programme are typically delivered by several applications: a combination of specialist packages and a business's existing applications.

Figure 10.1 and Table 10.1 describe a logical architecture for programme and project management systems, illustrating the building blocks of functionality that are required, and how they interrelate.

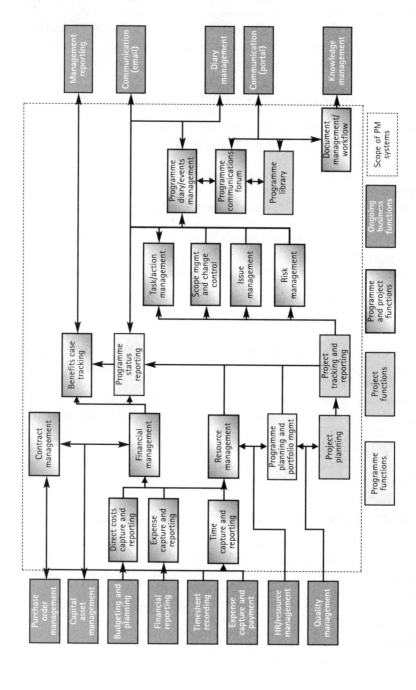

Figure 10.1 Logical architecture for programme management systems

Table 10.1 Explanation of the logical components

Logical component	Description
Project planning	Planning of projects by a project manager, incorporating task scheduling, dependency management and budgeting. Also includes ability to use template plans and estimating guidelines.
Project tracking and reporting	Monitoring of progress against plan by a project manager, including analysis of critical path progress.
Document management workflow	A solution to provide version control of documents and manage approval routes.
Programme planning and portfolio management	The ability to coordinate multiple projects with interdependencies, using the same resource pool. This includes both schedule and financial aspects of portfolio management.
Task and action management	The ability to assign and receive progress updates on tasks within aproject.
Scope management and change control	Controlling key project scope definition documents, and managing approval of any plan or budget changes arising.
Issue management	The allocation of responsibility for solving issues, and maintenance of an audit trail of issue progress.
Risk management	The identification and quantification of risks, assignment of a risk strategy and assessment of the impact of risks on the overall programme.
Diary/events management	The management of project meetings and calendars to provide effective coordination across the programme.
Communications forum	A programme 'workspace' where project resources can access key project documents, receive up-to-date information and discuss ideas.
Project/programme library	A document repository for key templates and standards, and also storage of controlled copies of final deliverables, key contract documentation etc.
Direct costs capture and reporting	The capture of all costs coming in via purchase orders/invoices from third parties.
Expense capture and reporting	The capture of out-of-pocket expenses incurred by project and programme personnel.
Time capture and reporting	The capture of hours worked by project and programme personnel, and reporting of this against budgets and to calculate project/ programme progress.
Contract management	The linking of contract requirements to milestones in the project plan (this is much smaller than the complete scope of contract management).

Table 10.1 continued

Logical component	Description
Financial management	The financial monitoring of the programme, including budgetary management, committed spend reporting, cashflow analysis and reporting for corporate requirements.
Resource management	The ability to assign resources to a project, manage pools of resource and allow operational managers to track their reports' commitments.
Benefits case tracking	The tracking of project outcomes against initial project objectives.
Programme status reporting	The reporting of project progress on schedule and financial bases to all stakeholders.

The role of existing business applications

Existing business applications (those used to manage the ongoing business) also have a key role to play in delivering an effective programme management systems solution.

To the left-hand side of Figure 10.1 are the elements of functionality typically delivered by financial or ERP applications, and the control processes that surround those. These are typically interfaced to programme management systems to provide a source of data, and may also take information back for reporting purposes. The benefits of relying on existing applications for this functionality include:

- the ability to rely on existing control processes in areas like procurement
- no need to implement additional processes which may be at odds with those already in existence
- integrity controls which should already be in place for financial data in existing systems.

To the right-hand side of Figure 10.1 are the existing collaboration and management tools that can assist programmes. Adopting existing systems and processes in these areas (where they have the required capability) can speed adoption of new processes due to user familiarity with existing systems, and ensure knowledge acquired during the programme will be available to the business after the programme has concluded.

One specific area where existing systems often do not have the required capabilities is knowledge management. Leading programme management solutions offer this functionality, with extended capability in the areas of most relevance to programme effectiveness: for example, methodology managers to capture project lessons and reuse these in future project plans.

Key characteristics of programme management systems

In addition to the specific elements of functionality considered above, there are certain characteristics that all effective programme management systems must possess:

- **Ease of use.** Programme management systems must be intuitive to all users (for at least their basic day-to-day requirements). For many people interacting with a programme, the activities of the programme are not part of their regular job. Even with good training, occasional users soon forget what they have learnt. Effective solutions usually provide a role-specific user interface that simplifies the functionality that the user sees, supported by online help.
- **Accessibility.** Programmes are typically distributed across locations, many of which may not be office-based. Solutions must cater for multi-user access by programme resources to the systems they need, ideally allowing for both online and offline working.
- **Single source of reliable data.** One of the major benefits of programme management systems is the access of all resources to a 'single version of the truth'. This is true for programme plans, programme metrics (progress, cost and so on) and key documents (scope, organisation charts and the like). This requires strong control over the integrity of data coming into the programme management system, and also good version control for documents and reports.

HOW DO PROGRAMME MANAGEMENT SYSTEMS ADD VALUE?

There are many ways in which investment in programme management systems can be justified. The major benefit drivers for programme management systems fall into three key areas:

- Reduction in programme risk (this is often phrased as 'improvement in business control', but a quantification of the reduction in risk/exposure is necessary to ascribe this a financial value).
- Increased efficiency of programme resources (this is a key benefit but is very difficult to quantify reliably).
- Reduction in programme administration overhead (the value of this benefit is often significantly less than the benefits above, but this can be the easiest benefit to quantify in monetary terms if it results in a straight headcount saving).

These major benefit drivers are considered in more detail below.

105

Additionally, there is often a need to define or justify the complete scope of a programme management systems solution, and the extent of integration with existing business systems. The business case drivers for each logical component of functionality are considered.

Finally, there is often a need to justify the requirement for integration to existing systems, as this can be costly. In many ways, integration is an enabler of the other benefits, rather than a driver of benefits in itself. This is also considered.

Reducing risk

Major strategic programmes can be a 'bet the company issue' – in terms of size of investment, competitiveness, and impact of issues on continuing operations. In these cases risk typically only needs to reduce by a few percentage points to justify the additional expenditure.

There are a number of key risks areas where the effect of programme management systems can be quantified. These typically occur at different stages of the programme:

1. **Procurement risk.** This occurs early on in the programme, where the main contractual costs are committed, and relates to obtaining best value for money from vendors who will deliver reliably. Fraud risk on major contracts is included in this risk area.
2. **Budgetary risk.** This occurs throughout the programme, and relates to the control of spend that is not committed in the upfront procurement. Fraud risk on ongoing expenditure is included in this risk area.
3. **Delivery risk.** This also occurs throughout the programme, and relates to the ongoing progress and coordination of projects within the programme.
4. **Scope risk.** The scope of the programme must be controlled carefully to ensure resources remain focused on the key deliverables, and to minimise the complexity and interdependencies.
5. **Transition risk.** This occurs towards the end of the programme, and relates to the effective transition to a post-programme environment with minimal disruption to ongoing operations. This risk is closely linked to delivery risk, but the programme management tasks become more complicated and business-critical as many of the component projects of the programme conclude concurrently, and hard deadlines for transition are set.

To quantify the benefit of risk reduction arising from the implementation of programme management systems, it is easiest to quantify the amounts at stake for each of the above risks, and quantify the anticipated potential reduction in risk by surveying the stakeholder group. (Mathematical quantification methods are more objective, but the data to perform calculations can be very difficult to source.)

Improving efficiency

Efficiency benefits that apply to all programme resources arise in a number of ways:

- Increasing the overall utilisation and focus of available resources. This arises from visibility of the projects that each resource is assigned to, and being able to view their actual allocation of hours. Under-utilised resources can be given greater workload, over-utilised resources can be relieved before burn-out, and any inappropriate focus on lower-priority activities can be corrected.
- Improving the deployment of appropriate skills: maintenance of skills databases, and scheduling of resources on the basis of skill-set, can increase overall efficiency.
- Improving planning and estimating efficiency and accuracy: many programme management systems include the capability to capture learnings from previous projects, and the ability to use previous projects and standard plan formats as planning and estimating templates. This reduces the time spent in planning and estimation, and increases overall plan accuracy. Across a programme with many interdependencies, the ability to plan each project accurately has a major influence on the ability to optimise the critical path and thus minimise the time and cost required to deliver strategic goals.
- Improving reuse of knowledge and deliverables.
- Improving efficiency of communication.

Streamlining administration

The key areas of programme administration where systems can help to increase efficiency are:

- **Reporting.** Complex programmes have many stakeholders and communities of interest, all of whom have their own specific reporting requirements. Compilation of these reports from multiple data sources can be a major source of administrative overhead. Also, manual compilation typically results in reporting delays, reducing the value of information, and also errors and lack of trust in the data. A systems architecture that delivers a 'single version of the truth', and enables report production, can eliminate the overhead while also improving the timeliness and quality of reports.

- **Scheduling.** Assigning resources to projects and tasks, and sourcing resources to meet forward estimates of workload, can be a significant management and administrative overhead. Systems can greatly improve the efficiency and effectiveness of scheduling.
- **Planning.** Systems can put more power in the hands of project managers for the preparation of plans and tracking of cross-project dependencies, reducing the need for dedicated planning resources. Correctly configured systems can also ensure that control over over-all programme timescales is maintained in a distributed planning environment.

Table 10.2 explores the business case drivers for each logical component.

Table 10.2 Business case drivers for each logical component

Logical component	Business case drivers
Project planning	*Reducing risk and streamlining administration.* Planning across the programme in a controlled, consistent manner, incorporating all dependencies and adopting estimating guidelines.
Project tracking and reporting	*Reducing risk and streamlining administration.* Project managers can only work with the information available to them. Also, if tracking is not up to date, programme milestones and dependencies cannot be monitored with any level of certainty.
Document management workflow	*Increasing efficiency and streamlining administration.* Document management, including version control, check-in/check-out and audit trail on updates, is key if several parties are working on the same document. This supports scope control and effective communication across the programme.
Programme planning and portfolio management	*Reducing risk and increasing efficiency.* Effectively monitoring the delivery of the programme, and ensuring that resources are optimally deployed and focused.
Task and action management	*Reducing risk and increasing efficiency.* Many resources will be involved, with many streams of activity, especially at the critical transition time. Having clear allocation of responsibilities, and a definitive picture of progress, is critical to the successful programme delivery.

Table 10.2 continued

Logical component	Business case drivers
Scope management and change control	*Reducing risk.* Any changes to budgeted spend should be tightly controlled. Also, any proposed schedule slippages will have knock-on effects across the programme, as will scope creep.
Issue management	*Reducing risk.* Systemising issue management increases visibility and management control.
Risk management	*Reducing risk.* Research has shown that effective risk management increases the predictability of programme outcomes by a significant amount. A 15 per cent increase in predictability in relation to a major programme can have a very large financial impact.
Diary/events management	*Increasing efficiency and streamlining administration.* Ensuring that people know what is happening when increases efficiency in itself, and the general feeling of organisation that a well-managed programme diary creates will bring additional productivity gains through focus of resources.
Communications forum	*Increasing efficiency.* This can make the process of induction and multi-site working much easier and make project resources feel more involved even if they only play a small part in the overall programme.
Project/programme library	*Reducing risk and increasing efficiency.* Storage of lessons learnt and programme standards enables the programme to estimate, plan, communicate and work more effectively; while having a central repository of key documents allows resources to easily find the information they need.
Direct costs capture and reporting	*Reducing risk and increasing efficiency.* Keeping control of external costs requires a tightly controlled purchasing process aligned with the project structure.
Expense capture and reporting	*Reducing risk and increasing efficiency.* Keeping control of expenses requires a tightly controlled process. Expense processing can also be a major administrative headache.
Time capture and reporting	*Reducing risk, increasing efficiency and streamlining administration.* For certain types of resource, the hours of effort give an indication of progress and overrun. Accurate time data allows management to ensure that employees are spending their time on the high-priority areas. Also, a manual timesheet process can be a significant administrative overhead.

Table 10.2 continued

Logical component	Business case drivers
Contract management	*Reducing risk.* Allows project managers to easily reference the contractual terms of delivery from contractors. Can also be used to link payment milestones to the completion of plan milestones.
Financial management	*Reducing risk.* This is essential for financial control and compliance with with external requirements (corporate reporting, audit, etc.).
Resource management	*Increasing efficiency and streamlining administration.* For certain types of resource, this capability can greatly improve efficiency and focus on important things. This capability also enables the business to identify forthcoming skills gaps in sufficient time to resolve them.
Benefits case tracking	*Reducing risk.* Monitoring the out-turn of the project against its expected benefits greatly increases the likelihood that the expected benefits will be delivered.
Programme status reporting	*Reducing risk and streamlining administration.* Enabling programme and executive management to take the right decisions in a timely manner, and ensuring that project managers and administrative resources are not excessively burdened with reporting requirements.

Business case drivers for integration with existing systems

The key value drivers associated with the integration of programme management systems with existing business systems include:

- Maintenance of a reliable 'single source of the truth' over a period of time. This does not release value in itself, but it is difficult to realise the reporting benefits listed above (reduction in reporting administration, reduction in manual information gathering) if the data is not integrated reliably.
- Elimination of 'dual-keying'. Data should be entered only once (wherever makes most sense) and then used everywhere it is needed. Systems integration enables this, and the benefits are increased data integrity (due to reduced opportunity for manual error) and savings in programme personnel.

SELECTING PROGRAMME MANAGEMENT SYSTEMS

Selection criteria

Many criteria must be applied in the selection of programme management systems. Meeting functional requirements is important, but other factors

110

such as ease of adoption and fit into existing technology can be equally important, particularly for programmes within and across existing enterprises. The key selection criteria, and how they interrelate, are described in Figure 10.2.

Selection process

Critical success factors for selecting programme management systems are:

- **Develop a balanced scorecard for selection.** This should incorporate the functional and non-functional factors outlined in Figure 10.2, along with a weighting of their relative importance.
- **Consider sets of solutions, not just single packages.** A complete programme management solution will typically incorporate several applications, including those already in use within an organisation. Consider alternative combinations of applications, and the relative ranking of these, to get the best total solution.
- **Ensure executive sponsorship from early on in the selection process.** Senior management should view programme management systems as their 'eyes and ears' in tracking the progress of programmes and the delivery of strategic goals. It is therefore essential that they are involved right from the start, so they have ownership and trust in the selected solutions.
- **Ensure involvement of key influencers across the business early on in the selection process.** Gaining adoption of programme management systems is always a major challenge. By gaining cross-business involvement from the start, and carefully choosing who to involve in the selection process, subsequent implementation activities can be made much easier.
- **Always progress the selection process to its conclusion** through demonstration and pilot stages, even if the best solution appears clear from initial functional rankings. The demonstration and pilot stages are key both to ensuring full buy-in and commitment from the user community and senior stakeholders, and also for learning about the selected applications and how they can best work together prior to committing to a full roll-out. A little extra time spent on these stages will repay time and cost in the full roll-out.

IMPLEMENTING PROGRAMME MANAGEMENT SYSTEMS

The major challenges in implementing programme management systems are rarely technical: most issues relate to acceptance of systems by users, and getting a consistent quality of data input. There is also an additional challenge if the systems are being implemented at the onset of a major programme,

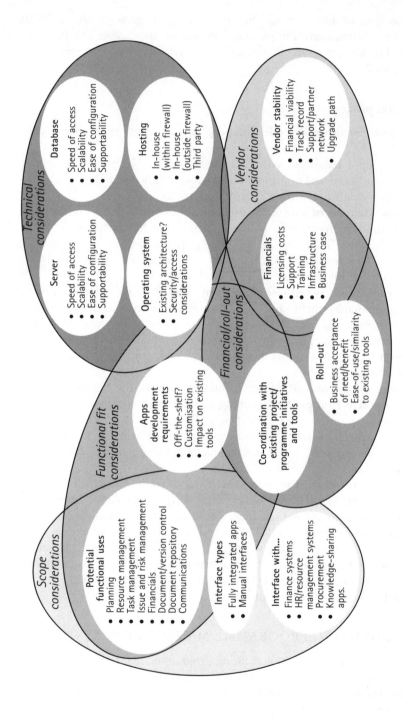

Figure 10.2 Selection considerations for programme management systems

Technical considerations

Database
- Speed of access
- Scalability
- Ease of configuration
- Supportability

Hosting
- In-house (within firewall)
- In-house (outside firewall)
- Third party

Server
- Speed of access
- Scalability
- Ease of configuration
- Supportability

Operating system
- Existing architecture?
- Security/access considerations

Vendor considerations

Vendor stability
- Financial viability
- Track record
- Support/partner network
- Upgrade path

Financial/roll-out considerations

Financials
- Licensing costs
- Support
- Training
- Infrastructure
- Business case

Co-ordination with existing project/programme initiatives and tools

Roll-out
- Business acceptance of need/benefit
- Ease-of-use/similarity to existing tools

Functional fit considerations

Apps development requirements
- Off-the-shelf?
- Customisation
- Impact on existing tools

Scope considerations

Potential functional uses
- Planning
- Resource management
- Task management
- Issue and risk management
- Financials
- Document/version control
- Document repository
- Communications

Interface types
- Fully integrated apps
- Manual interfaces

Interface with...
- Finance systems
- HR/resource management systems
- Procurement
- Knowledge-sharing apps.

getting sufficient time from programme personnel for implementation activities at the same time as programme mobilisation activities, and before programme resourcing has reached its steady-state level. Practical implementation steps to overcome these hurdles are considered below.

Adopt a phased roll-out approach

Programme management systems are best implemented and introduced in a gradual way, so that programme staff learn with the systems as they develop, rather than being presented with full functionality all at once. This is also a cost-effective way to roll out systems: although the implementation activities go on for longer, the later requirements are informed by early implementation learnings. This means that the system is ultimately a better fit to the business's requirements, and that functionality addresses real needs rather than those areas initially viewed as important from a less informed position.

Implementations typically begin with a pilot, and then gradually roll out functionality in easy stages, such as by groups of projects or groups of resources. Advanced functionality and reporting is also rolled out in a phased manner, as are interfaces to existing applications. (See Figure 10.3.)

Although roll-out in this way is gradual, there are certain aspects of functionality that should be in place right from the start: document templates, planning templates, programme resources and basic programme communications

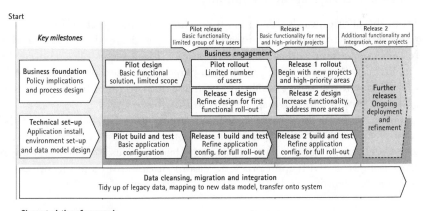

Characteristics of approach

- Phased roll-out of functionality with rapid deployment cycles gives faster delivery of benefits, reduced risk, better adoption by users.
- Roll-out phased by project or impacted community.
- Data conversion and integration continues until data completely transferred, all required interfaces in place.

Figure 10.3 Typical phased roll-out approach

113

should all be available within a system before it is released to users. Implementation of systems presents an excellent opportunity to gain consistency of approach across projects. If the disciplines are not there from the start, it is very hard to introduce them later, and the opportunity is lost.

Invest in training

Many programmes make the mistake of not investing in training for all systems users. They thus fail to realise the benefits and the control that the systems can bring. Training is essential, and should focus on programme management processes and techniques, with systems training wrapped around this. In this context, the training should be seen as an investment in the development of programme management capability, rather than just a requirement for roll-out.

Implement processes and systems simultaneously

Training should be delivered on a just-in-time basis, or else all of the key messages will be forgotten. Thus the training plan and the roll-out plan must be linked seamlessly, with staff being trained in new processes, techniques and disciplines at the same time as they are required to adopt those processes to perform their day-to-day activities.

Develop a 'change agent' community

From the pilot onwards, the initial users should be the greatest advocates of new systems (as well as the greatest critics!), and are the most effective resources to train and support new users. Ideally, the pilot should be resourced with personnel who will then play a super-user/change agent role in subsequent roll-out. This should be made clear to them from the outset, and they should be trained specifically in this role.

The concept of the change agent community goes beyond the 'train the trainer' approach recommended by many software vendors as a cost-effective way of delivering training. The super-users/change agents are specifically given an ongoing role (with appropriate development objectives and incentives) in addition to their day-to-day roles within the programme to:

- maintain a greater level of systems knowledge than standard users
- support their colleagues in the learning curve that continues after the formal training
- represent their user community in ongoing systems refinement
- communicate the implementation activities and benefits to their user communities
- lead by example in the adoption and use of systems.

114

HOW SYSTEMS ENABLE PROGRAMME MANAGEMENT PROCESSES

Core programme management systems

Programme management systems are only effective if they are part of a strong programme management organisation with clear, consistent processes, as described elsewhere in this book. Good systems cannot make up for deficiencies in the programme management structure, nor can they replace the key programme meetings and forums through which progress is discussed, risks are managed and issues resolved. The key areas in which systems do help include:

- capturing a reliable source of information on all aspects of the programme
- producing reports for key meetings and to enable resources to do their day-to-day tasks
- providing templates, examples and lessons learnt to all programme resources
- supporting communication across the programme
- automating programme management processes through workflow.

Communications infrastructure

One area of technology that does not fall strictly into the definition of 'programme management systems' but which can greatly assist the effective running of a multi-site programme is video conferencing and web conferencing. Given the one-off and developmental nature of many programmes, informal communications between programme resources are at least as important as formal communications.

Programme staff may be working as close colleagues with people on different continents that they have never met, and know little about, so informal communication needs to be promoted actively. On a large multi-site programme it is often impractical, if not impossible, to get programme staff co-located even once in the life of the programme. Thus it is important to make several channels of communication easily available, and persuade programme staff to spend time working with each other via all available communication media.

EXAMPLE APPLICATION 'FOOTPRINTS'

This section considers a number of generic application mappings to the logical elements of programme management system functionality, representing typical programme management system situations.

115

Stand-alone or cross-enterprise programme

A stand-alone or cross-enterprise programme is one where links into existing enterprise systems are not particularly important, or are impractical because of the potential need to link into the systems of several different enterprises. A typical scenario is a development programme (construction, systems or the like) performed under a consortium or joint venture arrangement. Under this arrangement no one party wishes to fully integrate the programme into its systems, and thus the programme requires a stand-alone infrastructure of its own.

The situation is slightly complicated if the programme vehicle is a separate legal entity with statutory reporting obligations. Under this circumstance additional accounting functionality is required, as illustrated in Figure 10.4.

Enterprise programme

For a programme that is performed substantially within the context of a single enterprise, the links into existing systems are far more important. In the first instance, user adoption will be much easier, and later on it is more likely that the new programme management capabilities will become successfully embedded if the systems deployed link seamlessly into 'business as usual'.

A typical application architecture in this scenario is outlined in Figure 10.5. The extent to which existing ERP/financial/MIS solutions are used to provide programme management functionality is largely dependent on the capability of the specific systems already in place.

CONCLUSION

Programme management systems are very valuable tools for supporting an enterprise programme management approach. To support multiple cross-organisational projects the systems must, in addition to planning, scheduling and resourcing, support workflow/collaborating knowledge management and management reporting. Integration of programme management systems with other business applications is becoming increasingly important to provide consistent and consolidated information.

Programme management systems add value by reducing risks, improving efficiency and streamlining administration. It is important to consider carefully the selection of appropriate systems, based on rigorous selection criteria including scope and functional fit, integration feasibility, business case, vendor suitability and technical considerations.

The following case study illustrates many of these points and shows the successful use of programme management systems in a multi-project global environment.

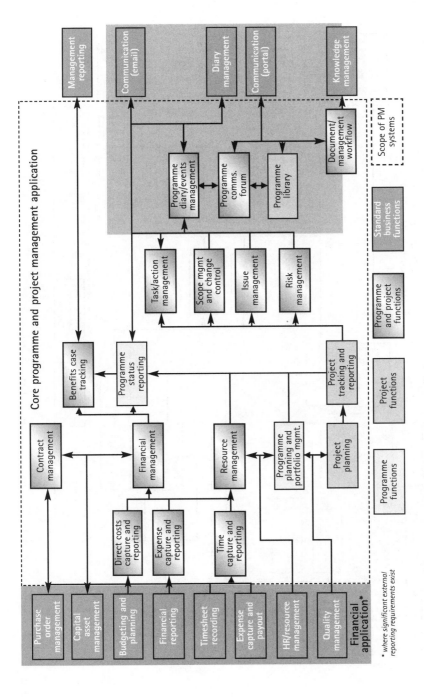

Figure 10.4 Logical architecture application mapping: stand-alone programme

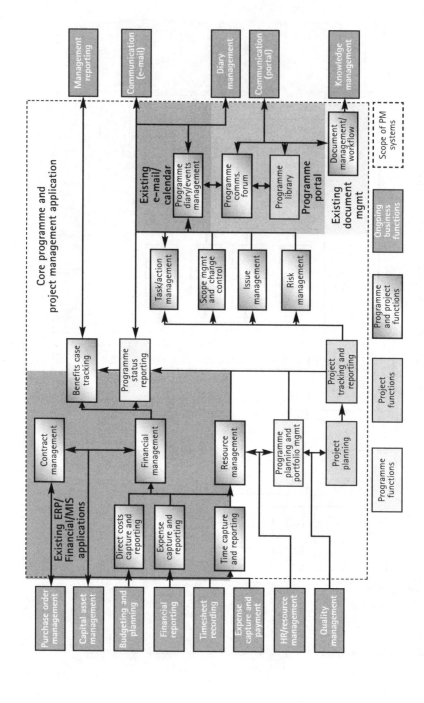

Figure 10.5 Logical architecture application mapping: enterprise programme

COMPAQ COMPUTER CORPORATION: GLOBAL BUSINESS SOLUTIONS ORGANIZATION

A Primavera Systems case study, February 2002

About Benchmarking Partners™

Benchmarking Partners is an industry analysis, consulting, and software firm based in Cambridge, Massachusetts. The firm is a leader in advancing strategic initiatives for CEO Teams. Since 1994, Benchmarking Partners has been a pioneer in the development and on-going value measurement of global best practices in key business processes.

Benchmarking Partners serves clients in three practice areas:

- Championship mobilization: supporting corporate champions in mobilising their own organisations to realise value from complex initiatives.
- Champion-centred selling: standing behind many of the world's most successful sales campaigns at the intersection of business and technology.
- Opportunity acceleration: working in partnership with leading innovators to create and succeed in new markets.

For more information, please visit www.benchmarking.com

Registered trademarks

Primavera, the Primavera Sundial logo, and Primavera Enterprise are registered trademarks of Primavera Systems, Inc. All other product names and brand names are trademarks (™) or registered trademarks (®) of their respective companies.

Benchmarking Partners, Championship Mobilization, Champion-Centered Selling, and DSET are trademarks of Benchmarking Partners.

Acknowledgements

Primavera Systems sponsored research performed in support of this case study. We would like to thank all the employees of Compaq who contributed their time and insights to this process.

Company profile

Compaq Computer Corporation, acquired by Hewlett-Packard Company in May 2002, was a leading global provider of enterprise technology and solutions. With annual sales of US$33.6 billion, Compaq was the third largest computer company in the world. Compaq designed, developed, manufactured, and marketed hardware, software, solutions, and services that were sold in more than 200 countries.

Global Business Solutions (GBS) provided Corporate IT support to the entire organisation. The Worldwide Programme Management Office (PMO) was created in 1999 to better control project management throughout the entire enterprise and was charged with developing consistent project methodologies and processes to improve project performance.

The Compaq PMO matrix consisted of 24 PMO offices across the enterprise responsible for over 1100 active projects. Over 1400 project managers and 3000 team contributors were part of this organisation (Figure 10.6).

Project background

PMO business needs:

- Manage multitude of projects across the enterprise
- Control costs
- Improve probability of project success
- Raise a level of project consistency

Challenges of corporate IT

Information technology (IT) executives around the world are facing increasing pressure to contain costs, manage operations more tightly, and create more visible value from disparate projects. In order to achieve these objectives, IT executives are treating their operations more like independent businesses – focusing more than ever before on project planning, disciplined delivery of services, and satisfying their internal customers.

For many global corporations, corporate IT managers are responsible for thousands of projects on a daily basis. At the same time, they are relying

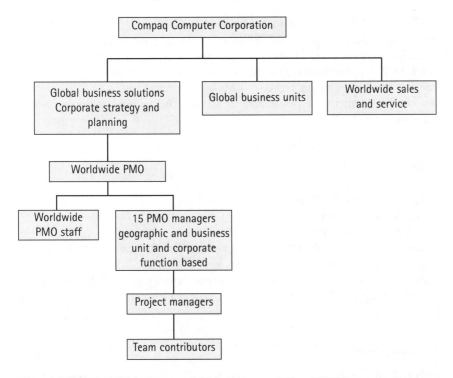

Figure 10.6 Worldwide Programme Management Office (PMO) organisational relationship to Compaq Computer Corporation

Source: Compaq Computer Corporation

on antiquated techniques (often phone calls, email and meetings) to prioritise competing programs and projects, deploy people, and monitor project performance.

In order to operate more like a business, corporate IT needed to gain visibility across all concurrent projects on which their personnel was working and ensure other offices worldwide were not duplicating projects with similar scope.

Compaq's senior management required a view of the entire range of projects to enable informed decision-making on funding and to align projects to the timing and direction of the business. With this visibility, the department projected that they could significantly improve cost control and return on investment.

However, the IT organisation needed more than visibility. In 1997 and 1998, Compaq acquired Microcom, Tandem Computer, and Digital Equipment Corporation. The merger activities significantly increased the firm's number of projects, and each company brought unique processes and procedures for project management. Compaq needed to prioritize the projects and set expectations consistently across the newly integrated teams.

IT needed somehow to manage the 2500 projects underway with 160,000 activities, 7500 resources, and 3000 users. They determined that a single, unified, enterprise-wide project management approach needed to be developed. In this environment, Don Kingsberry (Director of the GBS Worldwide Programme Management Office— PMO), in concert with a selection team, was charged with the responsibility to identify the optimal solution for the company's needs.

Key partner selection criteria:

- Multi-user, multi-project, multi-location
- Integrated and scalable
- Role-based functionality with ease of use
- Flexible for multiple plans, proposals, hypothetical scenarios, and real-time analysis
- Ability to integrate with third party systems (e.g., SAP, PeopleSoft and Microsoft)

Selection process

Robert Napier, Compaq's CIO, played an active role in the selection process because he believed that enterprise project management was central to the department's future direction. Napier, along with Kingsberry and a large number of worldwide PMO managers and project managers from the geographically dispersed PMOs (with dotted line responsibility to the Worldwide PMO) formed the selection team.

The selection team's activity was organised in four main steps:

(1) Determine selection criteria
(2) Research qualified partners
(3) Product demonstration
(4) Pilot

Compaq's selection criteria emphasised scalability. The solution needed to be able to handle up to 5000 users at any one time, with over 3000 projects running concurrently in over 100 locations. The solution also had to be adaptable to a variety of roles (from senior executives to peripheral team contributors) that compose the project teams.

Compaq required a solution with flexibility for real-time analysis of multiple plans backed by a strong, responsive service capability. Finally, in order to optimise enterprise functionality, the solution had to be capable of integrating with third party systems.

Based on analyst research and market share analysis, the selection team identified the top four players in the enterprise project management market. Despite some apparent similarities in functions and features, Kingsberry was unsure if any of the solutions could handle the volume of users Compaq anticipated.

To decide the final outcome, he tested the claims made by each product through pilot programmes. 'After the completion of each pilot program, Primavera TeamPlay® was clearly the winner due to its enterprise scalability, multi-user functionality, and vendor commitment to do whatever it takes', says Kingsberry.

The implementation

Compaq began implementation with the installation of Primavera's database and the convergence of existing project information into Primavera TeamPlay structures. During the pilot, the department, in close cooperation with Primavera, had clarified its needs for defined policies, procedures and guidelines on how to use Primavera TeamPlay, as well as training requirements and needs for system support plans.

Apr. 1999	Sept. 1999	Nov. 1999	Dec. 1999 to Feb. 2000	Mar. 2000	Nov. 2000	Jan. 2002
Started pilots concurrently with top four solution providers	Started Primavera TeamPlay Pilot	Completed pilots and evaluated performance	Developed methodology, planned implementation, configured system	Began rollout and training	Complete bulk of rollout	Complete integration with financial, and human resources

Figure 10.7 Functionality timeline

Source: Compaq Computer Corporation

Based on early positive results, John Buda, Vice President of Strategy & Planning, supported an aggressive schedule for a global rollout of Primavera TeamPlay on a phased basis. In addition, Buda played a key part in mobilising the organisation behind that effort.

By December 2001, over 3000 Compaq employees had been trained to use Primavera TeamPlay.

Miguel Peralta, the Operations Manager in the PMO, reports that the implementation process exceeded the unit's expectations. (According to an internal survey conducted by Corporate IT, 93 per cent of users were satisfied with Primavera TeamPlay's functionality and 96 per cent were satisfied with the process whereby their project activities were brought into Primavera TeamPlay. According to Peralta users no longer had to manually re-enter data. Projects and resources were, for the first time, all in one central database.) By agreeing, in advance, within their organisation on how they wanted to use the software,

Compaq was able to redirect its culture. Through the use of Primavera Team-Play, said Peralta, 'we were able to rapidly institute a whole host of changes that would not otherwise have been possible. This was our way of getting every-one on board.'

To show his support, Compaq's CIO, Robert Napier, signs every training certificate issued upon completion of the training programme. Napier sees his active involvement as contributing to each user's understanding of the necessity of the Primavera solution to achieving his wider objectives.

As the benefits of the Primavera TeamPlay implementation have been recognised throughout the enterprise, Kingsberry reports that other business units are expressing interest in using enterprise project management to improve their business processes. Several have purchased additional licenses and have begun to use the system for many different types of projects. Areas that include the solution in their processes range from Human Resources to New Product Development. In addition, Primavera TeamPlay has been fully integrated with Compaq's internal IT help desk software (Remedy) and is in the process of being integrated with SAP and PeopleSoft.

Benefits achieved

> Primavera TeamPlay has facilitated, in a way that was not before pos-sible, the Global PMO's goal of bringing its overarching principles into practice. 'Programme and project plans now accurately reflect the work our people accomplish.'
>
> Don Kingsberry (Director of the GBS Worldwide
> Programme Management Office – PMO)

Compaq reports multiple tangible and strategic benefits of the Primavera TeamPlay implementation in both the PMOs where the solution is in use and in the organisation as a whole. These benefits tend to overlap and extend beyond the business units where they have had the strongest impact.

At the highest level, Kingsberry reports that Primavera TeamPlay has facil-itated, in a way that was not before possible, the Global PMO's goal of bringing its overarching principles into practice. 'Programme and project plans now accurately reflect the work our people accomplish.'

Programme Management Office benefits

A standard for project performance

Compaq faced challenges in controlling its enterprise-wide project manage-ment. While many individual projects were properly managed, some were not formally planned and were managed with task lists. Project plans were not in a single database and actual project status was often unknown or unavailable.

Projects not being managed with a consistent methodology hindered comparisons and progress assessment. Executives or managers seeking actual project costs often found that they could not be determined with any certainty or timeliness.

By using Primavera TeamPlay, Kingsberry reports that the Worldwide PMO increased its percentage of projects meeting deadlines, budget and targets while accountability increased.

According to Kingsberry, 'The PMO's improved project performance is apparent even to people who are not Primavera TeamPlay users. Through web publishing, we are able to share our project plans and supporting documentation with our customers.'

ROI (return on investment) improvement

Compaq wanted a solution that would enable the group to determine actual project costs with certainty. By using data generated within Primavera TeamPlay, Compaq uses a standard return on investment (ROI) Calculator (developed in cooperation with Pricewaterhouse Coopers) on every project.

> Within the first year after the implementation, Primavera TeamPlay surpassed (by a factor of 15) the ROI that Compaq projected for the software in its Business Case. The Global PMO's business performance, also (measured by an averaged ROI) was significantly improved.

Don Kingsberry reports that the initial benefits of the TeamPlay implementation have far exceeded Compaq's expectations. Compaq does not publicly disclose its ROI numbers, but the calculator revealed that within the first year after the implementation, Primavera TeamPlay surpassed (by a factor of 15, according to Kingsberry) the ROI that Compaq projected for the software in its Business Case. The Global PMO's business performance, also (measured by an averaged ROI) was significantly improved.

Standardised reporting

Prior to using Primavera TeamPlay, the PMOs used a desktop solution that did not provide the level of project information that was needed on a large, global scale. The work involved in gathering information on project status was manual and required multiple updates from project contributors. The time it took to prepare this information was considerable and the results were insufficient to meet Compaq's fast-paced needs.

The PMOs were spending an enormous amount of time reacting to the needs of their internal customers. They often responded to 'fire drills', where project performance reporting was needed on an 'emergency' basis by various business units. Now, the PMOs use Primavera TeamPlay to standardise and update responses to such requests.

Originally, the PMO implemented the executive level program scorecard, a CIO Program Dashboard, with a manual process using a spreadsheet. Now this weekly executive reporting is generated directly from Primavera TeamPlay and the result is a web-based report that is easily viewable around the world.

Today, through TeamPlay features such as Reporting Wizard and Issue Management capabilities, the PMOs have been able to lessen the number of fire drills by proactively providing weekly scorecards in a more timely fashion. The scorecards created an objective standard for measuring project performance, which has become an increasingly important corporate requirement.

Instead of taking weeks to assemble specific project information, it now takes only a few hours. By dramatically reducing this unproductive time, the PMOs are now able to be more active in managing deeper levels of their projects and better monitor critical path issues.

Reduced resource costs and increased utilisation

Managers desired to have visibility into total resource utilisation. Primavera TeamPlay made this possible by providing a centralised view into resources which has helped the worldwide PMO make better decisions regarding resource utilisation and reduce overall payroll costs.

For example, Kingsberry reports that by being able to view resource requirements throughout the enterprise, the worldwide PMO was able to better utilise its offshore development partner. This, he said, helped reduce their high costs of outsourced labour and increased their internal utilisation rate.

Improved project management and risk mitigation

The reporting capabilities of Primavera TeamPlay have lessened the amount of rework that is required to provide project updates and, more importantly, to view resource utilisation. For example, to gain visibility into resource utilisation, project managers used to gather team members for project status meetings and enter the information into spreadsheet and a one-dimensional project management software. This process was tedious, and it was difficult to obtain timely information.

Team members are now able to enter timesheet information directly into Primavera TeamPlay, enabling project managers to quickly gain real-time resource utilisation information. Through this visibility, project managers are quickly identifying project risks and issues.

The tendency in the PMOs, as in any technically sophisticated environment, is to prioritise technology issues, but delay focus on project management until later in the process. Using Primavera TeamPlay, according to Kingsberry, Compaq's PMO is counteracting that tendency to:

1. Bring project issues to the fore earlier in the process
2. Expose potential problems more quickly
3. Maintain focus on the business requirements that are motivating the project activity

> Moving classroom training to the web enabled us to reduce the cost of training by 80 per cent.
>
> Miguel Peralta, Operations Manager in the PMO

Knowledge management, repeatability, and streamlined deployment

'We think of Primavera TeamPlay as a knowledge management system', Kingsberry said. Compaq is using Primavera TeamPlay to capture best practices and lessons learnt from projects all over the world. The worldwide PMO is using those lessons to build and disseminate repeatable, realistic best practices. For example, user acceptance testing for some large SAP projects was routinely scheduled for two weeks but actual data suggested four weeks was required. As a result of this enhancement, Compaq changed the planning template.

By not having a standardised project management approach, Compaq had put itself at unnecessarily high risk for loss of the accumulated expertise and knowledge, whenever a valuable employee was promoted, changed jobs or left the firm.

Through Primavera TeamPlay Methodology Manager, PMOs have been able to facilitate the transfer of many elements of project management expertise using project architecture plans. With this feature, junior project managers are now able to create plans based on the accumulated experience of Compaq's best, most senior project managers. This, reports Peralta, has reduced planning time and increased the speed of project staff deployment.

Reduced training costs

With differing and inconsistent project methodologies, Compaq could not train its personnel effectively. In shifting to Primavera TeamPlay with its web-based training as its single standard, Compaq was able to reduce classroom training and all its attendant costs (such as travel and work disruption).

'Primavera TeamPlay's web-based TeamPlay training is one of the best implementations we've seen,' says Peralta. 'With its dynamic screens, the users are actually performing the functions and the built-in tests confirm overall competency.'

'Moving classroom training to the web enabled us to reduce the cost of training by 80 per cent,' says Peralta. 'In addition, users are now able to access training independent of time and place, taking advantage of certain training modules only when needed and proceeding at their own pace.'

> A major benefit of Primavera TeamPlay is Compaq's ability to 'increase the percentage of its resources directed at the company's primary goals.'

Enterprise benefits

Portfolio management

Prior to Primavera TeamPlay, Compaq had no common executive level status reporting programme and no master plans for GBS programs.

Now, programmes are all instituted in a standardised format, using master plans accessible to senior executives and customers as appropriate. The standardised weekly scorecard generated by Primavera TeamPlay enables executive level reporting on every project that makes up the portfolio.

Portfolio management takes alignment to another level. The priorities of senior management are better able to influence both high-level decision-making and the most granular level execution.

Primavera TeamPlay helps managers, wherever they are located within Compaq's organisational structure, to consolidate disparate project information, to drill down into the details at whatever level is required and to take slices into varying layers of depth or breath.

Compaq has been able to improve its monitoring and decision-making on projects by systematically coding projects as strategic, legacy, or support. Similarly, Primavera TeamPlay allows Compaq to code projects based on their motivators (e.g., cost saving, revenue generating, direct business model support and compliance). Senior management is, thus, able to analyse the mix and learn what proportion of spending is going into each category.

A major benefit of Primavera TeamPlay, reports Kingsberry, is Compaq's ability to 'increase the percentage of its resources directed at the company's primary goals'.

Improved decision-making and flexibility

Prior to Primavera TeamPlay, IT management had to make decisions regarding project funding with information that was not always available or up-to-date. Since collecting the information was a time consuming process, PMO's were only able to provide about 10 per cent of the information they have available today, according to Kingsberry. With Primavera TeamPlay, the global PMO office has been able to provide much needed information to senior management.

> Primavera TeamPlay enables a vice president with responsibilities for Europe and a vice president responsible for the Global Business Units to view both an entire programme and all its constituent projects. Each can drill down for visibility into those aspects of the work that concern them the most.

Managers now have the ability to view their entire project portfolio and determine if there are duplications in project effort across the enterprise. In addition, as business needs change, they have the added flexibility to change the course of projects and replace those who do not address company needs.

For example, through portfolio management, the department has been able to redeploy resources to more strategic projects. In addition, they were able to better see when key project requests should be addressed, given the overall view into the programs they were supporting. And lastly, they were able to evaluate those projects that did not fit into the timing and direction of the current business agenda and cancel them before they were begun.

Overall, by having an enterprise view into corporate IT's project portfolio, reports Kingsberry, IT executives have been able to reallocate resources resulting in cost savings of US$15 million over the course of three business quarters.

With Primavera TeamPlay, Compaq has a better capability to shift the reporting responsibilities of entire teams without disrupting work and, at the same time, allow flexible visibility. Multiple vice presidents, for example, can simultaneously view the work of project teams whose output is important to them. Primavera TeamPlay enables a vice president with responsibilities for Europe and a vice president responsible for the Global Business Units to both view an entire program and all its constituent projects. Each can drill down for visibility into those aspects of the work that concern them the most.

Improved coordination

Primavera TeamPlay facilitates global management through its unified database, allowing units in Latin America or Asia, for example, to be managed together with teams closer to Compaq's Houston headquarters in ways that were not before possible.

Primavera TeamPlay has been a tool for both simplifying project categorisation and rapidly altering staffing when required. Jonathan Winfiele, a Project Manager and leader within the Global Business Unit Systems PMO organisation, reports that his unit was able to pare 200 programmes down to 65. In addition, Winfiele credits Primavera TeamPlay with facilitating the successful growth of his group, due to organisational changes, from about 300 employees to over 900 virtually overnight.

> With Primavera TeamPlay, every project can be audited in a consistent, commonly understood framework.
>
> Jonathan Winfiele, Project Manager

Compaq has, Winfiele says, embedded Primavera TeamPlay in the steering process. Now, with every project being reviewed in a standardised fashion, the basis for decision-making can be understood and appreciated by all concerned.

Alignment

Winfiele sees Primavera TeamPlay's standard reporting tool as a powerful unifier, often cutting through unintentional miscommunication with instruments such as Primavera TeamPlay's Project Lifecycle Reports, which Compaq prints out weekly.

Prior to Primavera TeamPlay, reports of completion levels were heavily dependent on subjective assessments. 'In one instance', he points out, 'a project was being loosely reported as being on the order of 60 per cent complete. Once we entered all the data into Primavera TeamPlay and ran the report, it was actually less than 10 per cent complete.'

Previously, Winfiele reports, it was not possible to get everyone to use the same project management approach and tools. Now, all Compaq IT Project Managers understand that for their work to show up on the single radar used by senior management, they must be in Primavera TeamPlay. Winfiele suggests that by using Primavera TeamPlay as they have, Compaq 'created a totally different atmosphere in managing new projects.'

The entire organisation is now influenced by using Primavera TeamPlay to standardise the format for consistently and comprehensively describing opportunities, scope, analysis, and decision-making. With Primavera TeamPlay, according to Winfiele, every project can be audited in a consistent, commonly understood framework.

Now, with a consistent system for all project reporting, everyone can rely on data with more certainty – for everything from budgeting through resource allocation to assessing progress in achieving both strategic and tactical objectives.

Enhancing competitive position

Compaq has built its respected brand over many years by bringing new products and services to market. By utilising Primavera TeamPlay, and enabling enterprise-wide visibility. Corporate IT has been able to selectively emphasize those projects that help Compaq to achieve technological, procedural and organisation innovation.

This strength was recently recognised by *Information Week* and listed in their *Information Week 500 Report*. Compaq received the honour as one of the most innovative IT organisations, and was the top ranking IT organisation within the hi-tech industry (Table 10.3).

Table 10.3 Compaq's ranking in the hi-tech industry according to *Information Week*, 2001

Rank	Company	Revenue in millions	Revenue change	Highest-ranking IT executive	Title	Industry
1	Owens & Minor Inc.	$3,504	9.7%	David Guzmán	Sr. VP & CIO	Health Care & Logistics
2	Continental Airlines Inc.	$9,899	14.6%	Janet Wejman	Sr. VP & CIO	Logistics & Transportation
3	Boises Cascade Corp.	$7,807	9.9%	Robert Egan	VP of IT	Metals & Natural Resources
4	Snap-on Inc.	$2,176	11.8%	Alan Biland	VP & CIO	Manufacturing
5.	Compaq Computer Corp.	$33,554	10.0%	Robert Napier	Sr. VP of Global Business Solutions & CIO	Information Technology

Being named to this list, far ahead of the next hi-tech organisation at #19, helps differentiate Compaq in the marketplace. Moreover, says Kingsberry, this department now views Primavera TeamPlay as a primary tool in facilitating the flexibility and adaptability that they depend on for competitive advantage.

Conclusion

Primavera TeamPlay is delivering tangible and strategic benefits to Compaq's corporate IT executives, PMOs, project managers and the company as a whole.

Compaq's Global Business Solutions organisation has quantified ROI in both its usage of Primavera TeamPlay and the overall project portfolio.

Using Primavera TeamPlay's capabilities for project standardization, standardised reporting and full project visibility, corporate IT has realised reductions in resource costs, training costs and project risk, with increases in resource utilisation, improvements in project management, process repeatability and deployment efficiencies.

As a result, corporate IT is able to run its operations more like a separate business entity and, simultaneously, increase the satisfaction of its internal customers. Both the corporate IT staff and senior management associate the implementation of Primavera TeamPlay with increasing sophistication of project management within the organisation.

Furthermore, the enterprise as a whole is deriving additional benefits from portfolio management enabled by Primavera TeamPlay. Specifically, they have been able to improve decision-making, flexibility, coordination, and alignment.

By using Primavera TeamPlay, Compaq's corporate IT division already dramatically and substantively improved its internal processes, qualitatively and strategically increased its enterprise-wide impact at the executive level, and enhanced Compaq's overall competitive position in the marketplace.

11 Managing programme risk

INTRODUCTION

Much has been written on the subject of managing risk in projects. The tools and techniques for project risk management are well documented and developed. Nonetheless many large, complex projects still fail because of a lack of understanding of end-to-end risk management.

In a large programme, not only are the difficulties faced by projects compounded, a whole new swathe of potential problems can be encountered. Conflicting objectives within the programme; demands on critical resources; maintaining balanced and sustained sponsorship; managing the 'business as usual' while focusing on strategic change; communicating the right messages; and managing risks across the extended enterprise are just some of the challenges.

This chapter provides an introduction to risk management, giving definitions of risk and risk management. Our approach goes 'back to basics' with a look at some of the fundamentals needed to close the gap between theory and reality. We look at some of the key challenges faced when managing risk across the programme, and identifies effective ways of rising to the challenge. Through discussion of appropriate techniques for identifying, assessing, communicating and managing risk, some developed from project disciplines, some unique to programmes, you will see what approaches are suitable for you. A case study provides a real example of what has worked for a successful business managing a successful programme. The experiences of delivering London's Congestion Charging scheme provides a framework for dealing with large, complex, time-critical and highly political programmes that have interrelated social, economic, environmental, political, financial and technological constraints. Without managing these risk factors proactively and pragmatically, the programme would be unlikely to succeed.

Throughout this chapter, emphasis is placed on the attributes required of programme teams, their management and their sponsors, and how to develop these attributes to deliver the desired benefits. Risk management is not treated as a management add-on, a function within the programme office. It is given its rightful place as an integral part of the programme, pertinent to programme objectives, crucial to programme strategy and decision-making, and practised by the programme executive.

WHAT IS RISK MANAGEMENT?

Figure 11.1 The scope of risk management

Promulgating a standard language around risk management and programme levels is a strongly recommended first step in beginning to establish the approach required for risk management to function effectively. We define risk as 'an uncertain event or set of circumstances that, should it occur, will have an impact, positive or negative, on the achievement of desired objectives'. This complements the Project Management Institute's definition of risk management: 'the systematic process of identifying, analysing, and responding to project risk'.

Prime Minister Tony Blair gives his own definition in his introduction to *Risk: Improving government's capability to handle risk and uncertainty,* a report by the Cabinet Office Strategy Unit in November 2002: 'Risk management – getting the right balance between innovation and change on the one hand, and avoidance of shocks and crises on the other'.

Our take on this is that risk management should aim to improve decision-making through the reduction of uncertainty, the identification and analysis of specific risks in relation to the goals and constraints of the enterprise; followed by the selection and implementation of an appropriate programme-specific mitigation or general enterprise control response in light of the criticality of the risk and the enterprise's risk tolerance. More simply put, it should equip decision makers with sufficient information to make timely and proactive choices to achieve the desired effect. The implementation and effectiveness of the response is then monitored, and adjustments are made as appropriate. Thus the purpose of risk management is not to remove all risk, but to remove avoidable risk, leaving the desired level of intrinsic risk. This approach also serves to reduce the uncertainty, or the 'unknown unknowns' that may exist in an business's external context.

While risk management may be easy to describe, it is very difficult to achieve. Recent history shows us that up to 70 per cent of programmes are late, over budget or ineffective, especially if the programme is large, complex, critical and incorporating major change.

MANAGING AND OPTIMISING THE DEGREE OF RISK AT EACH LEVEL IN THE ENTERPRISE

Risk management as a concept can be applied at all levels within the enterprise. However a differentiated *approach* is required, as each has a different purpose, scope and application.

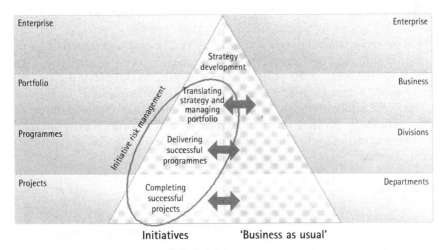

Figure 11.2 Enterprise-wide risk management

Before we take a closer look at the approach to risk management used by the Congestion Charging programme, it is important to understand the four different levels:

- enterprise (across the business)
- portfolio (multiple programmes)
- programme (multiple projects)
- project (multiple activities to achieve a defined output in a defined period).

At every level, there will be the requirement to integrate and link with the 'business as usual' risk.

Enterprise risk

At the enterprise level, we bring together the assessment and management of strategic risk within the 'business as usual' and initiative (programmes) sides of the enterprise to recognise dependencies, realise synergies, and integrate with the strategic risk management.

Portfolio risk

We see two types of risk within the portfolio. The first are simple, high-level faults that are generic in nature. These are often the cause of failure. Examples are a programme with inconsistent targets for delivery time, cost and performance, and programmes with incompatible targets. The other category of risk is detailed, project-specific risk that is not easily predicted or mitigated. At the portfolio level, the focus is the potential of the portfolio of initiatives (programmes and projects) to realise and implement business strategies within an effective and efficient approach. Figure 11.3 highlights the five key questions behind effective portfolio risk management.

The review of portfolio risk also includes aggregating and integrating the escalated individual project and programme risks.

Risk management at the portfolio and enterprise level represents a central component of strategic portfolio management. The principal steps involved in repeatable portfolio optimisation, of collecting information, analysing the portfolio, prioritising projects, and communicating and reporting, are supported by the risk management undertaken while monitoring the competitive environment.

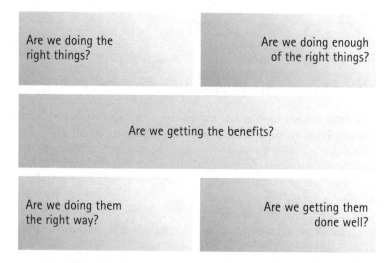

Are we doing the right things?	Are we doing enough of the right things?
Are we getting the benefits?	
Are we doing them the right way?	Are we getting them done well?

Figure 11.3 Five key questions for effective portfolio risk management

136

Programme risk

As mentioned earlier, risk management is fundamental to programme and project management. Within the programme arena, the principal balance is between investment, benefits realisation, and risk. Rapid top-down identification and mitigation early in the programme should run concurrently with the establishment and maintenance of programme lifetime risk management. Key risk responses at the high level include changing the programme scope, goals and approach, realistic re-planning, significant alteration of resources availability, amendment to the programme organisation, management processes and communication mechanisms. Key actions to reduce the intrinsic risk for the delivery of programme benefits include:

- ensuring adequate direction and inspiration from senior sponsors and stakeholders
- building a focus on delivery of value
- structuring the programme activity around an optimised programme approach
- explicitly managing all required resources: money, people, office space, infrastructure, knowledge
- encouraging appropriate capability transfer to build ongoing capability
- communicating more and better than ever before
- managing the programme through integration of benefits, cost, risk, reward, people and planning.

The initial routes for identification of risk are the explicit and implicit assumptions in the programme set-up; historical review of a programme's performance; analysis of the programme roadmap; and diagnosis of the programme management capability. The use of periodic external diagnostics/ validations is an extremely powerful method of risk reduction.

Project risk

At the project level the emphasis moves to strict time, cost, quality and scope criteria. Project risk management needs effectively to filter the identified project risks to identify those whose impact is critical at the programme level, or that could influence other projects across the programme.

THE PROGRAMME RISK MANAGEMENT APPROACH

Getting back to basics

Risk management is a relatively recent phenomenon outside certain specialised areas. It first developed as a formal process in the financial sector (insurance and banking), the military, and in audit and health and safety functions. More recently, partly attributable to the Turnbull Report, it has entered mainstream management activity across both public and private sectors. Risk has moved from being seen as a technical subject to being viewed as central to managing the whole organisation. There are strong parallels with other disciplines such as financial management and project management, which have increasingly become seen as necessary mainstream management skills (albeit supported by professional experts). In each of these areas the benefits of a systematic approach are well established and widely recognised.

Despite these advances, it is clear from the research and the experiences of programme managers that there is a significant gap between what is published in a plethora of risk management books and journals, and real-life programmes. The gap between reality and theory is often a chasm. This section presents a number of key themes that seek to bridge this gap:

- **Mind-set/culture.** Understanding the culture of the organisation and the stakeholders is critical. This requires heavy investment in time and political/emotional sensitivity.
- **People.** There is nothing more important than people: clients, customers or team members. All need to have a common understanding of risk management, and the risk team needs the right capabilities and skills to enable the processes to work.
- **Process – the six Ps. Prior preparation and planning prevent poor performance.** Processes are essential to get the right information to the right person at the right time. However, it is much more than appointing a risk manager or defining a new risk process - processes are enablers, not the product.
- **Tools: KISS principle, keep it simple and straightforward.** The paradox of programme risk management is that the simple often seems complex, whereas the trick is to make the complex seem simple. Good software tools can help to achieve this; bad tools can distract and confuse.
- **Structure.** The structure of the risk management organisation needs to reflect the needs of the programme. In other words, it should be as small as is needed to achieve its aims.
- **Communication.** The single most important factor is the maintenance of good communications. The best results come from having a strong emphasis on face-to-face communication wherever possible.
- **decision-making.** Risk management is a critical ingredient to effective decision-making. This requires fundamental changes in the decision-making processes and priorities, especially at the senior management level.

THE APPROACH TO BUILDING THE FOUNDATION FOR EFFECTIVE RISK MANAGEMENT

Often we find that risk management in practice is concerned with just two factors: process and tools. This greatly limits the potential value to be gained. We believe risk management requires a much broader set of capabilities. It is enabled through the interrelationship of five parameters (people, process, tools, structure and information), all guided by the culture and mindset of the enterprise and stakeholders involved, for the purpose of making and optimising specific decisions.

These are represented in Figure 11.4 by three parallel planes: the Ends, the Ways and the Means. The right-hand plane is the decision-making plane (the Ends), where decisions are made, either direct risk management decisions or more general business decisions. It is termed as the 'Ends' because this is where risk management has greatest effect, enabling decision makers to maximise positives and minimise negatives. The left-hand plane represents the general enterprise and programme culture, and specific mind-set of those involved in risk management (the Ways). In the middle, the enabler plane provides the necessary capabilities (the Means) to undertake risk management.

Plane 1: Mind-set and culture (the 'Means')

The correct risk management mind-set is a critical but frequently neglected component of risk management: critical because it shapes the effectiveness

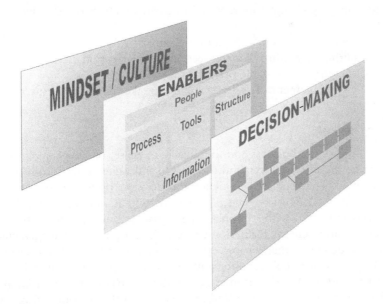

Figure 11.4 Three planes of risk management

139

and focus of risk management, neglected because it is difficult to engender and intangible.

Recognising risk

The nature of the industry, competitive position and shareholder expectation will be major determinants in the appropriate mind-set, culture and focus of risk management. This will allow a view of the necessary risk appetite (target degree of risk) and tolerance (limits of unacceptable risk). This is most effectively realised through embedding in the mind-set, rather than through enforcing a methodology. This requires an emotional connection with the risks and business objectives.

Some cultures encourage the proactive identification of challenges and risks; in others this is tantamount to an admission of failure. The most important factor is the matching of environment, expectation and action. The quest for higher returns requires the acceptance of greater risk. The demand for faster benefits realisation is incompatible with the emphasis on cost minimisation or the elimination of uncertainty. For some, these require major mind-set shifts.

In most situations there is usually a warning signal that leads to a chain of events, which may or may not be noticed. Sensitivity to pick up signals, or the absence of signals, is required for optimal decision-making in dealing with risk.

The following changes are required to create an effective risk mind-set:

- improving the sensitivity to warning signals
- establishing a culture of direct learning and reflection
- encouraging accountable risk-taking
- the encouragement of contra-thinking to take the wider perspective.

Managing risk

The culture of the business and the specific mind-set of the people involved determine the priority given and the quality and value derived from the risk management enablers, and influence the decision options and outcomes. Risk management must be seen as important, and an ongoing responsibility. It must integrate with the planning, goal setting, progress tracking, resourcing and benefits realisation elements of programme management. It must be much more than a paper exercise, undertaken to be seen to meet the regulated management requirements. Ownership of risks must be real, proactive and meaningful. Immersion by the risk team and the programme leadership team in the purpose and the methods of the customers is essential to creating the right foundation for risk management.

Being nominated as a risk owner must be seen as a serious responsibility and potentially a personal opportunity. Risk management is not the sole domain of the risk manager: he or she is present to facilitate, monitor, structure and validate the process and the risks raised, not to take direct responsibility for mitigation. For all concerned the culture must show reward, and support the notion of faster and better risk management.

Plane 2: Enablers (the 'Ways')

Process

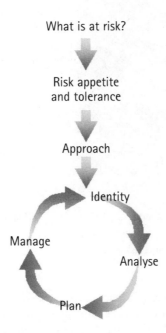

Figure 11.5 The risk management process

Processes using the six Ps (prior preparation and planning prevent poor performance) are essential to get the *right information to the right person at the right time*. It is difficult to overestimate the importance of completeness of process in risk management.

What is at risk?

In order for the identification and analysis of risk to be meaningful it is necessary to have a clear understanding of what is at risk. This requires a clear definition of goals, objectives, scope, strategy and the programme environment.

Risk appetite and tolerance

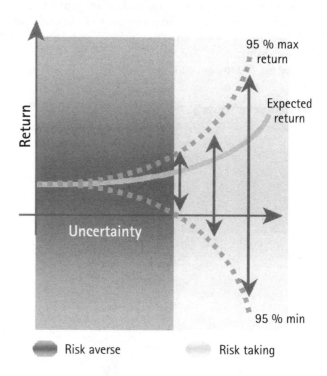

Figure 11.6 Risk appetite and risk tolerance

It is necessary to have a clear definition of the organisation and programme's 'risk appetite' (target) and 'risk tolerance' (limits) in order to define the most suitable risk management approach, and calibrate risk sensitivity and risk criticality. The definition of appetite and tolerance will include the definition of certain outcomes which must be prevented from happening. An organisation must also measure levels of uncertainty, and look to transfer uncertainty into manageable risk where possible.

Risk approach

The approach to risk management will depend on all the above decisions, and will define the scale, scope, resourcing and importance of risk management. The output from this step will be confirmation that the proposed approach is appropriate, and a documented description of the risk management approach, plan and processes.

Identify

The risks should be identified as comprehensively as is possible, yet this should be achieved in a practical and cost-effective manner. Confidence in the thoroughness of the identification process is necessary to give the risk management process validity. Normally all stakeholders should be included in the identification process. Wherever possible, lessons learnt from previous programmes or general enterprise experience should be sought, assessed and utilised.

Analyse

The risks and responses need to be described and characterised sufficiently to allow effective risk planning to be conducted. To the extent that is practical and value-adding, quantitative and qualitative assessments need to be made of the probability of occurrence, impact (time, cost, performance, related risks and issues) and time to impact (net of mitigation lead time).

Typical tools include the probability, impact, and time grid to both communicate risk criticality and prioritise risk activity. These can prioritise time or scale of risk (and benefit). Simultaneously, risk management should be identifying the principal uncertainties in the baseline activity plans and cost schedules.

Plan

The typical responses of mitigate, monitor and ignore need to be considered for each risk. The chosen risk response plans provide a direct input and revision to the programme and work package plans. Contingency planning should be undertaken for critical risks, and these provide supplementary plans to the base plans. Contingency planning must include defined triggers and structured decision rules for initiating reactive contingency responses.

Manage

The key aspects of this iterative phase are implementing the risk action plans, and frequent, meaningful monitoring of programme progress, risk action progress and the underlying residual risk, driven by unambiguous allocation of responsibility to nominated individuals. This is the area that is most frequently inadequate. We believe that risk management, although well understood in theory, has yet to realise its full potential in many companies in practice. As part of the ongoing risk management process, it is important to monitor the effectiveness of the process and compare the risks arising with the original estimates of likelihood and probability.

	Project: Programme level and occupation					Sort by L-I rating					Active, Monitor, Closed		
	Updated: 09-May-02			%; 2 1–20%; 3 20–50% 4 50–90%; 5 > 90 %		Standardised to 0–100% = L^(1/2)*I					Avoid, Reduce, Monitor, Ignore		
				Post mitigation									

Risk no.	Risk area	Risk cat.	Title Description, inc. cause impact and assumptions	Likelihood	Impact	⬆	L-I rating This month	Last month	Initial	Owner entity	Respon. person	Status	Adopted strategy	Management action with named action owners
84	Occ	Migration	Insufficient DR capacity in xx: although there will be plenty of space at HDC, no production migration can occur unless DR is in place at HH or xx. There is a risk, given the environmental constraints, that this constrains the migration to a dual site strategy and embarrassingly prevents businesses taking advantage of the xx capacity.	4	5		89%	89%	63%	ES		Active	Reduce	ACTION: forecast space (power, heat) requirements understand problem better ACTION: identify initiatives to significantly increase spare capacity
61	Occ	Migration	FSU delivery: the FSU project currently has insufficient planning and coherence which is delaying implementation of the FSU. This has dramatically reduced the number of consolidations from xx, resulting in increased migration costs, and some businesses finding alternatives to the FSU. The delay, assuming this leads to no FSU consolidations, will significantly increase the total PUAM cost.	5	4		89%	80%	46%	ES		Active	Reduce	ACTION: get agreement on who will own the project, and provide resources ACTION: highlight dependencies on FSU
74	Occ	Migration	Intelligent space planning: There is a risk that space allocation is sub-optimal, if no single person owns all allocation, if the xx process is not fully integrated with that person, and if migration allocation is not integrated with new kit.	5	4		80%	80%	54%	ES		Active	Reduce	We need to ascertain who will do the intelligent space planning and allocation; and then integrate with xx and the xx team ACTION ON xx space planning guidelines still in progress
77	Prog		Purchase authorisation: The delayed procurement authorisation for the xx kit needed to migrate from xx has significantly delayed the migrations and put at severe risk the vacation of xx by the end of June. The remaining xx storage elements that are still subject to approval and if delayed will impact the migration from xx and other locations, as well as impact the credibility/utility of the SAN.	3	5		77%	77%	72%	ES		Active	Reduce	xx are reviewing the procurement process for x related kit/services - chase up ACTION: more clearly identify time critical purchases; track their way through the system; ensure no blockages within the x team
115	Occ	Migration	Last minute cancellations: There have been a number of last minute cancellations, often due to preventable reasons. This is partly due to an apparent lack of timely communication with all.	4	4		72%	72%	89%	ES		Monitor	Reduce	ACTION: ensure authorised business representatives communicate to all involved ACTION: ensure much more urgency in responding to the?

Figure 11.7 Risk action plan example

Tools

The use of risk tools is a significant enabler for long-term success. This includes quantitative analysis of plans, cost breakdowns, risk logging, prioritisation and tracking, risk action management and reporting. The appropriate tool may be an Excel spreadsheet, an Access database, a commercially available programme risk management tool or an enterprise-wide risk tool, depending on the size, complexity, duration, criticality, risk appetite and risk management maturity of the initiative and enterprise under consideration.

We frequently see inadequate use of standard tools, reducing efficiency and effectiveness, or alternatively the implementation of risk tools without the shifts in behaviour required to drive through an effective risk management approach. Tool implementation may offer an opportunity to embed the culture and ways of working required around it.

The paradox of programme risk management is that the simple often seems complex, whereas the trick is to make the complex seem simple. Good software tools can help to achieve this; bad tools can distract and confuse.

People

The skill-set, capability and motivation of an organisation's people are critical to the successful function of risk management. Inconsistencies, gaps and deficiencies in skills, motivation and training must be addressed to create the capability for risk management to function. The selection of risk management staff must be done with due consideration.

Structure

For risk management to be effective, a continuous self-sustaining process for risk management must permeate all levels of the organisation, ultimately driven by the board and the CEO. Key to the establishment of a dynamic risk management system is an appropriate governance structure through which to feed relevant information and make decisions. Imperfect organisations create new risks for themselves, and tend not to manage existing risks as well as they could.

The risk manager is a core part of the overall programme and portfolio management. In a programme environment, the risk manager works day to day with the PMO (at project or enterprise level), facilitating the risk management processes, working with the programme team in identifying and analysing new and changed risks, and liaising with those responsible for planning, resourcing and benefits within the PMO. The links to planning and benefits management are particularly critical.

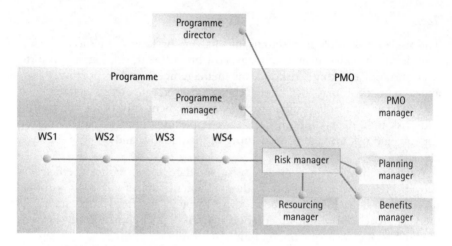

Figure 11.8 Governance structure for risk management

Additionally, the risk manager should have regular risk reviews with the programme manager and/or director (as this is often the only way to achieve the real benefits of risk management). Risk owners must be in a position to facilitate and manage the risk mitigation actions.

Information

The availability of up-to-date and accurate information, and the ability to analyse and aggregate, are key to helping the risk management decision-making process: garbage in, garbage out. Elements of the information may be held in a central repository created from the various tools available, as discussed in the tools section.

The single most important factor is the maintenance of good communications. The best results come from having a strong emphasis on face-to-face communication wherever possible.

Plane 3: decision-making (the 'Ends')

The point at which a decision is made, or should be made, is the point of impact for risk management. What does this mean? This is where risk management has traction and must be integrated with the general decision-making mechanisms within the project, programme or portfolio. Effective risk management will be apparent through the contribution of risk thinking to existing business decisions, and the addition of extra decisions solely because of the outcome of risk analysis and planning.

The principles of project management can be applied to decision-making, and the balance between speed, cost and quality of decision can be managed to suit circumstances. This will shape the decision-making chain complexity, duration and inclusiveness.

The appropriate selection will depend on the impact of the identified risk, probability of occurrence, time till impact, cost and lead time of mitigation options and the complexity of the decision. Remember that typically the value of a course of action decays with time, and hence a more rigorously analysed decision is not necessarily a better decision.

There are a number of well-documented psychological traps that are particularly likely to undermine business decisions. These include the anchoring trap, where the mind gives disproportionate weight to the first information it receives; the status quo trap, a bias towards decisions that maintain the status quo; the confirming evidence trap, where supporting information is gathered and contradictory information is avoided; and the estimating trap, where most people are over-confident in the accuracy of their predictions. These are especially important after a significant issue has arisen or event has occurred. In the panic that follows, mistakes can easily be made again, procedures forsaken and the overall risk increased.

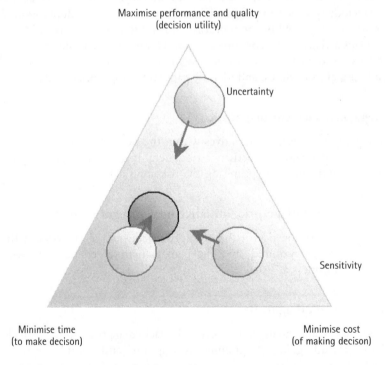

Figure 11.9 Dimensions for decision-making

TOOLS AND TECHNIQUES FOR IMPLEMENTING PROGRAMME RISK MANAGEMENT

We have discussed the components of a best practice risk management system, but how do you implement this? How can you realise the benefits of risk management? The first priority is to diagnose the key risks, and the effectiveness of the risk management process. All too often we see partially complete and under-performing risk management systems. The greatest shortfall is typically seen in the definition of the key desired outcomes and the risk tolerance; together with full analysis of the risks and ongoing management of the risks. Of course best practice risk management cannot be achieved overnight.

An overview of risk management options is given below. There are three levels of intervention: effective implementation from the start; a diagnostic and assurance of the current environment; or longer-term ongoing risk management implementation, either stand-alone or as part of a broader portfolio/programme/project management service.

Enterprise diagnostic

This is performed to identify the risks to and within the project portfolio. These include risks of poor alignment, conflict, omission and duplication. This diagnostic is supported by the transformational alignment matrix (TAM). The TAM maps activity to the core objectives and targets of the business. The TAM allows us to identify the contribution of the portfolio to the desired key organisational capabilities, and identify gaps and inappropriate focus.

Strategic management diagnostic

This activity prioritises all initiatives within the portfolio for the purpose of focusing risk management activity and general management attention. This is a direct contributor to optimising the risk approach.

Change overload diagnostic/initiative management maturity

This is to address the risk of the enterprise being unable to cope with the degree of change required, and the management of change necessary in relation to 'business as usual'.

Programme risk diagnostic

This identifies and analyses the key risks facing a programme (top-down analysis), including key programme assumptions and confidence in likely mitigation effectiveness.

Programme management diagnostic

This reviews the underlying programme management capability to deliver its planned outcome. This diagnostic uses the eight programme leadership dimensions as the framework for review and development of a continuously improving capability programme.

Risk management maturity diagnostic

This identifies the current maturity of the risk management capability in the organisation. It addresses the risk that the risk management itself is poor, insufficient or inappropriate. It uses the three-plane model and process methodology as the basis for diagnosis, and hence reviews mind-set, process, people, information, tools, structure and decision-making capability.

Cost and benefit component analysis

This is performed early in the programme lifecycle to build a relatively simple, Monte Carlo cost model; enabling the identification of key risk components and facilitating meaningful scenario analysis and budgeting activities.

Hot spot analysis

Once initial network charts and Gantt charts are available, the hot spot analysis highlights the critical and riskier activities within the plan, to allow proactive mitigation and contingency planning. This takes into account critical path analysis (CPA), but has a far broader range of inputs and outputs than CPA. The focus is proactive amendment to the planning on the basis of confidence in completion.

Decision management

Effective decision-making is critical to delivery of the desired outcomes, whether they are strategic, programme or at a project level. Treating decisions as critical mini projects can significantly speed up and improve decision-making, and we have a number of tools to do so, including a decision-making diagnostic. This can remove a significant amount of systemic risk.

MAKING IT HAPPEN

Implementing business-wide change to create the risk management mind-set and culture requires a structured approach to enable individual stakeholders to understand the logic behind the risk management system.

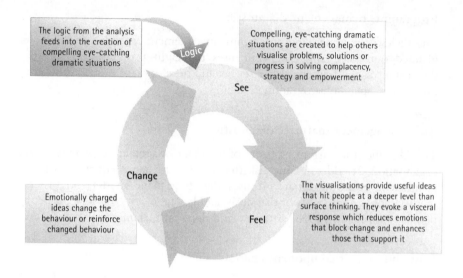

Figure 11.10 Creating a risk management mindset

This approach is based on the 'See, Feel, Change' model (see Figure 11.10) developed by Deloitte. It aims to enable and motivate individuals to recognise the importance of risk management within the business through visualisation, dramatisation creating emotion and then changed behaviour.

RISK MANAGEMENT IN ACTION AT LONDON CONGESTION CHARGING

Background: the challenge

Road user charging is an increasingly popular approach to reducing road congestion. The benefits associated with this include reduced traffic volumes, congestion and travel time; increased travel time predictability; increased road safety; additional revenue for the charging authority; an alternative policy to road or vehicle taxation; an improved environment; and improved quality of life.

Along with New York and Tokyo, London is one of three world cities that was being brought to a halt by a failing transport system. In 2002, traffic travelled at the same speed in London as did horse-drawn carts in the nineteenth century, with vehicles typically spending half their journey time in queues. Road congestion was costing London's business community around £2 million per week.

In 1999 the UK government gave the Mayor of London the go-ahead to introduce congestion charging, which is a charge on motorists for using congested roads. Ken Livingstone, the first elected Mayor of London, made proposals for the introduction of congestion charging in Central London a key element of his summer 2000 manifesto and his *Transport Strategy* of July 2001. This was the world's largest congestion charging scheme, involving:

- A 21 square km charge zone.
- An 18 month consultation process consisting of presentations, public meetings, and public exhibitions.
- A network of over 600 enforcement cameras (fixed and mobile), Europe's largest camera and telecommunications contract, sited at the 174 entry/exit points as well as sites within the charging zone.
- Daily monitoring and charging of approximately 200,000 vehicles.
- A broad range of innovative payment options including SMS text messaging from mobile phones used by some 100,000 people per day.
- UK's largest public information exercise since British Telecommunication's 'Ask Sid' privatisation campaign.
- Europe's largest traffic management schemes to ensure that the traffic flowed at its optimum volume and speed, while minimising any negative impact on the boundary. For example, in a single borough (Westminster City Council) there were: complementary traffic measures; automated traffic monitoring sites to give real-time data on traffic volume and speed; new major bus schemes and new routes with new bendy-buses; traffic signs and road markings; and real-time traffic management schemes which provided the police and traffic planners with immediate visibility and awareness of traffic flow patterns, to enable proactive management to avoid traffic queues.

As programme managers, we helped establish eight work streams that managed the 45,000 tasks needed to deliver the scheme by 17 February 2003. The key ingredients to the successful integration of the work streams (with over 430 separate projects) was having the right processes and tools to get the right information to the right manager at the right time, in order to allow a timely decision to obtain the most benefit from the situation.

To enable the team to remain focused on the primary aim of achieving 'go live' on 17 February 2003, the management of risks and issues became fundamental to maintaining tight timelines in a constantly changing environment. One of the primary success factors of the programme management methodology was the ability to identify risks proactively, analyse their likely impact, and employ mitigation strategies to minimise negative effects, or maximise positive impacts.

The success

To the credit of the Transport for London (TfL) directors and their team, Central London Congestion Charging Scheme went live on 17 February 2003 on time, within budget, and achieved the technical specification to meet the required customer service levels. Heralded as a huge success, it has reduced traffic in Central London by a steady 16 per cent within the zone, shortening delays by 40 per cent and generating revenues of up to £3 million per week. All net revenues are to be reinvested into London's transport infrastructure.

So what was the risk methodology underpinning the programmes' successful programme risk management?

Implementation planning and risk management

Risk management played a vital part in the planning process. Given the scale, complexity and political profile of the project, it was important to model the uncertainties and risks in the programme cost and duration. One of our initial tasks was to build a high-level Monte Carlo cost model (using Pertmaster and @Risk) to determine potential cost variance. As the implementation plan developed, Monte Carlo analysis and probability curves were also used to ensure critical analysis of task durations, to identify the criticality/likelihood of achieving key milestones, thereby enabling proactive management to ensure timely go lives.

Contingency/continuity planning

In anticipation of Scheme Go-Live, we helped TfL to make the transition from a focus on project and implementation risks to active contingency planning. Key operational risk scenarios, along with appropriate owners, mitigations and contingencies, were identified through a series of workshops, interviews and discussion documents. Advanced modelling simulation was also used to test results. Contingencies were signed off by project sponsors to enable a swift response in the event that a risk scenario arose during live operations. These scenarios were entered into a customised version of the central Risk Register for ongoing reference.

Stakeholder interest in the Congestion Charging Scheme was very high, and responding to it was an important part of our role throughout the procurement and implementation phases. We managed a comprehensive consultation process, first engaging key stakeholder organisations, including London boroughs, the emergency services and business representatives, and then engaging the general public. The public consultation included distributing leaflets, articles in newspapers, broadcasts on radio and television, public meetings, notices, an exhibition and a call centre to answer any

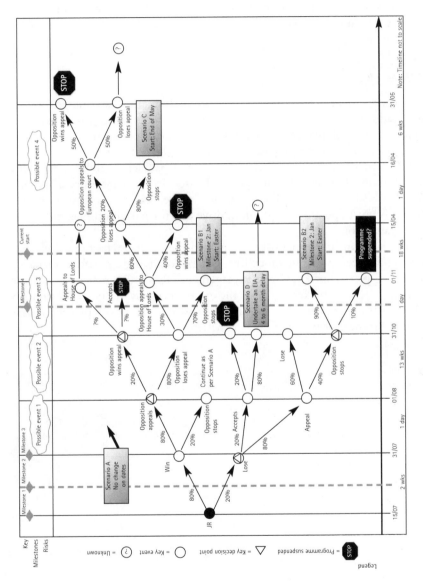

Figure 11.11 Outcome decision tree analysis for contingency planning

queries. As part of the ongoing risk mitigation strategy, the programme continues to work very closely with key stakeholder groups to ensure that the scheme meets the needs of specific customer groups such as drivers of black cabs, people with disabilities and fleet operators. The provision of comprehensive reports to the Greater London Assembly's scrutiny committee has also been an important aspect of ensuring that the scheme meets stakeholder requirements.

SUMMARY

Risk management is an approach to creating competitive advantage, opportunity and flexibility while minimising risk exposure and nugatory expense. Fully effective risk management will shape the plans of the business, test the plans of the business and realise learning from the outcomes.

Risk management depends on a number of parallel capabilities, and this often requires fundamental changes in the decision-making process and priorities, especially at the senior management level. People, process, mind-set and tools must operate as a system to drive executive decision-making within the organisation.

Thus it is concluded that risk management is an integral part of the change programme, central to its objectives, crucial to strategic portfolio management and programme delivery management. Risk management is key for enabling decision makers to take the right decisions at the right time to ensure delivery to schedule, quality and cost criteria, whilst protecting the existing business or organisational activities.

12 Benefits management

INTRODUCTION

Analyses and post-mortems of programme failure tend to concentrate on whether the programme delivered the product as specified on time, on budget and to a certain quality. In other cases, a post implementation review may conclude that the programme has been delivered successfully, the team are successfully redeployed, suppliers have been paid and the impacted users or stakeholders are reasonably happy. Much more rarely does the most pertinent question of all get asked: that is, did the programme really deliver the benefits that were outlined and predicted when the investment was sanctioned? A 'successful' programme that does not deliver the intended benefits is akin to that cliché of medical black humour, 'the operation was a complete success; unfortunately the patient died'. This chapter on benefits management discusses the processes required to ensure that the survival of the patient is identified as a key success measure, that the pulse is taken throughout the course of the operation, and the patient's well-being is monitored for a relevant post-operative period of time.

The Office of Government Commerce estimates that 30–40 per cent of projects designed to support business change deliver no benefits whatsoever, and one must assume a not dissimilar percentage fail to meet the anticipated benefits. Benefits management is challenging, and often overlooked, not least because it spans a time period greater than what is often seen as the overall lifecycle of the programme. Thus the enterprise programme management pyramid view, topped by the business strategy of the organisation, is a useful framework with which to consider benefits management. Benefits management begins with benefits identification before a specific programme is initiated, and continues with measurement even after the programme has delivered and 'business as usual' has reasserted itself. To add to the difficulty, benefits management may require different skill-sets and mind-sets from those needed for other aspects of programme delivery.

Benefits management, within the enterprise programme management context, directs business change towards valuable, desired results by translating business objectives into identifiable, measurable benefits and systematically tracking and communicating the results.

155

HOW DOES BENEFITS MANAGEMENT FIT INTO THE ENTERPRISE PROGRAMME MANAGEMENT FRAMEWORK?

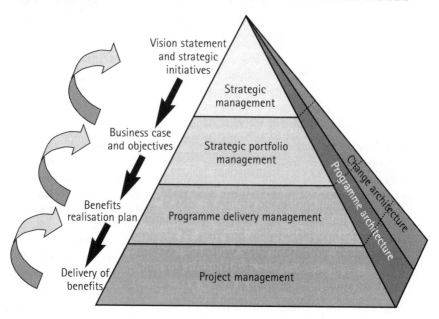

Figure 12.1 Benefits management with the enterprise programme management framework

Benefits management has application within all dimensions of the enterprise programme management pyramid. The enterprise programme management approach recognises that change initiatives do not take place in isolation, and the integration of mechanisms for delivering programmes and projects with the existing operational structures, processes and systems is key.

At the **strategic portfolio management** level, a continual process of creating, managing and evaluating a portfolio of strategic initiatives aims to focus on delivering lasting results and benefits. This is where the benefits management strategy is defined and executed. Processes include validating the direction of the programme initiatives, articulating the value propositions and business cases, and defining the goals, objectives, benefits and other criteria for success. Portfolio management ensures that the initiatives are continually managed and tracked. Finally the benefits and results of initiatives are reviewed in order to measure the progress towards realisation of the business strategy. The benefits must continue to be relevant and aligned to the initiatives. At this level, the key objective is to ensure that all change initiatives are aligned with the strategy, and are managed in an integrated way to deliver the desired benefits.

Programme delivery management uses the results of the strategy and portfolio alignment to link strategy with operational activities. This ensures that the delivery of the benefits is coordinated and that processes, tools and methods are used consistently and efficiently. The planning, executing and controlling processes define, implement and track the benefits delivery.

Project management addresses the operational activities where results are actually achieved. Specific measurable benefits are delivered and controlled, project teams are managed and incentivised to focus on the delivery of the benefits as set out in the business case, and anticipated and realised benefits are communicated.

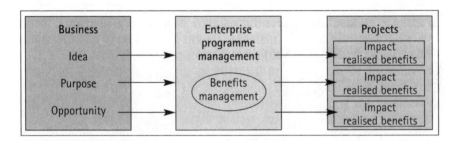

Figure 12.2 Linking project benefits with business objectives

It is often the case that once a business case defining benefits is signed off, the emphasis becomes on managing delivery time and cost. One of the reasons for this is the isolation of business case development from the resulting delivery of the programme. The other usual stage in the traditional approach is the post-delivery or post-implementation review. Again, this is too often done in isolation and fails to reveal the true benefits from the programme, focusing instead on time, cost and quality of the programme delivery. Establishing a continuous programme management approach, where the business case is integral to the business outcomes, can mitigate these risks.

A benefits plan that is quite separate from the programme management process is a common pitfall. The two must be aligned, dynamic processes with reporting on benefits integrated into the programme reporting process from the start. The integrated plan needs visibility and ownership at the sponsor level, as well as at the delivery level.

The scope of the process for managing the benefits of a programme will vary according to the type and size of the programme, and the organisation in which it is being implemented. There are however some fundamental principles that apply to all change programmes, which we will discuss in this chapter. We look at the overall approach, key tools and techniques, required roles and responsibilities, and highlight some common pitfalls.

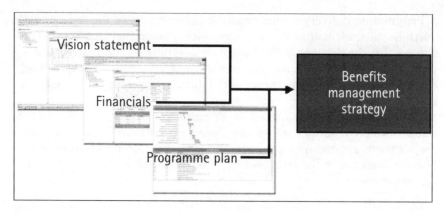

Figure 12.3 Integration of the benefits management strategy

WHAT IS BENEFITS MANAGEMENT?

Benefits management is the identification of potential benefits, their planning, modelling, tracking and reporting, and the assignment of roles and responsibilities from programme initiation through to realisation of benefits. The term 'benefits management' is sometimes replaced by 'benefits realisation' in some industries. We have deliberately stuck to the term benefits management to emphasise that it is a continual process of planning, identifying, structuring, tracking, reviewing and evaluating processes in order for them to be realised.

Key features of a successful benefits management approach are that it will:

- identify expected benefits that will be delivered by a programme
- establish a benefits management structure defining processes, relationships, communications, roles and responsibilities
- develop models to structure the programme benefits, including intermediate and final outcomes
- define the benefits, including their value, attributes and measures, owners and risks
- assess how the benefits are interrelated
- develop a benefits realisation plan, including a schedule for delivery, review points and interdependencies with other projects or programmes, and business change processes for implementation and delivery
- establish accountability for realisation and a means of tracking benefit realisation, including any performance management requirements for programmes and businesses.

Quantifying benefits

Privately, programme sponsors and managers sometimes admit that benefits management does not receive the focus it should because quantifying benefits is simply 'too difficult'. Similarly, being on the hook to deliver benefits quantified by a strategist keen to receive programme sign-off is just too painful or too risky.

Quantification can be made easier by having a clear understanding of the categories into which benefits can fall. Ensuring involvement and continuity of the relevant stakeholders throughout the benefits management process also enables ownership and buy-in to quantified benefits.

Many different types of benefits may accrue to an organisation, enabled by the introduction of new ways of working. The importance attached to individual types of benefits will depend on what the organisation is trying to achieve. These are the outcomes that the organisation is seeking – not necessarily a saving in cash terms, although it will often include this. Identifying and quantifying potential benefits can be difficult when you start to look away from just the return on investment benefits. A robust approach is therefore needed, a prerequisite of which is understanding and communicating what the intended benefits are.

Benefits fall into three categories:

- direct financial benefits: those that can be quantified and valued (tangible)
- direct non-financial benefits: those that can be quantified, but are difficult or impossible to value (tangible)
- indirect benefits: those that can be identified but cannot easily be quantified (intangible).

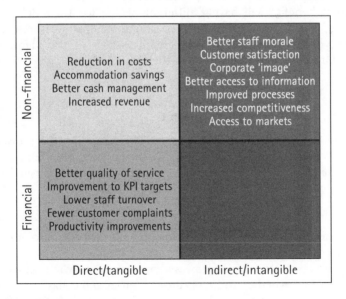

Figure 12.4 Types of benefits

159

Tangible benefits

Financial and direct non-financial benefits are relatively easy to identify and quantify. Direct financial benefits can be compared with each other in cost terms, or to other potential investments (to assess the opportunity cost). Non-financial benefits, such as improving market share percentage, must be justified more aggressively to ensure stakeholder buy-in. Gartner Group points out that implementing automated computer systems will not necessarily result in direct cost savings, but has enabled many other benefits to the organisation to be realised, such as an improvement in productivity. To fully assess the overall contribution, it is important to identify, measure and value benefits in terms of their contribution to business value.

Intangible benefits

Indirect or intangible benefits must be identified and prioritised, even though there may be no common currency between them. To do so requires that their contribution to business objectives be assessed. For a clear meaningful linkage to be made, the objectives themselves should be stated in the most specific and measurable way possible. Even so there will remain a qualitative aspect to documenting and comparing intangible benefits.

During the benefits management process, intangible benefits must be tested continually against business strategies and objectives in order to ensure they are robust, relevant and in some way measurable, even if against an artificial scale aligned to a business objective.

Different benefits will have a different profile for their delivery and realisation, and this profile in terms of timing, ease of measurement and likelihood of achievement will be defined as part of the identification process. This will be used to input to the timing and structure of benefits reviews.

Objectives, success criteria and benefits

Objectives, success criteria and benefits are different ways of expressing the outcomes that the programme is trying to achieve. Confusion between them can obscure the benefits management process. Although very similar, they have some distinct characteristics which are clarified below:

- The objectives define the overall programme aims and reasons for investing in change. These will not normally change throughout the length of the programme.
- The success criteria are key measurements which, when achieved, are indicative of whether the task/project/programme has accomplished what it was set out to do (the stated objectives and benefits). These are

subject to tolerance levels and do not change regularly unless key performance indicators are changed.

- The benefits are the advantages delivered by the specific programme or project plan. The benefits describe how the successful achievement of the programme objectives will impact the business, the staff, and customers. Once the original benefits are delivered it is possible to identify and deliver additional benefits from the new capabilities provided by the project or programme.

The high-level objectives of a benefits management strategy within a programme are to:

- define the investment costs and benefits (the business case)
- estimate additional benefits and probability factors
- develop an implementation plan for realising the benefits
- identify those who will be accountable for realising the benefits
- assist those accountable in implementing the plans.

APPROACH

The key steps in an effective benefits management approach begin before the programme is initiated and continue throughout the lifecycle of the programme and even beyond it.

- Initial **planning** for how the benefits will be delivered. The programme and project business cases should describe how the organisation wishes to manage and achieve benefits. This should include key benefits statements and stakeholder analysis, benefit models, the benefits register and schedule for delivery, and alignment with other programmes or projects and the business case. **Structuring** the phasing of the projects and benefits delivery should aim to maximise the speed of delivery of benefits while taking into account resource constraints and risks.
- Benefits **identification** and **definition**. For each programme, the benefits must be tied back to the overall strategic business objectives. The needs and expectations of the stakeholders, which may not be explicit in the programme definition, must be understood and defined. This involves assessing what the programme outputs will actually mean in business terms, understanding their dependencies and linkages, and prioritising them using appropriate measures.
- **Realising** and **tracking** benefits. A process for developing detailed action plans for the delivery of benefits should be developed. The progress against the benefits realisation plan should be reviewed throughout the programme lifecycle. This should continue after the delivery of the usual project deliverables and post implementation organisation changes.

- **Review** and **evaluation** of benefits. This process measures the benefits achieved against the targets and measures set out in the benefits plan. Additional or unplanned benefits should also be measured throughout the life of the programme at 'gateways', as well as at the end of projects, to assess those benefits achieved.

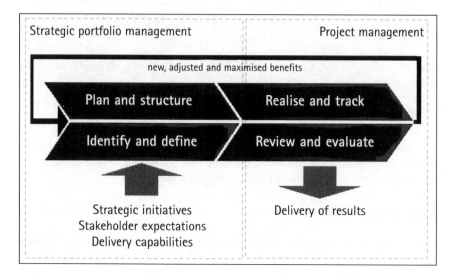

Figure 12.5 Key steps of benefits management

Key steps

Plan and structure benefits management plan

The benefits management process needs to be anchored to the vision and strategic objectives of the organisation. A vision statement for the programme should be produced to describe how the implementation of the programme will contribute to the achievement of these objectives.

For each programme, an appropriate benefits management strategy should be framed, to answer the following questions:

- Why is the programme being undertaken and how does it align to the vision and strategic objectives?
- What are the anticipated business improvements from the programme?
- Can these be quantified and is there a financial value?
- Who should be responsible for delivery of each benefit or improvement?
- What changes are needed to obtain it?
- Who will be affected by the changes?
- How can the benefits be achieved?
- When can the changes be implemented?

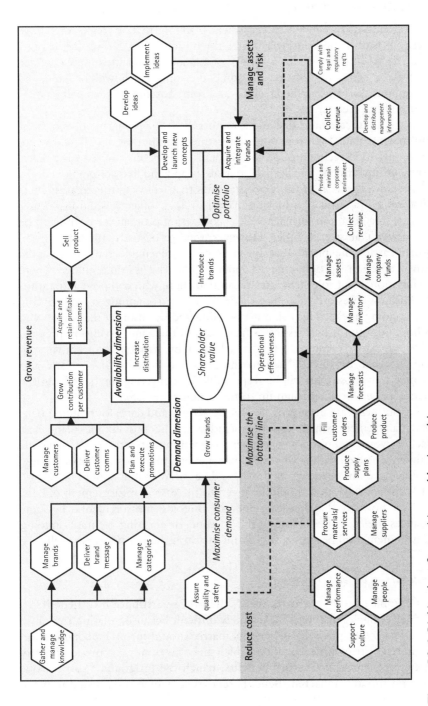

Figure 12.6 Linking benefits to vision and business drivers

Business case development

The key output of benefits management planning that addresses the above questions is normally considered to be the business case. However, the business case will need to fulfil a variety of functions, and in some cases may comprise a series of documents, some dynamic which will be amended throughout the programme lifecycle, and some baselined which will serve as fixed points of reference.

The business case must first and foremost act as the primary source of decision-making data for programme investment authorisation. To this end, commonly used techniques of cost–benefit analysis, discounted cash flows, return on investment hurdles, value analysis and the like are employed. To facilitate the selection of those programmes that will yield the greatest combined return in terms of achieving overall strategic objectives, business cases must be in a common format to allow competing programme options to be considered against each other. However, the use of a structured, common format carries the pitfall that business cases are engineered to meet the known criteria of programme acceptance. This risk is compounded where organisational and role structures mean that those who compose and authorise business cases are too often those who have something to gain by the project going ahead. This risk must be mitigated by ensuring that those who author and sign off business cases have 'skin in the game' to ensure they are delivered. Most commonly this is achieved by structured incentive programmes that are directly tied to the predicted benefits. It is clearly also essential that those who will be responsible for delivering the benefits in the operational environment sign up to the benefits predicted.

The business case must provide specific actions and dates for ongoing benefits management which can be included in the programme plan. Best practice would require some element of contingent actions, or 'what if' analysis associated with key benefits management milestones. That is, if these benefits have not been achieved by this date, what actions should be taken?

Finally, consideration should be given to the ease of measurement of benefits, for both the baseline case and the ongoing measurements. In some instances the cost of establishing the baseline, or ensuring accurate ongoing measurement, will become a significant factor in the business case itself.

Structuring benefits tracking

In a complex business environment, the precise attribution of benefits to particular change or action is extremely difficult because isolating the cause and effect is not possible. A benefits matrix should include a combination of directly attributable benefits (which may be minor, or predominantly intangible), and contributory benefits, which the programme can reasonably said to have impacted. Benefits reporting (which is discussed in more detail below) requires qualitative commentary as well as a quantitative element. The definition and estimation of benefits definition will require updating if and when external forces outside the remit of the programme significantly impact the benefit measures. The important thing is that a structure process is in place to revisit and update predicted benefit measures, and then to feed this result into the strategic portfolio management process to verify that the portfolio of projects is still optimal to achieving strategic business goals.

Identify and define benefits

Defining benefits

Benefits can be defined and documented in several ways, including using a benefits profile or a framework. A standard categorisation system and template for recording benefits reduces the time spent, can stimulate ideas, and facilitates comparison of benefits across alternate or competing programmes. Typically a benefits framework will be derived from the business balanced scorecard, with benefits aligned to the scorecard components. The framework may also prompt for benefits in the form of 'new benefits', 'improved benefits' and 'disbenefits to be reduced or eliminated'. The framework must also include who will own the delivery of the benefit, the measurement method and measurement frequency, and key performance indicators that can give early warning of the impact of the programme on the intended benefit.

At a high level, all benefits could fall into the categories shown in Table 12.1.

In addition, risk avoidance should always be considered as a further benefit. In some instances risk avoidance can be the main driver for change. For example, financial services organisations will ensure their anti-money laundering processes are robust in order to avoid fines, prosecutions and negative publicity.

Table 12.1 Categories of benefit

Tangible	Intangible
Cost avoidance	Strategic alignment
New income	Competitive advantage
Additional income	Competitive response
Reduced working capital	Management information
	Employee satisfaction
	Improved customer service

Source: C. Worsley, *Project Justification*, Project World Seminar, 2002.

Establish baseline

Establishing a baseline involves collating key organisational, financial and operational metrics against which improvements can be measured objectively, and the establishment of a control tool or mechanism for managing changes to costs and benefits through the implementation.

Key activities and tasks to establish the baseline are:

- Devising a strategy for the collection of baseline data (questionnaire, interviews, reports by location and organisation structure).
- Confirming a baseline date with the relevant authority to determine a relevant starting point for benefit quantification.
- Establishing a collection template and set minimum information requirements.
- Nominating appropriate resources to manage the distribution, collection and collation of data.
- Reviewing the quality of information and information gaps and addressing gaps.
- Designing and develop a change control mechanism for holding baseline data and identified costs and benefits.
- Inputting the baseline data into a database.
- Signing off baseline data.

Where baseline data is not available, an initial programme phase for collection of data, with a checkpoint for authorisation to proceed after it is collected, should be considered.

Identify target baseline

Target measures that can be achieved as a result of the redesigned process and systems are set, and the estimated costs and benefits quantified and refined.

Key activities and tasks to identify the target baseline are:

- Establishing target baseline and performance measures based on outputs from redesign workshops, best practice and benchmarks.
- Assessing process interdependencies.
- Conducting further research/analysis to clarify workshop outputs where required.
- Quantifying the net benefit.
- Determining supporting infrastructure needs and high-level implementation steps to support achievement of the target baseline.
- Reviewing cost estimates and revise where appropriate.
- Obtaining agreement on the target baseline, quantified benefits and costs from stakeholders.

Resistance among business owners to accepting the target baseline is not uncommon, particularly where step change improvements are anticipated. However, gaining the buy-in and understanding of the key stakeholders at this stage is critical to the whole benefits realisation approach.

Prioritise benefits

A key input to programme planning will be the prioritisation of benefits delivery. For example, proof of early benefits may be essential to secure continued programme funding, even though delivering early benefits may have a higher cost than a programme approach that defers them. Similarly, programme activities that relate to benefits impacting business areas or objectives that are subject to change may be scheduled for later in the programme.

Prioritisation of benefits should be a structured process that compares a number of options, or analyses one option based on the benefits and the likelihood of realisation. Benefits should be analysed according to a number of criteria, typically including:

- alignment with strategy
- short and long-term expected results
- required resources versus capability: is the expertise readily available?
- probability of success (the benefits management interface to the risk management process).

The aim of this analysis is to get the best pace of programme, taking into account the investment needed and resistance/acceptance to change.

Set performance management targets

Realistic measures, agreed by those who will be responsible for delivery, should be derived using a number of sources such as:

- organisation and business unit strategy
- management forecasts
- industry best practice
- internal and external service level agreements.

Realise and track benefits

Tracking and reporting on the realisation of benefits encompasses two distinct areas: first, tracking and reporting on the likelihood and achievability of benefits, and second, tracking and reporting actual benefits realised. The former will always be required within the lifecycle of the programme; the latter may be relevant within this timescale, or may only begin after the programme has formally delivered.

Tracking and reporting on the likelihood and achievability of benefits requires more than reporting on the status of programme delivery; it needs to include the influence of factors external to the programme on the benefits that are predicted. This reporting should be regular and periodic, though generally less frequent than programme status reporting. It requires revisiting the business case, having an understanding and familiarity with those factors and initiatives that will impact the anticipated benefits, and applying analysis and reporting skills. The output from the process will feed into the benefits review and evaluation.

Tracking and reporting actual benefits realised may take place while the programme is still in the delivery phase, or may commence after delivery. In either case, giving responsibility for tracking and reporting actual benefits to the business unit impacted yields a number of benefits. This approach encourages ownership of the solution and associated benefits within the relevant business area, reduces the risk of 'optimistic' reporting from within the programme delivery team, and enables the benefits reporting to be assimilated within regular management reporting. Where the programme is still in the delivery phase and actual benefits are being measured, a feedback loop mechanism to programme planning needs to be in place to ensure variance from expected results can be used as an input to programme planning.

Review and evaluate benefits achieved

Formal benefits reviews may occur at any suitable time during the programme, prompted by the scale and timing of delivery of the benefits. These will typically take place after the realisation of any major benefit or group of benefits. The purpose of the review is to:

- inform the stakeholders of progress in benefits delivery
- identify further potential benefits
- assess the performance of the changed operations against original performance levels
- assess the level of benefits achieved against the benefits profile or baseline, and advise on the effect on the programme's business case
- review the effectiveness of the benefits management strategy, and implement improved methods based on the lessons learnt
- provide an opportunity to publicise progress and successes.

Roles and responsibilities

The need for clearly defined responsibilities, and assignment of these to roles and individuals, is heightened within benefits management because of the

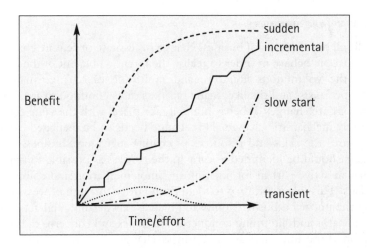

Figure 12.7 Review and evaluation of benefits achieved

potential ambiguity between tasks for the delivery team, and tasks for the operational business. Moreover, as alluded to above, there is a benefit in recognising the difference between a delivery capability, and a capability that seeks to assess whether that delivery has resulted in the intended benefits. This is not to say that the benefits management process needs to be run by individuals outside the programme delivery function, in a checking or auditing capacity; only that the different roles and behaviours required must be recognised even if they are to be enacted by the same individuals.

Key roles that are required for successful benefits management are described below.

Business benefits manager

This role within the programme delivery teams acts as the key interface between the team and the business units who will be impacted. The role requires the holder to work closely with the individual managers of business areas involved in the change programme, who will be responsible for actual benefits delivery in their area. It is therefore essential that the business benefits manager has knowledge and credibility with the leadership of the business areas to be impacted by the programme. The business benefits manager owns the benefits management process, from the planning and structuring phase through to review and evaluation. (Responsibility may pass from one individual to another, but the role and recognition of its importance must remain.) The business benefits manager will work closely with the programme manager, but it is advisable that the two roles are not performed by the same individual, and that the business benefits manager does not report to the programme manager, but rather to the sponsor or a similar business-focused executive.

Business change managers

Virtually all programmes of business change necessitate or require changes to the way people behave in order to realise the intended benefit of the change. Despite the voluminous literature and multitude of 'change managers', 'people specialists' and the like, many business cases continue to assume that the appropriate changes of behaviour will take place, with the same certainty of a purely mechanistic change. This change needs to be managed carefully, and requires the skills and resources of change managers. Business change managers should be identified as early in the process as possible so that they can play an active part in formulating the implementation and communication plans. This role is required to identify and drive through process change, involve the impacted business units and increase ownership, and act as a key communicator and 'lightning conductor' for issues and concerns of the individuals in those impacted areas. Business change managers must be fully committed to the achievement of the benefits, need good knowledge and credibility from the business areas they represent, and should be empowered to make decisions on behalf of their respective business units or process areas.

Sponsor

As the champion and ultimate owner of the programme and associated business case, the sponsor must look beyond delivery of the programme to delivery of the associated benefits. The sponsor's role in scope setting and issue resolution must be informed by the likely impact on the programme benefits. The sponsor must also exercise leadership in the communication of the anticipated benefits, and the required 'benefits focus' from the programme delivery and operational teams.

Programme manager

The programme manager is a vital role within the benefits management framework, because he or she will be responsible for flexing, amending and fine tuning the programme plan in response to the outputs of the benefits management process. The programme manager will work closely with the business benefits manager, since the analysis of programme status with regard to likely achievement of benefits will require the input of both. As part of programme delivery, the programme manager is responsible for ensuring the stakeholder management and communication mechanisms are in place to facilitate continued buy-in to the programme through a focus on business benefits.

VALUE OF BENEFITS MANAGEMENT

Without a proactive approach to benefits management, programmes risk taking on a life of their own and becoming an end in themselves rather than a means to an end. Benefits management helps ensure that the best portfolio of projects to meet the strategic objectives of the business can be selected and maintained. Structured benefits management is thus a vital navigational aid on the journey to achieving strategic objectives.

Benefits management addresses the risk of operational areas failing to commit to the benefits, by involving key stakeholders from these areas throughout the process. This in turn reduces the likelihood of unrealistic benefits being forecast at programme inception in a desire to secure investment. In addition, benefits management lends the ability to fine tune, replan or even abandon programmes that do not look as though they will achieve sufficient benefit. As projects and programmes become an increasing part of many business endeavours, benefits management provides a key input to the learning organisation, helping build a knowledge base of the characteristics of programmes that deliver sustained business benefits.

To increase the likelihood of gaining the value from structured benefits management, the following can act as an essential checklist.

Insist on a robust, realistic business case

The business case should be put together as the key input to the initiation and approval process, not as retrospective justification for a decision already taken. The business case must be a key programme document throughout the life of the programme; it must be realistic, and committed to by key stakeholders who stand to gain or lose by its success or failure.

Create benefits ownership

The right people, with a real stake in the outcome, need to be involved throughout the benefits management process. It is essential that there is continuity of accountability through the business case and delivery.

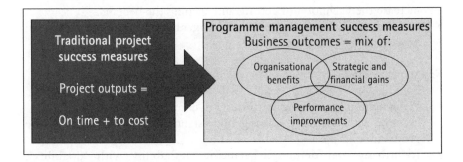

Figure 12.8 The value of benefits management

Ensure priority of benefits realisation

Executive ownership will ensure that the programme team has some authority to make organisational and process changes in order to realise the benefits. Programme and business leadership must actively support, and be seen to support, the benefits management process and the philosophy of programmes aligned to benefits aligned to strategic objectives.

Manage expectations

Do not assume that all stakeholders will be as committed to benefits management and realisation as the programme sponsor and team. Stakeholder management and ongoing two-way communication of anticipated and achieved benefits are vital if benefits management is to be accepted throughout the enterprise.

Track benefits and risk

Factors contributing to the erosion of possible benefits must be identified at an early stage. Revisit the business case early and often, and revalidate based on programme progress and changes to the business environment outside of the programme.

SUMMARY

Benefits realisation is a structured, repeatable process applied to corporate initiatives to maximise the likelihood of achieving the expected business benefits. Benefits management includes:

- a robust approach to identifying and quantifying potential benefits
- key enablers to establish corporate ownership and accountability of key business processes
- a repeatable process for continuous performance improvement to increase the likelihood of getting and keeping the benefits
- a structured approach for guiding the organisation through the required process and organisation change.

Key steps include:

- Planning and structuring: rigorously defining the desirability of a programme and projects. Ensuring understanding of the purpose of the programme/project.
- Identifying and defining: balancing desirability with 'doability'. Identifying the business targets with measures and values. Forecasting all

potential benefits. Linking all benefits to business targets. Developing an action list for delivering the benefits.

- Realising and tracking: measuring the value of the benefits, and monitoring the progress and received benefits.
- Reviewing and evaluating: continuously tracking the benefits, not just the time, effort and activities.

There are many obstacles to implementing a successful benefits management approach, and too often the process is de-emphasised, haphazard, glossed over or ignored. In order to achieve a sustainable, robust benefits management framework, the following foundations need to be in place:

- unambiguous support of senior management and key stakeholders
- a clear distinction between projects and programmes
- supporting knowledge management framework
- a systematic view of resources and timeframes
- programme alignment to vision and strategy
- openness to change and restructuring of priorities in order to achieve the intended benefits.

Applying and ingraining a structured benefits management framework cannot of course guarantee that programmes yield the anticipated business benefits. Moreover, if applied successfully programme failure, curtailment or cancellation will be painfully visible. The benefits, however, in terms of visibility of results, the early warning of programme deviation, and the savings from directing effort and investment to those endeavours yielding maximum business advantage, make benefits management a vital component of successful enterprise programme management.

13 Managing suppliers

INTRODUCTION

It is rare for any one organisation to possess all the people it needs to deliver a programme. This is particularly the case when a programme brings together information technology (IT), processes and organisational changes to achieve an overall strategic business imperative. The larger the IT element, the more likely it is that the programme will need to bring together a multitude of internal organisations and external service providers (ESPs). IT-heavy programmes tend to have the most common requirement for significant involvement of multiple ESPs – very few organisations have all the skills, experience and resources required to deliver a large and complex IT solution for an overall strategic business change.

It is one thing delivering a programme involving multiple internal organisations, with the usual conflicting priorities, organisational boundaries, internal politics and 'history'. When it comes to working with external providers, particularly multiple ESPs, in a business change programme with tight commercial and delivery demands, there are a huge number of new challenges for the programme team to understand and manage. These challenges arise from differences in style, cultural, contractual and commercial pressures, as well as more familiar problems such as coordination and issue resolution.

In this chapter, we consider the practical approaches that programme leaders should adopt when managing suppliers in a complex, integrated and IT-heavy programme. We consider the lifecycle of supplier engagement from initial sourcing strategies through to managing deliverables and post-launch support. The context for this chapter is complex and integrated business programmes with a significant element of IT delivery, concentrating mainly on the IT suppliers. These programmes tend to be most complex from a programme management perspective, and also have most likelihood of going wrong.

We will follow through a recently completed programme that involved many internal and external IT service providers to deliver a new online Internet business for an existing global travel and leisure company. The Solution Build Stream of this programme involved 22 separate service providers working over 18 months. In this chapter we will use this programme, and the Solution Build Stream in particular, to highlight five approaches that are key to successful ESP management:

- Recognise and accept capability gaps in your own organisation and formulate approaches on how to fill the gaps and the type of ESPs you will engage.
- Contract in the right way. This includes commercial/legal consideration, solution design and programme processes.
- Integrate everyone into one united programme team with shared understanding of key processes, tools and working methods.
- Manage and behave as an integrated team covering business, process and IT.
- Clearly understand cross-ESP issues, risks and changes, and actively micro-manage to resolve them before they become showstopper issues.

Before we explore these topics in detail, let us provide you with an overview of the case study.

CASE STUDY: A LARGE INTEGRATED PROGRAMME, LAUNCH OF MYTRAVEL.COM ONLINE BUSINESS

Mytravel plc is a global travel and leisure business offering everything from budget flights to luxury cruises. Mytravel has operations in the UK, Scandinavia, Germany and the United States, operates using over 50 brands, and has multiple sales channels which include brochures, call centres and high street shops. Historically, Mytravel had a range of transactional and brochure-ware web sites, each with their own 'look and feel' and customer experience.

On 27 November 2001 Mytravel.com was launched, completing one of the biggest online initiatives ever attempted. Mytravel.com is an umbrella brand linking several tour operators, their brochures, call centres and high street shops, and replacing existing websites into one seamless travel provider. Mytravel.com is a new business for the online sales channel, covering the UK, Scandinavia, Germany and the United States, and provides more travel products (real time) than any of its competitors.

The programme to deliver Mytravel.com included three main work streams, covering:

- Business launch: this stream covered organisation, commercial and fulfilment processes for the new business.
- Content management: this stream covered transactional content relating to purchasable products (for example, price and availability) and 'brochure' content to promote, inform and push products to customers (for example, resort guides and accommodation details).

- Solution build: this stream covered the IT elements to develop, deliver and integrate the online transaction site, the content management platform, the network and server infrastructure, together with the integration of the solution with the existing reservation systems.

The technical solution for Mytravel.com contained five major integrated subsystems.

- Engage, a content management and publishing solution
- Broadvision for the website presentation and personalisation engine
- a MOAI-based auction sub-site
- integration with four different reservation systems
- a managed service hosting and network infrastructure.

These subsystems and related components (such as content feeds, testing and systems management) were designed and delivered by 22 different external service providers.

DEVELOPING A SOURCING STRATEGY

All programmes will, to one extent or another, need resources with the right expertise to complete the various programme work packages or deliverables. The first issue for the programme leader is to understand and develop a sourcing plan. There are essentially three options open to the programme leader:

- Use your own people and potentially supplement with specialist contract or secondment staff where gaps exist in your own capabilities or availability. This approach keeps most of the programme activity internal to the organisation, helping with post-programme support and increased business integration, and builds programme delivery capability within the organisation. This approach is similar to the in-sourcing approach adopted by some organisations for their IT.
- Appoint a single supplier to undertake all of the work packages. The appointed supplier may engage the services of other suppliers to deliver its contractual commitments. This approach is similar to an outsourcing arrangement. This type of arrangement has been common for some large and complex programmes, particularly in the public sector, where a prime supplier is appointed to deliver the overall programme.
- Appoint a series of suppliers based on the 'best of breed' approach, where the overall programme is parcelled up into a series of packages or work streams, and suppliers contract to deliver one or more of them. This arrangement is similar to selective sourcing, whereby a supplier is engaged based on the unique specialist expertise it brings to the programme.

This type of arrangement has attracted a lot of backing more recently, particularly in the private sector and financially constrained times.

Most programmes have an element of insourcing supplemented by either the outsourcing or selective sourcing approach. Organisations need to retain control, even if it is limited to financial or contractual management, over the programme delivery. Furthermore, in any large-scale business change programme, this approach provides the umbrella structure that ties together the various business, IT, process, organisational and change pieces into a single cohesive programme. The outsourcing and selective sourcing strategies on their own cannot deliver business change.

The main differences between the outsourcing and selective sourcing strategies are the extent to which a single supplier can be trusted with all the capabilities required for the programme, and the level of change in the business the programme is expected to deliver. In most cases, the selective sourcing strategy is adopted for the simple reason that most suppliers just do not have all the expert resources at the right price to deliver complex integrated programmes.

In considering any of these strategies, another factor should also be considered: the use of offshore suppliers. This area has had a tremendous impact on the IT industry in the United States and UK. Offshore IT providers have changed the sourcing game by:

- undercutting traditional suppliers by as much as 90 per cent on price alone
- demonstrating very significant credentials and capabilities (for example, many Indian offshore organisations can demonstrate a SEI-CMM Level 5 rating)
- overcoming the cultural and geographical issues by having local presence and the ability for their staff to work locally on site.

This book does not focus on offshore suppliers: an entire book could be written about this subject alone. The key point is that a selective sourcing strategy should consider the use of an offshore supplier, particularly for the IT element of the overall solution. The more traditional professional services organisations can then focus on the business and process pieces and the support for the programme management team.

DEVELOPING AN ENGAGEMENT PLAN FOR EXTERNAL SUPPLIERS

Using a high-level design and planning process as a way of driving out supplier engagement

The delivery of a large-scale programme, particularly involving a large degree of IT, means suppliers will be trying many approaches to get involved. They will be pushing their particular product, service or people offerings. Their ultimate aim will be to secure the most business (and revenue) that is possible without putting themselves at too much risk. As a programme leader, you need to be wary of such tactics, and ensure the supplier scope is consistent with your needs and their experience or cost. Yet at the same time, involvement of suppliers in the early stages of the programme formation is critical to success:

- They gain a much better understanding of your specific business, the objectives and priorities of programme and the overall context.
- You will gain an early view of their strengths and weaknesses, and their product or solution offering.
- The supplier can provide early input into the planning and solution design, resulting in a richer solution with the best of breed, and a much more realistic programme plan and timescales, as well as good understanding of issues, risks and early concerns that need to be managed.
- The supplier is able to take ownership and understand its commitments, resulting in much better contractual arrangement between the supplier and programme.

However, this can be difficult to achieve in a situation where competing organisations may be jostling for position against other providers for a greater slice of the pie. And yet without the early involvement of suppliers, the programme is likely to be much more difficult to deliver. So how do achieve this?

There are three principal techniques to managing the involvement of suppliers in the early, perhaps pre-contractual stage, of a programme:

- **Establish a strong core programme team comprising at least a solution architect, programme planner and programme office support**. The solution architect will own the master blueprint of what the programme will deliver: for example, containing view of the business structure, organisation, applications, integration, high-level data and infrastructure. With this view, the programme team can ensure the involvement of suppliers is appropriately focused.
- **Set up a physical space for programme planning and collaboration among suppliers**. We have found this aspect to be a critical success factor. During the early stages of the programme, the different suppliers need to get to know each other in a working environment. At the same time, the planning and set-up often needs to be done quickly to maintain overall momentum, and to avoid suppliers spending significant resources in a pre-contractual stage.

- **Retain overall ownership of the solution blueprint and plans through coordination and involvement of each supplier**. Facilitation skills are key in this stage. The programme team needs to guide each supplier to think through its specific area of involvement, its scope, approach and issues, while maintaining the cross-dependencies and resolving cross-supplier issues and decision-making. This is one of the most difficult stages of the programme. Get this wrong and it will hurt in the delivery stage.

Within the Mytravel programme, a number of specific steps were undertaken early in the programme to engage with suppliers.

1. The programme team facilitated brainstorming, planning and decision-making workshops to build the overall solution design and plans. Each supplier was asked to complete a common project initiation document (PID) to detail its scope, deliverables and activities. The programme team maintained and shared the overall scope with everyone, deliverables and plans, including the key dependencies across suppliers.
2. The solution design and planning was completed over an intensive six-week period, with the main suppliers co-hosted into a common space. The space was partitioned to provide a semi-degree of privacy for each supplier. A common web-based collaboration and sharing facility was established by the programme office to allow suppliers to see common documents, schedules and announcements.
3. The programme team played a leadership role for the overall solution architecture blueprint and programme plan. The team had in place people with experience and skills, to challenge suppliers on many aspects of the solution and integration, force suppliers to constrain themselves to focus on the right areas, and manage overall risks in the programme. There was a tendency for some suppliers to 'bite off' more than was desirable. There was also the need to ensure that everything that was required from the collective set of suppliers was covered by someone, and that no gaps could arise in the future. For example, the interface between Broadvision and Engage had to be defined tightly by both suppliers through the programme to ensure that both suppliers delivered components that could work without further development work by the client or programme team.

As a result of this planning phase, the programme team was confidently able to define its resource needs from the internal business and IT organisations as well as each supplier. Each supplier was then able to contract with the right understanding of its commitments.

Do not forget to plan knowledge management and transfer

An often neglected area is the process of transferring knowledge and know-how from the suppliers to the internal organisation. This is often put in by suppliers as an 'end of project activity' that in reality gets squeezed as delivery pressures become significant. Failure to achieve effective timely knowledge transfer can lead to operational issues as well as significant cost implications. The programme leader can help significantly in this area through a number of simple activities:

- Treating knowledge management and internal capability build-up as a specific programme stream.
- Creating a coordinated plan for recruitment, induction and involvement of new people into the programme.
- Organising specific learn and share sessions, sometimes also referred to as 'brown-bag' sessions.
- Incorporating specific knowledge transfer activities into the project plans of suppliers (as part of the PID development process).
- Using a common team room, both physical and virtual, to encourage learning and sharing.

CONTRACT IN THE RIGHT WAY

Create 'joined-up' contracts

One of the features of a large and complex programme is the need to integrate everything together: not just IT but also the delivery processes. By this we mean that the programme should bring together the statement of work, legal and commercial aspects (the things the supplier is going to deliver) with the programme processes and solution architecture (that is, how the supplier is expected to work within the programme). This important factor is critical if the programme team is going to be able to manage the overall programme as an integrated programme using common processes. It is no good if one supplier has a different set of acceptance criteria from another, and does not fit in with the programme agreed standard.

While this may sound obvious, it does not often happen in reality. The legal representatives of the supplier and the internal lawyers spend many hours debating specific points of the termination and indemnity clauses which, while it is recognised they are important, have nothing to do with the mechanics of delivery. Within the Mytravel programme, the programme team included a legal expert who was integral to the design of key programme processes such as acceptance, observation reporting and change control. His job was to ensure that the contracts being drawn up reflected these processes while at the same time flexibility was maintained in the contract. In many cases, the standard supplier contract required substantial changes to fit in with the programme processes and overall solution.

Do not contract too early

One of the tendencies, particularly driven by the suppliers, is to enter into the contractual negotiations too early in the programme. While a supplier may want a signature on the contract and recognition of a closed deal, this is not in the best interest of the programme. The programme team should get the key processes in place, perform a pilot or test case, and prove some of the downstream process (such as the strategy for testing and acceptance). This takes time, and if rushed will lead to problems later on. The programme team should define the key strategies and plans for these processes, and then ensure they are factored into the contract with the supplier.

On Mytravel, the testing approach caused particular difficulty with the supplier contracts. The testing approach defined the numbers of individuals required from each supplier during end-to-end integration testing. However by the time the approach was developed, the contract with one of the suppliers had already been signed, and it did not accommodate sufficient resource to support the testing phase. After many protracted discussions and negotiations, the programme team was left with either a change order to the contract very early in the programme, or constraining the testing approach to be consistent with the contractual commitments. In the end the second option was adopted, leading to a sub-optimal testing phase.

Spell out clear reporting lines and roles

One of the main areas of difficulty with the Mytravel programme was the contractual arrangement. The suppliers were contracted on a selective sourcing arrangement without any one prime supplier. It would have been difficult to find any one supplier to take the overall risk on this programme. The programme management team also included resources from an ESP.

This caused many difficulties. The programme team had no direct management control over the suppliers other than through influence and gentle coaching of the suppliers. While this was a good outcome for Mytravel, it did present difficulties that can occur with multiple reporting lines.

On the positive side, the contract did include regular supplier review meetings, scheduled alongside key programme milestones and set timing. This provided an opportunity for the programme team and the commercial/legal representatives to present a consolidated view and approach. In addition, the programme sponsors made it clear to the suppliers that the programme team would need to sign off on deliverables before payments could be made. These simple steps gave the programme team significant power to manage and direct the suppliers in the context of the programme.

In one incident, a project manager from one supplier was significantly under-performing. The programme leader raised this with supplier account management, and within a short period of time a new, much improved project manager was put in place.

INTEGRATE EVERYONE INTO THE PROGRAMME

Working together is difficult

The critical success factor in delivering an integrated solution is to ensure the people involved in the delivery work in an integrated fashion. There is a commonly used saying that 'integrated people and processes lead to integrated solutions'. So why is this hard to achieve?

- Each supplier team has its own culture, approach and processes. No two suppliers are the same.
- The legal and contractual frameworks often prevent openness and flexibility for the greater good.
- There are individual capabilities, styles and positional jockeying, as is often the case on any project.

So what can you do? This is where the programme leader and programme office can make a major difference.

Induction role

The programme team should always have on hand a current pack of information for introducing new people into the programme. This should detail the structure of the programme, the teams and key individuals, the various programme processes, current status and forward plans. This pack is critical not just at the start of the programme, but also during delivery. For example, on Mytravel the programme started with around 40 people and added an average of 10 people each month, reaching something like 150 people directly involved and some additional 30 to 50 with minor roles or interests. The programme induction pack served as a key tool for delivering a consistent picture of the programme and its forward plans. The programme team also encouraged the individual suppliers to use the pack as they brought in their new people behind the scenes.

Coaching, mentoring and support role

Another critical aspect of the programme team is to coach, mentor and support the individuals in the programme. This goes beyond administrative support. When you have a larger number of people working intensively over a long period of time, the strengths and weakness of each individual should be understood, and development encouraged. This will not directly support the delivery of the programme, but it makes the process a positive and developmental one for the individuals involved. This may appear to conflict with the contractual arrangements, but without it the contract will become a stumbling block to the success of the programme, which ultimately depends on the performance of individuals in their specific roles.

Within Mytravel, the programme team took several steps to promote this kind of behaviour:

- It built on role models and good examples. The team often made a small positive contribution or success into something very big, and then used it as an example of individual behaviour to encourage others. As an example, the way the wider team worked together to agree the web page design was highlighted to others.
- It supported supplier team leaders with facilitating key meetings and workshops. This is a skill often lacking among very technical people, but key to engaging with a wide range of business and IT people.
- It provided formal feedback directly to individuals and their leaders, around specific development needs or areas to improve in the context of the programme.

Standards and process role

The adoption of common tools and processes to direct, track and report progress from suppliers is critical to the smooth running of the programme. This is important as programmes typically last between one and two years. Having a common tool set will not only make everyone's life easier, but also encourage integration of teams and solutions. Within Mytravel the key programme processes included:

- status and deliverable reporting
- issue and risk tracking and resolution
- change management
- problem definition and management (during testing)
- interim deliverable sign-off.

Even with these processes and standards in place, some suppliers will fail to deliver. For example, on Mytravel one supplier was contracted to deliver a solution design document (SDD) for the content management engine. The structure and content of their document was significantly below required standards because it had failed to follow the programme guidelines. As a result the users, sponsor and programme team all started to lose confidence in the supplier's ability to understand the requirements and deliver the solution. However, with a strong senior-level push, the situation was managed and the SDD delivered effectively.

KEEP THE END INTEGRATED SOLUTION IN MIND

The difference between programme and solution

The programme team has a difficult job. It has to manage not only the schedule and cost but also the solution, weaving and joining together the various components to deliver an integrated IT and business solution. This requires two types of skilled individuals:

- A programme manager, a commercially minded individual who provides strong delivery.
- A solution architect with strong technical and architectural skills to govern the overall design and integration.

The solution architect should be the custodian of the detailed blueprint that each supplier is meant to be delivering against. This is a critical role. While the programme manager owns the delivery processes, there need to be individuals on the programme team who own and can resolve the solution-related issues, be these technical, infrastructure, data, processes or business.

The basic premise for the programme team should be that the individual supplier teams will be focusing on their specific component of the solution, and pushing as much as possible onto other suppliers. The role of the solution architect is to focus each supplier's solutions to achieve an overall integration. Again, this will be helped tremendously if the contract has been set up with a degree of flexibility.

In the case of Mytravel, a key element of the solution was the interface between the content management solution being delivered by one supplier and the Broadvision subsystem being delivered by another supplier. The initial interface was defined at a high level during the early phase of the programme. As is often the case, the devil is in the detail! The mapping logic in the interface can only be done at one end or the other. Once the programme reached the implementation stage, there was significant friction between the two suppliers. Each supplier was pushing the other to write the logic. The role of the programme team was critical. The solution architect micro-managed each issue, and worked in detail with each supplier through negotiation and compromises. The programme solution architect was able to find and build on a sufficient basis to move each supplier in different areas to deliver the overall solution. Looking back, it would have been better to contract with one supplier to perform the intelligent processing, and the other to act as the dumb recipient/sender of data.

Architects, architects ...

They say that everything is created twice, initially on paper (such as an architect creates the plan for a house) and then in real life (as a builder and project manager build the house). It is important for the programme to pull together technical representatives from each major supplier into a technical design authority (TDA) to make decisions and resolve issues around the overall solution. The TDA should also include the overall solution architect from the programme team.

Who is the integrator?

The biggest challenge in any complex integration programme is to ensure all the sub-systems come together at the right time and in the right way to deliver an integrated solution. This can be achieved with a strong oversight solution architect role, and the programme team conducting joint planning and actual delivery of key common streams.

Within Mytravel, the programme team managed the central programme plan and milestones (under change control), and tracked project team plans and deliverables. Weekly progress meetings were held for the Solution Build Stream with representatives from each supplier. Overall and dependent deliverables were tracked and managed at a programme level.

The programme team directly managed the data, infrastructure and integration test streams of work. These streams culminated in the bringing together of the various independent components into a single integrated environment for end-to-end testing and release to the business. The individual suppliers were required to demonstrate that they had reached a certain level and quality in their own individual components before delivering into the end-to-end environment. This included, for example, suppliers working together on a point-to-point basis to test interfaces formally prior to delivering. The end-to-end environment was not meant to be the first time two suppliers had formally tested their integration.

The end-to-end environment was also the first opportunity for suppliers to work with real test data. This proved to be a stumbling block for one of the suppliers. Its own testing prior to delivery had made too many incorrect assumptions about the data model. When delivered, the solution did not work with real-life data. This was pushed back before further integration testing was performed with the other suppliers, which would have wasted significant time for everyone involved.

MANAGE AND RESOLVE SUPPLIER RISKS, CHANGE AND ISSUES

This is where the programme team really proved its worth when working with suppliers. While each supplier manages and resolves its own issues and risks, the role of the programme team is twofold:

- Enforce the timely identification and reporting of issues within a supplier stream that could impact the overall delivery. These issues are relatively easy to resolve since the supplier can usually be forced to resolve them through its contractual obligations.
- Do the same for cross-stream/supplier issues. This requires real focus and attention since these kinds of issues will not be easily addressable through individual supplier contracts.

The programme team needs to be on top of all the important programme issues and issues.

Plan to manage change in supplier contracts

Another complexity for the programme team is changes to scope and requirements. This is unavoidable in any large complex business programmes. Change is inevitable but must be managed appropriately. Supplier contracts will be written to deliver specific products well before the overall solution has been designed, and well before multiple suppliers have created their own specific designs and interfaces.

The process of managing change is critical. Within Mytravel, the programme team established a robust change process that included:

- a simple change order form that could be raised by anyone proposing a change
- the programme team acting as the central control for change logs and workflow
- a change board comprising the programme team and the supplier account managers.

Change is also a difficult subject: a change from one supplier may impact timescales and costs for another supplier. It is also usually an emotive subject. A clear and robust process coupled with programme management leadership will help.

When things go wrong

It is inevitable that no matter how well the programme is structured and managed, there will be issues that need to be addressed with suppliers. The most important aspect of effective supplier management is to identify the issues promptly and focus the necessary resources to resolve them. One of the primary reasons given for poor programme performance and failure is that issues known about early in the programme were either ignored or not dealt with promptly, thereby coming back to bite when they were much more difficult to resolve. For example, a design or integration issue with supplier deliverables will be much more difficult and costly to fix during integration testing.

We have come across two effective techniques for managing programme-level issues with suppliers:

- **Micro-management:** the application of substantial management time and resources to manage and resolve 100 per cent of the details. For example, in the case of the Broadvision and content management interface, both suppliers were raising issues associated with the other suppliers' provision and processing of data in the interface. The programme team quickly determined the underlying problem to be related to the physical implementation of the data model in both systems. The programme team then applied significant focus and resources to micro-manage:
  - the list of issues
  - the decisions that had to be made that could impact functionality
  - the scope and contractual changes
  - testing and test data changes.
  One could argue that such an issue should not have arisen in the first place. However, this was inevitable. When the logical data model and the interface were agreed between the two suppliers, neither supplier team had a complete and full understanding of the other's detailed solution.
- **SWAT:** in this case, a formal sub-unit or team is created to clear a backlog or complete a specific deliverable. The team is created with full-time individuals, hand-picked from the existing team members. This is usually a special team, working together to complete a specific outcome. In the case of Mytravel, this approach was applied to the completion of the web HTML design. This was initially planned as a serial activity, with the Mytravel in-house team completing the design and a supplier team completing the implementation. However, the programme team soon realised that this was not working. The designs were late, they did not always match the scope, implementation was running late and often did not have much resemblance to the designs. The programme team created a single SWAT team, co-located in the same space and containing all the Mytravel web developers and supplier resources involved in this area. The team was led by the programme management and lasted for six weeks, after which the deliverables were completed and agreed. The team was then disbanded into the original involvements.

Contractual versus doing the right thing

This is perhaps the most sensitive area of working with suppliers. There is always a natural tension between the team on the ground and their management back at base. The team on the ground will be part of an integrated programme focused on delivery under the guidance of the programme team.

If the programme management has done a good job, then the supplier team will be working and behaving as part of one overall team. However, back at base, there will be pressures to manage tightly to contract, look for opportunities for additional revenue through scope changes, and at the same time manage any internal delivery or people-related problems at arm's length from the programme leadership. The question is, how do you manage in this environment?

- As we have mentioned elsewhere, create a one-team environment with open, impartial discussions and reporting.
- Manage the human aspects of the team effectively, to win over the supplier's team and its loyalty. This means tending to the team's personal, development and social needs as well as the formal contractual role. In Mytravel, the programme team considered its role to be as much as team mentoring and coaching as overall delivery. This also helped the team on the ground to be much more open and clear about progress and issues.
- Build a strong relationship with people at base, for example through formal review meetings, status updates and social gatherings. It is just as important to ensure the account/relationship management team of the supplier is well integrated into the programme so that issues can be resolved quickly without unnecessarily complex contractual hurdles. In Mytravel, regular supplier meetings kept the account managers copied in on progress reports, and they were invited to key meetings and socials. In this way, they were directly involved and could be called upon to resolve issues.
- Be very clear about contractual commitments, and the authority invested in the programme team. The programme team has to ensure it does not cross the line between managing the programme, and making key design or contractual decisions without proper consultation. It is very easy to make remarks that could be taken by a supplier as approval of a change request or scope change. It is also easy to become too friendly and lose the impartiality of the programme leader role. This a balance that needs to be struck by the programme team members, based on their individual style and the nature of individuals involved in the programme.

The programme leader needs to be able both to manage the contract and to operate with a team mind-set. This is a subtle area: getting it wrong can cause all sorts of issues. Getting it right will help smooth the path delivery.

SUMMARY

In this chapter, we have outlined a number of approaches to working with suppliers as part of a large integrated programme. In summary, the key to successful engagement of suppliers is to balance the team and contractual management with a focus on both the delivery processes and the final solution. We recommend programme leaders and teams ensure they address the following areas in any programmes involving one or more suppliers:

- Establish an appropriate sourcing strategy.
- Create the environment for suppliers to work with in-house staff on the design early in the programme.
- Include the solution design and programme processes in the contractual agreements with suppliers.
- Treat suppliers as part of the programme team.
- Ensure someone in the programme retains an overall integration oversight.
- Step in early to resolve cross-supplier issues, risks and changes.

Managing relationships, both contractual and interpersonal, with suppliers is a key capability required to deliver programmes and projects within our enterprises.

14 Building a communications capability

INTRODUCTION

Consider for a moment these recent business trends:

- increasing merger and acquisition activity
- a greater number of strategic alliances, even between competitors
- blurring of lines between industries and regions
- emerging power of the individual in the war for talent
- industry shake-ups due to regulatory pressures
- increasingly complex customer needs
- shorter and shorter product lifecycles
- continued integration of technology and business
- increasing pressure on senior executives to deliver.

These trends mean that today's organisations are spending more money, more often and on bigger programmes. You have probably had some level of involvement in these initiatives, perhaps as a project manager or as a recipient of the change. However, greater experience with change may not always necessarily mean that you are better able to deal with it and deliver maximum benefits.

As discussed in earlier chapters, a startling number of programmes still fail to deliver the expected value. They go over budget and over time. Probable reasons for this are:

- Programme team members often do not understand the interdependencies of their work and so cancel out each other's efforts.
- The intended changes to employee work practices do not always happen, or occur grudgingly only after extra time and expense.
- Board members do not understand where the programme is up to, and are unconvinced of the value of the work.
- Shareholders fail to support a resolution to release funds to allow the programme to continue.
- Suppliers are not aware of procedural changes and think the business is failing to respond to their queries, so they focus their efforts on other accounts.
- decision-making is slow and windows of opportunity are lost.

These outcomes are often the consequences of failing to communicate effectively with those who influence the programme's success: team members, employees, sponsors and decision makers, shareholders and business partners. These people have the power to make or break an initiative. Their involvement and buy-in is critical.

So effective programme communications is about communicating with the right people at the right time in order to secure their involvement and buy-in (whether they are employees being impacted or senior managers who will need to make key decisions). It means understanding what is important to those who have an influence over the programme, and interacting with them in an engaging and effective way. It also means establishing communication mechanisms that are relevant to the programme, rather than just using 'business as usual' techniques (which are made for 'business as usual' situations, rather than complex cross-organisational changes).

Importantly, programme communications is not just about sending the right messages, it is also about tapping into ideas and expertise that exist outside the programme team, then using this feedback to improve the programme.

Effective programme communication underpins the enterprise programme management (EPM) model, and has multiple touch points, including programme architecture, change architecture and project management. It is a key capability to develop, and will help drive organisational agility.

Overall, we believe that the ability to communicate with the organisation as programmes are implemented is an essential capability in today's market. Developing and using this capability will not only help you achieve the goals of the programme, it will also help you deliver long-lasting and sustainable change within your business. In addition, a communications capability is just one

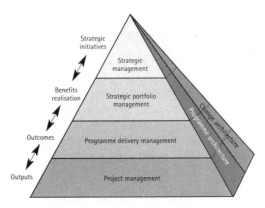

Figure 14.1 The enterprise programme management framework

characteristic of high-performance programme teams, teams that can act as a competitive edge for your business, as discussed in earlier chapters. The objective of this chapter is to help you build this capability by laying the foundations for a robust communications strategy and plan.

WHAT WILL YOU GET OUT OF THIS CHAPTER?

There are a number of organisational players who have varying levels of interest in programme communications. To get the most out of this chapter, you should identify the outcomes or objectives that are important for you.

For example, if you are a programme manager, you will want to understand how best to share the programme vision, goals and progress with those who will impact, and be impacted by, the programme. You will want to secure buy-in of key people as soon as possible, and hence secure resources to develop and execute a robust communications plan. If you are responsible for change management for a particular initiative, you will want to develop and deliver a detailed communications plan that will help achieve the business objectives.

You may be part of the internal communications department, in which case you will want to understand the process that programme staff go through in developing and delivering their communications plan, and then identify opportunities to leverage existing channels and media. Or you may be a programme team member who has regular contact with the wider organisation. You will need to know which messages to communicate at which point in the programme, often informally and alongside the more visible communication methods.

Whatever your role, take a few minutes to identify why programme communications is important to you, and what you hope to achieve by reading this chapter. This will then help you to focus on those topics that will have the most impact on your job.

WHAT DO WE MEAN BY 'COMMUNICATION'?

In general, good communication is about exchanging meaningful information with other people, often aimed at influencing beliefs or actions. Programme communications is no different: it is about exchanging timely and useful information with programme stakeholders (such as team members, senior executives and employees) in order to secure their buy-in and involvement. Examples include face-to-face discussions, formal presentations by senior managers, regular progress meetings, email distributions and intranet sites.

THE BENEFITS OF PROGRAMME COMMUNICATIONS

The benefits can be defined at the organisational and individual level.

Organisational benefits

- Provides clarity around communication roles and responsibilities.
- Contributes toward developing appropriate levels of commitment to the programme.

- Creates an underlying foundation of trust, as communication becomes frequent and meaningful, needed to engage all levels of the organisation.
- Minimises destructive rumour mills.
- Energises people for change.
- Builds credibility in the programme's solution.

Individual benefits

- Prepares and manages expectations about the upcoming changes.
- Facilitates a sense of community.
- Promotes morale and feeling of value.
- Links management to employees.
- Builds buy-in and ownership for change.
- Helps people understand how they fit into the change, are impacted by the change and what they need to do to contribute to the change.

The rest of the chapter will show how these types of benefits can be obtained by developing a programme communications capability.

USING COMMUNICATIONS TO MANAGE RESISTANCE

Programmes usually mean change, and change affects people in very significant ways. This creates turbulence and uncertainty. People can react strongly and unpredictably, often resisting the change. This in turn affects the stability and performance of the business during the programme and beyond.

Having worked with many businesses going through change, we have seen first hand what resistance can do, whether it comes from shareholders, senior executives, employees or even unwilling programme team members. Resistance can come in a variety of guises: a failure to commit resources, missing meetings, complaining about the project (all 'active' forms of resistance), and not advocating the change or not asking questions in meetings (both 'passive' forms of resistance).

Why do people resist change? Change is very situational, and people oppose change for a wide range of personal and organisational reasons. In general terms, however, resistance is often driven by three states:

- Not knowing: people do not know about the change.
- Not able: people do not have the ability to change.
- Not willing: people are not willing to change.

You may hear this referred to as the 'resistance pyramid'. Within your company, different people will be at different states, or levels, of the pyramid. In fact, they may be in more than one state at the same time. Programme

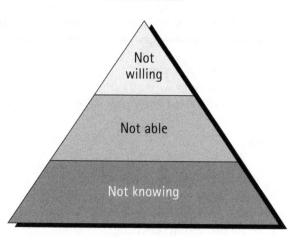

Figure 14.2 The resistance pyramid

communication is directly relevant to targeting and overcoming these states of resistance, and building the commitment needed for successful programmes.

Nearly every communications plan focuses, at least in part, on 'not knowing'. Sharing information about the programme vision, strategy, rationale, approach and progress helps to remove uncertainty and fear of the unknown. This state is often the easiest (relatively speaking) to deal with.

The state of 'not able' is more complex. Here communication activities need to focus on two issues: first, understanding why people think they cannot make the change, and second, taking actions to help overcome this view. In some cases, people are not aware of the fact that they already possess the knowledge and skills to make the change. They may also not be aware of the extent of support available. In these cases, information and two-way communication activities can reduce resistance. However, in other cases, barriers such as lack of skills, an inappropriate organisation structure or lack of funding may mean that people really are not able to make the change. In these cases, the broader programme resources will play a role in helping develop the skills, structures, processes and systems to enable the change. Whatever the scenario, programme communications can play a supporting role.

The third state, 'not willing', is the most difficult to overcome. In these cases, people may already understand the need for the change and its impact on them. They may even have the knowledge, skills and support to make the change, but are reluctant to do so. Here, the role of communications will be to understand people's needs (which will differ up and down the organisation) and to deliver communications that address these needs. Communication needs at this level often include:

- Reassurance: people often believe the worst.
- Business strategy: people need to know that there is one.
- Direction: where should they focus their efforts.
- Involvement: wanting to feel part of the programme and having a real impact on the results.
- Expectations: what can they control and manage?
- Performance and reward: what is in it for them?

Effective communications addresses all three states, hence it is important to remember them as you work through the programme's communication needs.

ALIGNING COMMUNICATIONS WITH CHANGE ACCEPTANCE

The resistance pyramid focuses on the reasons why people are not buying into the programme, allowing you to employ specific techniques to address different problems. This is a reactionary, yet valuable, approach. But when building buy-in to the programmes, it is just as important to employ a proactive approach – to progressively help people to commit to and own the change. As discussed in Chapter 7, each person who is involved with, or impacted by, the programme will go through a personal process of acceptance of the oncoming change. This is true of a wide range of stakeholders, including programme team members, employees and business partners. The stages these people go through usually range from a lack of awareness of what is happening up to an internalisation or ownership of the change.

Those responsible for communications must be aware of the acceptance process that stakeholders are likely to go through, and tailor communications messages and roles accordingly. Figure 14.3 provides an example of what this process might look like. The focus on communication activities must align to the relevant stages of the change acceptance process.

As you can see from the figure, the five 'types' of communications activities are:

- Advertise (tell people about the programme in general terms).
- Counsel (tailor messages to address people's concerns).
- Involve (work with people to gain their input and buy-in).
- Educate (help people build the skills and capabilities to be successful in the new environment).
- Support (provide ongoing coaching to sustain commitment).

At different points in the programme, you will need to initiate different types of communications activities, although usually more than one type in parallel. Bear in mind, however, that people within your organisation are likely

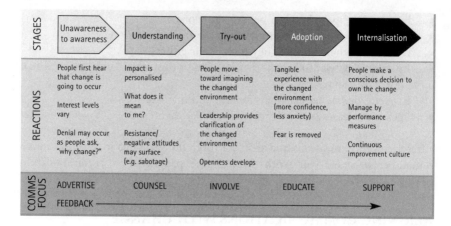

Figure 14.3 Stages of reaction to change

to be at different stages of the change process at any one time. Even people within one audience group may be at varying stages. As you will see later in this chapter, it is important to focus on both general and individual face-to-face communications to address this issue.

As we move through the remainder of the chapter, keep two concepts in mind: the resistance pyramid (responding to resistance issues) and the change acceptance process (proactively building commitment). Building these concepts into your communications approach will help you deliver meaningful and practical communications.

BUILDING A PROGRAMME COMMUNICATION CAPABILITY

Effective programme communications relies upon three key outcomes:

- Developing a communications strategy that is aligned to the programme strategy and goals.
- Creating a comprehensive and practical work plan that outlines the who, what, when and how of all communication activities.
- Organising resources and processes to create, manage and deliver the strategy and plan.

This chapter is about helping you to build and deliver a communications strategy and plan for your particular programme, but we know that no two programmes will have the same communication needs, even within the one company. There is no 'one size fits all' approach for effective programme communications. For this reason, we focus on posing questions that will help you to define your requirements, and suggest tools or techniques that you will find helpful. In addition, we include some examples to bring the ideas to life: a merger of two companies, a technology implementation and a customer-focused brand re-launch. To achieve these outcomes, this chapter will guide you through the process shown in Figure 14.4.

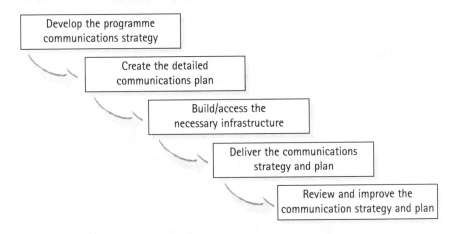

Figure 14.4 Building a programme communications capability

DEVELOPING YOUR COMMUNICATIONS STRATEGY

The quality of your communications strategy is the key factor in building an effective programme communications capability. The strategy must reflect the goals of the programme and the context of your business. It must pinpoint those people who will be impacted by the programme, and isolate the best way to communicate with them. As a strategy, it will set the direction and tone of the subsequent communication activities. This is an important document and you need to get it right.

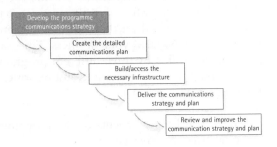

Figure 14.5 Developing a communications strategy

The elements of a good communications strategy are split out into the following ten sections. Take the time to think through and write down your answers to the questions within each section. This is not a textbook exercise to be done in 20 minutes. It will take time, effort and consultation with your colleagues, but the end result will be a documented

197

programme communications strategy – one that meets the specific needs of the programme and business.

Before you get started, decide who to involve in the development of the communications strategy: your peers, team members or just yourself for now. Whatever you decide, it will be critical to allow opportunities throughout this development process to test and confirm your ideas with others.

Step 1: Define your high-level objectives

Think through the rationale and objectives of the programme itself:

Why are you doing this programme?

What is the programme strategy? What are the programme goals?

At a high level, who will be impacted by the programme, and in what way?

What will happen if the programme fails?

Once you have a solid grasp of the programme strategy and goals, translate these into the high-level communication requirements:

As a result of the above, what are the preliminary communication objectives and priorities?

Overall, what general types of communication are likely to be required (advertise, counsel, involve, educate and/or support)?

These questions are designed to provide the initial direction; the answers will be refined later. Moreover, the answers to these questions are very situational. They depend on the nature of the programme you are undertaking and the context of your business. For example, Table 14.1 lists some priorities identified by three different programmes.

Once the high-level objectives and priorities have been defined, consider the next set of questions:

What will be the benefits to the programme and the business if these objectives are achieved?

What issues will be critical to the success of programme communication?

What are the existing barriers that programme communication must overcome?

The answers to these questions will form the opening section in the programme communications strategy document. You will want to revisit and

Table 14.1 Sample communication priorities

Type of programme	Communication priorities
Merger of two companies	Decide and communicate structure and leadership quickly (*advertise*) Deal with the 'Have I got a job?', 'What is my role?' questions (*counsel*) Shape the future strategy and business priorities (*educate*)
Technology implementation	What will happen and when (*advertise*) How roles will change (*educate*)
Customer-focused brand re-launch	Understand how internal behaviours reinforce the brand (*educate*) Communicate what needs to change at an organisational and individual level (*advertise, educate*)

review these answers once you have analysed the detailed communication needs of the business.

You should of course create a document that works for you and your business, but as a starting point you may want to reproduce each of these section headings in your own document.

Step 2: Agree guiding principles

This strategy will set the direction for the later development of the communications plan and content. Think through the guidelines that would need to be shared with those responsible for developing and delivering the plan:

What are the principles that should guide effective programme communication in your business?

For example, when one of our clients undertook a brand relaunch, some of their communication guiding principles included:

- 'The timing, integration and presentation of communications to Customer Service, Marketing and Operations staff will be established and agreed by consultation with the Steering Group, the leadership team and key stakeholders (identified as Level 1 in the Stakeholder Directory);

- Communications will be regular – monthly at a minimum. Even if there is little new information to share, we will continue to reinforce key messages and minimise staff anxiety;

- We will communicate the latest thinking wherever and whenever possible (after consultation with the Legal Department with regard to commercial sensitivity);

- Internal and external communications will be aligned and consistent. Our communications team will work closely with Corporate Affairs;

- Line Managers will be accountable via the performance management system for delivery of communications to their staff.'

Your communication principles might be quite different from the above, perhaps more general or more detailed. The critical step is to define those that make the most sense for the programme and business.

Step 3: Identify the needs of stakeholders and audiences

Identifying who's who with respect to the programme is one of the most critical steps. This can also be labour intensive, so you may want to enlist support if you have not already done so.

There are two broad groups of people who will be important to the programme. Stakeholders are key individuals who can make or break a project, and usually need to be managed on an individual basis. Examples are the managing director, trade union officials and unofficial leaders. Audiences are groups of people who will be impacted by the project and who need to buy-in to the upcoming changes. Examples are employees, customers and suppliers. The way you manage stakeholders and audiences will often be quite different.

> Who are the stakeholders of this programme, both internal and external to your business?

> Who are the audiences that will be impacted, both internal and external to your business?

Your two lists might be drawn from the following, but remember to be as specific as you can (naming names where possible).

Possible stakeholders and/or audience groups

- programme management
- programme team members
- board and senior executives
- middle management

- team leaders
- employees (usually distinguished by function)
- trade union representatives
- suppliers
- customers
- shareholders
- city analysts
- government or regulatory bodies
- local community.

Once you have compiled your two lists, ask yourself:

How will this programme affect them?

Are they currently showing resistance to the programme? If so, what is driving this (not knowing, not able, not willing?)

Where are they currently on the change acceptance process (lack of awareness to awareness, understanding, try-out, adoption, internalisation)?

Where do you want them to be?

Based on the above, what type of communication activities will best build their commitment (advertise, counsel, involve, educate and/or support)?

Stakeholders and audiences that have common communication needs could be grouped together. Initially these audience segments may be quite broad. The audience groups can be segmented further as the programme progresses and the impact on different audiences is further understood.

For a recent technology implementation, we helped our client to populate the matrix shown in Table 14.2. You may find it helpful to capture this information in a similar way. When populating this matrix, remember to revisit your stated objectives, priorities and guidelines. Later on this matrix can be used as a basis for the more detailed communications plan.

Answering these questions can be challenging. In general, there are two methods that can be employed to determine the attitudes and needs of the stakeholder and audience groups:

- 'Rough and ready' assessment, where the programme manager, communications specialist or other key individuals involved in the programme undertake an assessment of resistance and change acceptance levels of stakeholders and audience groups according to observed behaviours and attitudes of those groups.
- Qualitative assessment, where the stakeholders and audience groups are asked to complete a questionnaire on their thoughts, feelings and understanding about the programme.

Table 14.2 Sample audience/stakeholder matrix

Audience/ stakeholder	Impact from the programme	Influence on the programme	Evidence of resistance	Current stage of acceptance process	Desired stage of acceptance process	Communication needs (advertise; counsel; involve; educate; support)	Action steps

Which one do you choose? Consider the advantages and disadvantages listed in Table 14.3.

Table 14.3 Advantages and disadvantages of communication needs assessment methods

Method	Advantages	Disadvantages
Rough and ready	Quick Fit for purpose (internal project management document) Based on observed behaviour rather than espoused behaviour.	Subjective Does not allow the person/people being measured the opportunity to 'have their say' Confidentiality/data protection issues?
Qualitative assessment	Asks the person/people being assessed to provide their own thoughts and feelings which can make them feel involved and listened to Better quality information	Takes much more time People may not be willing to be involved May be difficult when there are groups of people being observed

Step 4: Review current communications capability

Understanding the current communications capability will help you to decide the extent to which it can be used for the programme, or whether additional development is required.

> What are the current communications channels used within your business?
>
> How effective are they?
>
> Who in the organisation is responsible for developing communication content, and managing activities and infrastructure?
>
> What messages have already been communicated about the programme – how have they been received?

To answer these questions, a communication audit should be undertaken to gather information about current channels, ownership, messages, audiences, processes and resources, feedback loops and sign-off routes. This will also help to identify the barriers and enablers of the existing communication infrastructure.

Channels vary between organisations. However the following list can be used as a starting point:

Formal:

- steering committees
- annual general meetings
- team progress reports
- annual reports
- intranet/Internet
- general emails
- magazines and newsletters
- bulletin boards
- general memos
- general voicemails.

Face to face:

- team meetings
- one-on-one coaching sessions
- senior management briefing sessions
- training courses
- video conferences
- management walkarounds.

Personal:

- one-on-one coaching sessions
- personalised voicemails
- personalised emails
- the grapevine.

For a recent merger programme, we helped our client to populate the simple matrix shown in Table 14.4. You may find it helpful to capture this information in a similar way. Once the assessment is complete, validate the information with people from all levels within the business. These meetings can also serve as an opportunity to elicit information about the hot topics within the business.

Table 14.4 Sample communication channel matrix

Communication method/ channel	Current fre- quency	Advantages	Drawbacks	Opportunities	Assessment (use, develop, scrap)

Ultimately, you need to decide the extent to which you can use the existing communications infrastructure to meet the programme needs.

> Which methods already in place will communicate the programme strategy and goals most effectively?
>
> Which channels will need to be developed or improved?

When identifying the most appropriate communication methods to employ, keep in mind the levels of the resistance pyramid. For example, if key groups 'don't know' about the programme, then look for methods to gain maximum exposure. If some stakeholders 'aren't willing' to support the programme, look for methods to involve them in an appropriate way.

Also, based on our experience it appears that the greater the degree of personal change expected, the better people respond to face-to-face and personal communications. Build these considerations into the plan by looking for methods that involve one-on-one, personalised interaction.

Step 5: Define the key messages

What are the vital messages to communicate to stakeholders and audiences?

To answer this question, refer back to your objectives, priorities and guidelines as well as the stakeholder and audience assessment. For example, during a recent merger of two multinational businesses, the priorities of the communications plan were to communicate the leadership structure quickly, deal with the 'Have I got a job?' and 'What is my role?' questions, and share the future strategy and business priorities. As a result, the communications team identified key messages that would need to be transmitted via the various channels:

How do you know what the relevant messages are? In most cases, you will use the knowledge of programme personnel and senior management to identify the most appropriate messages. These messages must support the programme's vision and strategy, as well as being meaningful to the recipients (see Figure 14.6, and your stakeholder and audience analysis for ideas).

Strategy
- Strategy of the firm and how we are working to achieve this
- New value proposition and resultant action plan

Building community
- How we are, and should be, working together to achieve the new strategy
- Networking opportunities

Performance
- Wins and successes in the marketplace
- Performance against plan and utilisation figures

Aspirational/motivational
- Why this is a great place to work
- Why you should want to stay with the firm

Marketplace
- Updates on what is happening in the marketplace
- Competitor performance
- Forward view of 'order book'

People
- Career progression
- Promotions
- Reward and recognition

Figure 14.6 Possible key messages

Step 6: Consider style and tone

How you communicate is just as important as what you communicate:

> How should the key messages be communicated?
>
> Will the communication styles be simple or flashy?
>
> How do you want the audience groups to feel about communication?
>
> How important is it that your messages are consistent in style and tone?

Consider language and style use. The language used is one of the most powerful factors in whether people understand the message or not. As a general rule, keep it simple.

A useful tip is to get someone from the intended audience to review each communications piece before it is published. Opportunities for this will depend on the content and confidentiality of the message. This is a good technique for weeding out any jargon and ensuring the communication messages are explained in a way that can be understood by the target audience.

Step 7: Align communications with programme milestones

> At what stage in the overall programme do key messages need to be communicated?
>
> At a high level, what is the logical sequence for communicating to different stakeholders and audiences?

An effective programme communication strategy will be aligned to the overall programme and its milestones, and should run in tandem with it. Work with programme management personnel to understand the key stages and milestones of the programme, and adjust the communication calendar as appropriate. This will be an ongoing activity.

Step 8: Be able to measure the effectiveness of the communication strategy

The communication needs of the programme will change over time. Similarly, the audiences will change their perceptions and requirements over time. The programme itself may be redefined. For these reasons, it is critical to establish a feedback process that works for the programme.

> How will you know if your communications are sufficiently proactive and clearly understood?

How will you identify if the sponsors and executives are committed to the programme's objectives?

What mechanisms can you use to determine whether the communication strategy is achieving the programme's objectives?

How will you ensure that objectives are achieved and the working philosophy is adhered to?

There are various forms of formal feedback, such as questionnaires/feedback forms, focus groups, annual surveys and telephone surveys. Informal feedback routes include project teams, management findings when 'walking around' and feedback from human resource management staff. During a recent technology implementation, we helped the client to establish an intranet-based feedback mechanism. This proved to be a valuable source of information for the programme team.

It is also important to understand the informal routes that already exist in the organisation, which can be used to gather feedback either on programme communications to date or on what people would like to hear. Informal routes include the grapevine and casual chats over the water cooler or lunch table.

Step 9: Establish a lasting communication framework

Developing a programme communications capability is a long-term goal, rather than a short-term fix, so consider the way that you can sustain the capability across the business.

Have roles and responsibilities been clearly defined in order to achieve long-term goals?

Have line managers been provided with the skills and involvement to enable them to conduct regular face-to-face communication with their teams?

Will those affected by the programme be involved in a continuing programme of two-way communication, enabling them to contribute their experience and ideas to the improvement of the implementation process?

During a recent customer-focused vision and brand relaunch programme, we helped the client to develop internal communication capabilities, and gradually transferred knowledge from consultants to employees. As part of this, we jointly established a regular review mechanism to sustain the quality of programme communications.

Step 10: Gather support for your strategy

By this point, a draft programme communications strategy should be in place – one that focuses on the specific needs of the programme and business. However, the job is not yet over. Be sure to test the content with others within your business and make the necessary refinements. You may want to obtain formal sign-off from key stakeholders such as the steering committee, programme manager, human resource director and internal communications staff.

Once the strategy is in a good state, the process of translating it into a detailed communications plan can begin. In reality, the strategy will be a dynamic document. It is likely that it will be revisited throughout the life of the programme.

CREATING A COMMUNICATIONS PLAN FOR THE PROGRAMME

Completing the above steps will place you in a strong position to now develop the detailed communications plan. The programme communication plan should include the following major sections:

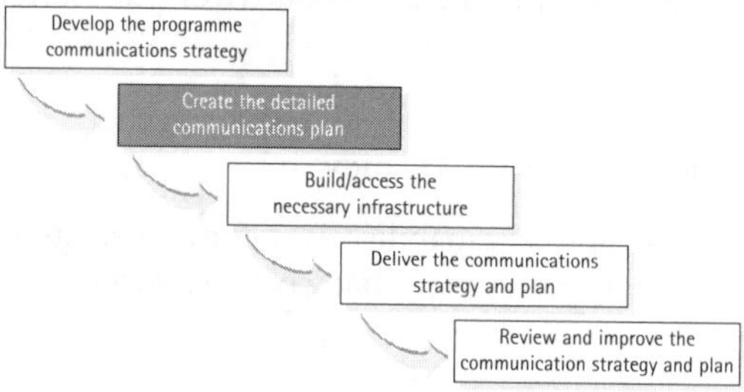

Figure 14.7 Creating a programme communications plan

Message

What messages are needed: recommended messages that need to be communicated to the audiences, and the purpose for providing them with this information.

Desired outcome

Why these are needed: the desired result we hope to achieve by sending the communication.

Audience(s)

Who needs information: specific audiences being impacted by the business transformation.

Event

Where the message is going to be communicated: the event that gives the sender the opportunity to communicate the required message.

Timeframe

When each message should be delivered: recommended timeframe for implementing each communication vehicle during the implementation.

Method

How these messages can be delivered most effectively: recommended communication vehicles for delivering these messages to the appropriate audiences.

Feedback mechanism

How the information is to be gathered: the most effective way to gather feedback from the audience regarding the communicated message.

Developer

Who will develop the message: specific person(s) responsible within your business for preparing the message and the material needed to present the message.

Sender

Who should send each message: specific person(s) most effective in communicating each message to the appropriate audiences.

The plan can take many forms; however a spreadsheet matrix or project plan is probably the easiest to manage.

At this point, the strategy and planning phases – often the most time-intensive phases – should be complete. The next three phases are simply about turning those plans into reality. This involves working out the resources and infrastructure needed, executing the plan, and reviewing and improving.

BUILDING YOUR COMMUNICATIONS INFRASTRUCTURE

Once your communications strategy and plan are in place, the appropriate infrastructure needs to be planned. Early on in the process, you will need to assign responsibilities for the design and delivery of programme communications.

Do new programme roles need to be created?

Can existing communications infrastructure be utilised?

How do you ensure that management takes responsibility for communications?

Consider the following principles.

Figure 14.8 Building the communications infrastructure

Ensure roles and responsibilities are clearly defined

Communication must be an integrated part of the project. One or two people who are not involved in design or process work cannot effectively communicate to audiences on their own. There needs to be a strong link between the design teams and the communications team/ person.

It is important to ensure roles and responsibilities are clearly defined. Communication is more than content, it is process and delivery too. It is often too easy to assume other people doing something that they are not.

Consider joint working with other teams

There may be other programmes or projects running in parallel with your own. It is imperative that you find out what other activities are happening, and consider these in your work. You do not want to send conflicting messages. You might also want to tap into the communications resources being used elsewhere.

Make sure you include, or link to, external communications

Depending on the organisation, you may find that employees find out what is happening by reading it in daily newspapers before you have had a chance to communicate it internally, especially if there are leaks. Similarly, you may find the public relations (PR) people are communicating messages externally that differ from the ones you are generating internally. Sometimes this happens because PR is in one department such as marketing, and internal communications is in another department such as HR. If this is the case, you may want to include a PR person in your joint communications group.

Consider using an editorial team

Do not underestimate how long it takes to publish and distribute communications material. If there is a lot of change or many impacted audiences it may be worth establishing an editorial team. This team could be responsible for developing the detailed plan, and act as a sounding board for communication activities and messages. Ideally this team would be representative of the organisation, know what is happening at the grassroots level of the business, have the ear of the organisation, and could spend time reviewing communication materials at short notice.

Additionally, consider if there are other people the team needs access to, such as copywriters, creative experts, conference organisers or market research agencies.

DELIVERING THE COMMUNICATIONS STRATEGY AND PLAN

By this stage, you should have a validated communications strategy and plan along with a view on the resources and infrastructure required. To now deliver and implement the strategy and plan, the following activities should be undertaken:

Figure 14.9 Delivering the communications strategy and plan

1. Mobilise the communication team:
    -   Are the required resources in place?
    -   Do they have the necessary skills?
    -   Have performance measures been established?
2. Develop communication content:
    -   Based on your previous analysis, what are the detailed communications messages required by stakeholders and audiences?
3. Deliver the communications:
    -   Is the plan flexible enough to change as the programme evolves?

REVIEWING AND IMPROVING

Implement the feedback loops developed earlier in the process. Remember to:

-   Gather feedback about communications from stakeholders and audiences:
    -   How effective is the communication process?
    -   Are the key messages still relevant for the needs of the stakeholders and audiences?
    -   What are people saying about the programme?

- Review the communication team:
  - How effective is the team?
  - Are team members achieving their objectives?
  - Is there a need to build further capability?
- Review programme status:
  - Does the communication strategy still reflect the needs of the programme?
  - Is the communication plan still aligned to programme milestones?
  - Adjust the strategy and plan as necessary.

A checklist for effective communication

By this point, you should have a good understanding of the communication needs of the business and the best way to meet them. If you have a programme in play right now, then you may also have established the necessary communications infrastructure.

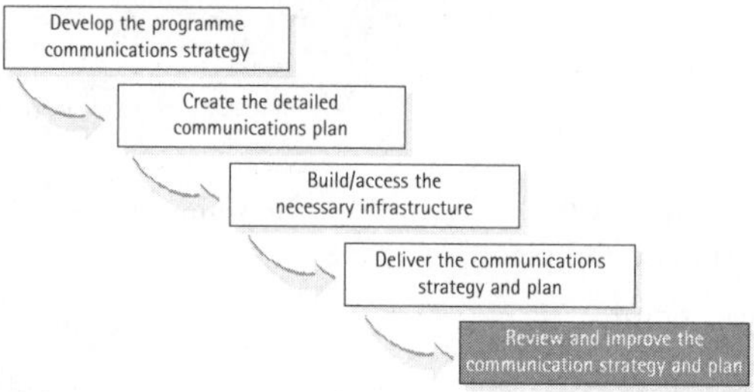

Remember that communications is situational: the strategy, plan and infrastructure need to fit your organisation. Moreover, the requirements of your organisation will change as the programme progresses. But here are a few final bites of communication know-how that are widely applicable:

Figure 14.10 Reviewing and improving the strategy and plan

Communication strategy

- Segment and assess the impacted change on audiences and stakeholders.
- Conduct a communications audit.
- Develop and document an overall communications strategy for each phase of the change process.
- Assess the effectiveness of the communication strategy on a regular basis.
- Assign somebody to be responsible for the overall execution of the strategy.

Communications plan

- Be clear on what messages to send, when.
- Increase message credibility by using the appropriate sender and involving leadership.

- Use the most effective methods to convey messages: this often means using existing channels where buy-in already exists.
- Set up effective feedback mechanisms to help the sender understand whether the message was received and how it was accepted.
- Document and regularly update your plan.

Communications infrastructure

- Ensure roles and responsibilities are clearly defined.
- Utilise existing communications resources where possible.
- Link to external communications.
- Consider using an editorial team.

Delivery

- Mobilise the communication team with the necessary skills and Key Performance Indicators (KPIs).
- Develop communication content based on previous analyses of stakeholder and audience needs, particularly the stages of change acceptance and resistance.
- Ensure that the communications plan is flexible enough to cope with future changes.

Review and improve

- Gather feedback on a regular basis from stakeholders and audiences, both formally and informally.
- Review the communication team and help build capability.
- Ensure that the communication strategy and plan continues to reflect programme needs.

SUMMARY

Effective programme communications is about communicating with the right people at the right time in order to secure their involvement and buy-in to the programme. It means understanding what is important to those who have an influence over the initiative, and interacting with them in an engaging and effective way. Securing their buy-in can help the programme to achieve its objectives and deliver the intended benefits.

But achieving this buy-in requires careful thought as to the most appropriate communications strategy, plan and infrastructure for the programme at hand. It means establishing communication mechanisms that are relevant to the programme, rather than just using 'business as usual' processes. The high-level process outlined in this chapter can help you achieve this:

- Develop the programme communications strategy.
- Create the detailed communications plan.
- Build or access the necessary infrastructure.
- Deliver the communications plan.
- Review and improve.

Overall, the ability to communicate with your organisation as you implement programmes is an essential capability in today's market. Developing and using this capability will not only help you achieve the goals of the programme, but will also help you deliver long-lasting and sustainable change within your business.

CASE STUDY: TUI, USING COMMUNICATIONS IN SUPPORT OF A FINANCE FUNCTION TRANSFORMATION

Resignations of key personnel. Decreasing employee morale. Dips in productivity. These concerns are enough to make most managers nervous about communicating a significant change to the wider business. This anxiety is further increased if there is a risk of redundancy, requiring communication with employee representative groups. There may also be concerns about how city analysts, customers and suppliers will react to the news – whether they will perceive that the programme will be of benefit. A robust approach to communications can meet these challenges.

To illustrate some of the concepts covered in this chapter, here is an example of how a communications strategy was put into practice as part of TUI's recent programme to implement leading-edge technology across the business and build a new Finance Shared Service Centre.

Company background

In 2000, Preussag AG bought Thomson Travel Group, Thomson being the largest travel group in the UK. In 2002 Preussag AG formally changed its name to TUI AG, and Thomson Travel Group became TUI Northern Europe. The UK-based operation, TUI UK, has remained the largest travel and tourism company in the UK and is the name behind many popular brands. Its retailers include Lunn Poly, Travel House and Manchester Flights. It also owns tour operators including Thomson Holidays and the Specialist Holidays Group, with brands such as Magic, Crystal, Thomson and Austravel. TUI UK had revenues of £3270 million in 2001 and over 10,000 employees UK-wide.

Programme background

The travel industry has been hard hit in recent times, with significant world events sending holiday bookings on a downward spiral. As profit margins have been eroded, travel organisations have been forced to reduce the overall costs of their business, with a particular emphasis on reducing back-office infrastructure costs.

Deloitte worked with TUI Northern Europe's senior management to transform the finance organisation, enabling it to reduce costs across the business and support greater business consolidation. The initiative was called Project Enterprise. Achieving these strategic objectives involved:

- Implementing standard business processes, state of the art technology and information systems.
- Designing and implementing a new Shared Service Centre (SSC) organisation that would provide consolidated financial processing for multiple business units.
- Building a strong customer service capability within the new model.

The programme team realised that effective communications would be critical to achieving the above. While space does not permit a full account of the wide-ranging communication initiatives that were implemented, the following paragraphs highlight some of the key aspects.

Using the communications strategy to guide team efforts

The team recognised that it was vital to develop a coordinated and consistent approach to communications early on in the project. The scale of the change also meant that all team members had to recognise and accept their responsibility for effective project communications – this activity could not remain the sole responsibility of an HR manager or the Executive Steering Group. If the project was to be a success, all team members needed to start talking directly to employees as they collected information for the upcoming design phase.

By developing a comprehensive communications strategy, the team ensured they were able to achieve their goal of making everyone who would be impacted by the project aware of the proposed changes. Below is an example of some of the initial guidelines issued to all team members:

- Provide finance employees with timely, honest and useful updates on Project Enterprise, facilitating their understanding of the need for the changes.

- Provide group wide audiences with updates, as and when necessary, to facilitate their overall understanding of the impact Project Enterprise will have on them (for example, changes to employee expenses; purchasing process).

- Target senior managers within the finance team to obtain their buy-in and support to ensure effective management of the finance teams during the project.

- Minimise any negative press coverage that may arise as a result of following Project Enterprise recommendations (for example, moving to SSC model and corresponding redundancies).

Figure 14.11 helped explain the principles behind the Project Enterprise communications strategy:

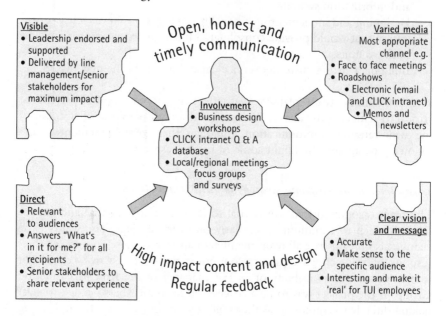

Figure 14.11 The Project Enterprise communications strategy

Creating a comprehensive and practical work plan

The comprehensive nature of the communications plan for Project Enterprise is captured in Figure 14.12. Not only was this high-level plan translated into a detailed diary that outlined the specific communication activities key stakeholders would be involved in each month, it also confirmed the supporting activities that the project communication team would be working hard to deliver throughout the duration of the project. This was a vital document for encouraging detailed discussion about how the communications strategy would be put into practice.

By developing and sharing this high-level plan at the start of the project, everyone knew the headlines about what, and when, things would be

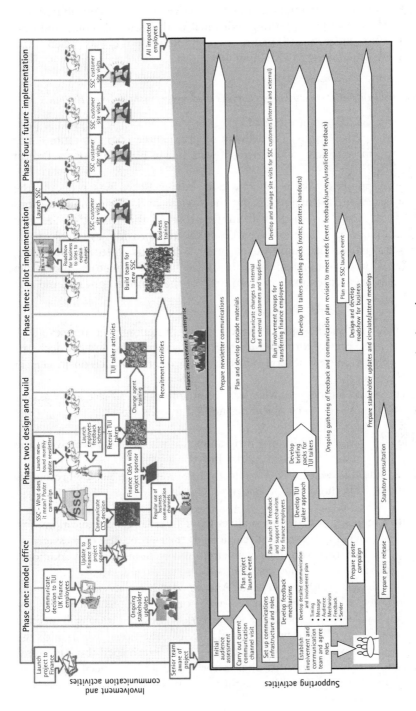

Figure 14.12 Project Enterprise's involvement and communication plan

happening from a communications perspective. This plan contributed to a successful project by supporting individual work stream planning, and outlining the sequence and nature of communication events when team members would need to give input.

Organising communication resources and processes to deliver the plan

The detailed communications and involvement plan clearly assigned responsibilities for the design and delivery of programme communications, but what specific resources and processes were put in place to support Project Enterprise?

The appointment of a separate Stakeholder Board was probably the most significant factor influencing the success of TUI's communications approach. This was distinct from the role of the Executive Steering Committee, which was more typically engaged in providing strategic direction and giving final approval to project decisions. Instead, the Stakeholder Board comprised local business finance directors and some cross-business representatives from each of the impacted groups, and was established to:

- ensure key business people were involved in signing off processes
- provide a regular forum for discussing project progress and key decisions
- formalise communication between the project and decision makers in the business
- ensure the business got what was required from the project, and was part of decisions where compromises needed to be made.

Table 14.5 was used within the programme to help distinguish between the Steering Committee and Stakeholder Board.

In addition, Project Enterprise effectively leveraged existing TUI resources to support its communication efforts. The team:

- Met regularly with representatives from Internal Communications and Public Relations to test out reactions to their proposed key messages.
- Utilised existing web sites, newsletters and bulletin boards as additional methods to get the message across to the wider audience.
- Established a Question and Answer database accessed from the intranet, which provided a two-way communications mechanism for employees to let the team know those questions that still needed answering. Measuring the similarity of questions asked and the frequency with which specific queries were 'hit' helped the communications team to prioritise their efforts, and address specific points of interest to employees that might not have been covered effectively in previous events.

Table 14.5 Project Enterprise: Steering Committee and Stakeholder Board

	Steering Committee	**Stakeholder Board**
Expectations	Allocate time to understand and resolve issues and risks presented by the project Deliver any allocated tasks as part of the decision-making/ resolution process Keep the project informed of any strategic decisions which may impact upon Project Enterprise	Allocate time to assist and to provide feedback Own and facilitate the communications with employees Deliver any work allocated, as part of the Stakeholder Board involvement
Actions required	Apply knowledge and expertise to resolve difficult project issues Use knowledge gained in the Steering Committee to input into other roles 'Walk the Talk' – be seen to support the project in public Attend monthly meetings as scheduled Partake in ongoing informal communication and involvement with Project Sponsor/Project Managers	Apply knowledge and expertise to help design the solution Partake in interviews and maybe workshops Satisfy themselves that they/the business will get what is required Attend monthly meetings as scheduled Partake in ongoing informal communication and involvement with key project team members (SSC, Change, Process, Applications, Interfaces, PMO) Gain and provide feedback from process representatives 'Walk the Talk' – be seen to support the project in public

Overall, the Project Enterprise team utilised a number of the communication concepts covered within this chapter. The result was an effective translation of their communications strategy into a comprehensive plan, which they successfully implemented to deliver a series of well coordinated and informative activities.

15 The enterprise programme management office

INTRODUCTION

Leading enterprises today have established and mature organisation structures which reflect the core skills and capabilities the organisation

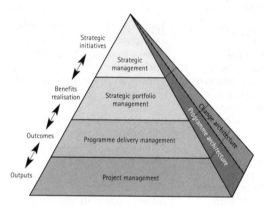

Figure 15.1 The enterprise programme management framework

possesses, and are focused on efficiently delivering the core products or services that the organisation exists to produce. In this book we have discussed at length the idea that the core capabilities that enable and support the everyday business are inadequate to enable organisations to manage complex programmes of change.

This chapter examines the role, benefit and value of an enterprise-wide programme management office (EPMO) in providing, maintaining and developing an organisation's programme management capability and infrastructure. In using the term EPMO we are referring to an enterprise programme management function and capability. This deliberately goes beyond the traditionally accepted definition of a programme management office (PMO).

An EPMO enables organisations to develop and integrate the essential disciplines described in the PM framework.

Strategic portfolio management

An EPMO coordinates all project and programme activity within the organisation and ensures that a 'line of sight' is maintained between an organisation's strategic imperatives and its investment in projects and programmes.

Programme architecture

An EPMO is an organisational function which represents the portfolio of change programmes with authority and voice at the most senior levels of an organisation's leadership. The EPMO is also responsible for establishing the systems and infrastructure that the organisation needs to be able to deliver change programmes consistently and efficiently.

Change architecture

The EPMO function maintains a 'big picture' perspective of all change activity in an organisation, and uses it to plan and manage the implementation and acceptance of change within the organisation.

Programme delivery management and project management

The EPMO function should develop standard good practice programme delivery and project management tools and methodologies spanning all activities within the organisation.

This chapter includes:

- an overview of the varieties and types of traditional programme management offices
- shortcomings of traditional PMO models
- role of an EPMO
- rationale and justification for establishing an EPMO
- implementation considerations for establishing an EPMO.

PROGRAMME MANAGEMENT OFFICE TYPES

PMOs have been commonplace and routine, in project and programme environments, for many years now. Traditionally a PMO has fulfilled the following roles in support of project and programme activity:

- Provides **administrative support** to projects.
- Develops **project management standards**, tools and templates which are then applied consistently across projects within a programme.
- Provides a point of **coordination** for planning, prioritisation and resource allocation across multiple projects and competing demands.
- Assists in **communication** within the programme and project teams and externally to other stakeholders.
- Applies **consistent tracking** processes and standards, enabling visibility and comparability across different projects and programmes.

- Provides software **applications, tools and templates** to enable project teams to work efficiently and in a consistent way.

The first PMOs were mainly supportive and administrative structures. However it is now increasingly common for PMOs to take direct management authority over projects, thereby adding the following roles to those described above.

- **Owns** project management resources and assigns project managers to projects.
- Provides **quality control** checks and audits on projects.
- Holds project **budgets** and act as gatekeeper for access to critical resources.

Reach and lifespan of a typical PMO

The reach or span of a PMO traditionally follows one of two models.

- **Programme-specific PMO:** many PMOs are set up to support one particular programme. The reach of such a PMO extends to all projects within that programme but not to projects outside it. The PMO is in existence for the length of the programme, which may be significant but is unlikely to be permanent.
- **Subject-specific PMO:** often certain business functions establish PMOs to bring the benefits of coordinated programme management to all projects occurring within that area of the business. This tends to occur in business units that have a high degree of project activity, and is common, for example, in information technology departments. These PMOs tend to be more permanent structures whose scope extends to a wider variety of projects.

The degree to which the modern PMO has arisen out of relatively new and project-intensive business functions, such as IT, cannot be overstated. The pressures for project speed and success upon such functions have supported the evolution of the PMO concept.

In summary, modern PMOs have typically arisen either to support specific temporary programmes or to support specific project-intensive functions. In both scenarios the PMO represents a tactical investment (or overhead) put in place to support delivery of a specific set of results. In neither case has the PMO arisen from a need to support a *sustained* strategic advantage.

SHORTCOMINGS OF TRADITIONAL PMO MODELS

Traditional PMOs can be very effective in supporting the delivery of project and programme activity. However, traditional models often fail to contribute as much as they should to the development of an organisation's overall programme management capability, for a number of reasons.

Multiple PMOs with narrow focus

Traditional PMOs are focused on one specific programme or specific business area, and do not reach across all project and programme activity in an organisation. This results in some major shortcomings.

- Traditional PMOs fail to support business executives in making decisions regarding priority of initiatives and skill and capability development needs.
- Multiple PMOs within an organisation are often blind to each other's existence, leading to duplication of effort and reinvention of the wheel in attempts to establish programme management good practice.
- Different PMOs in an organisation often adopt different standards, policies and systems.
- The same project may be under way in more than one part of the business, with its members oblivious to a duplicate endeavour occurring elsewhere.
- Senior management have no visibility regarding what project/ programme activity is occurring across an organisation.
- Senior management have no way of linking today's results with the expectations and business cases set for yesterday's projects and programmes. In short, benefits tracking is impossible.
- Pockets of programme management excellence develop in particular areas of the organisation, but their value is not capitalised upon, and extended to help develop the programme management capability of the wider enterprise.
- Different parts of an organisation do not work effectively together on projects and programmes, as different ways of working clash and compete.
- PMOs do not have access or visibility of the best resources in the business unless they are local to the PMO's area of focus.
- Poor economies of scale are realised in investment in project and programme management.
- Programme management activity is managed using very basic tools and systems, which are poorly integrated, if at all, with established business systems.
- It is impossible to cost-justify meaningful investment in developing a programme management capability. This can be illustrated by reference to the business case for programme management IT systems, discussed in Chapter 10. The better programme management IT systems can be costly, and therefore very difficult to justify on just a sub-set of an organisation's project or programme activity.

The situation of having multiple PMOs in an organisation is analogous to a hypothetical situation of a business having many unique and separate human resources and finance departments scattered throughout the enterprise. If this unlikely scenario were to occur, it would undoubtedly be exorbitantly costly, confusing and inefficient. Meaningful management information would be very difficult to obtain, and management control of the business would suffer.

No one individual finance or HR unit would ever be able to justify investment in enterprise management software systems, purely on its own needs, and the likely result would be an entire organisation managed using basic spreadsheets and simple desktop applications. This may sound a ludicrous scenario, and would rarely be allowed to occur for any modern business function, yet it is the most commonplace distribution of programme management capability within organisations today.

Fragmented PMOs focus on programme delivery in silos

Traditional PMOs focus (and justifiably so) on programme delivery and project management. However the traditional PMO is ineffective and poorly placed to exercise the strategic portfolio management processes that ensure scarce resources are focused and prioritised on the initiatives that deliver the most value. This results in some or all of the following major shortcomings.

- The PMO is distant from the strategic portfolio management processes that ensure that the right initiatives are pursued.
- The PMO focuses on delivery of projects, not the measurement of and realisation of benefits.

In short, the traditional PMO may enable the exceptional delivery of the wrong project. and in the process, miss critical dependencies and fail to deliver the expected benefits.

Inconsistent interfaces with other essential capabilities

No PMO works in isolation from other business functions and capabilities. Projects and programmes almost always require contributions from most or all of the following business areas.

- **Finance:** for programme budgeting, financial tracking and accounting.
- **Human resources:** for programme resource allocation and recruitment, and assisting with the people impacts resulting from projects.
- **Facilities:** providing suitable accommodation for project and programme teams and providing access to sites, canteen facilities, telephony, IT equipment and so on.

- **Legal:** assistance with programme contracts and other legal matters.
- **IT:** Provision of development and/or support services.

Where multiple PMOs exist in an organisation, it is likely that many interfaces will exist between the PMOs and the business support capabilities. In this scenario there is no overall coordination regarding the nature of involvement or the level of involvement. It is likely that programmes will be served in an ad hoc and inefficient way. Worst still, there will be no mechanism to plan for developing these business support capabilities so that they can adequately support both project/programme demands and business as usual demands.

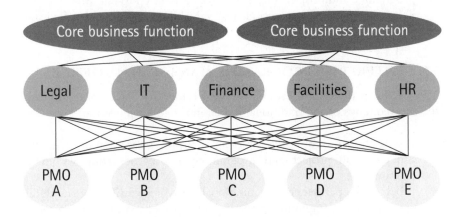

Figure 15.2 Difficulties with multiple PMOs in an organisation

In our experience, it is commonplace that supporting capabilities in an organisation provide excellent service to routine 'business as usual' needs, but fail dramatically in supporting projects and programmes.

Inability to develop programme management professionals

It is likely that the people working within the regular business have well-defined career paths, training and other career development opportunities, and a performance management framework that aids their development and rewards their contribution appropriately. However, many organisations are yet to recognise the need to support, train, develop and reward people undertaking project and programme roles. In the case of an organisation housing multiple programme management structures with a narrow focus, the following problems can occur.

- People get pulled into project roles from the regular business and end up losing the career and personnel infrastructure that they had. This can act as a disincentive for all but the least effective individuals to undertake project and programme roles.

- Project and programme management does not get recognised as a distinct expertise in its own right. Good technical staff end up getting reassigned to project management, with little support, and end up becoming lousy project managers.
- Rewards may be inconsistent across equivalent roles on different programmes.
- People are not trained and developed for programme and project roles.
- People with exceptional business skills may be redeployed into unfamiliar programme and project roles where they are set up to fail. All too often, in our experience, organisations lose valuable motivated and skilled staff and gain demoralised and ineffective programme and project managers.

THE ENTERPRISE PROGRAMME MANAGEMENT OFFICE

The EPMO is the logical evolution of the traditional PMO, and addresses the shortcomings of the traditional model in the following ways.

- It is positioned right at the top of an enterprise's organisation structure, and spans all project and programme activity occurring within an enterprise.
- It becomes a permanent organisational entity, responsible for the development of the programme management capability within the enterprise.
- It is headed up by a strategic programme director (or equivalent) who is part of the organisation's main leadership team and accountable to the CEO for execution of the business strategy through projects and programmes.
- It supports the ongoing development of the business strategy and the strategic programme portfolio.
- It coordinates the involvement of the core organisational functions and the supporting organisational functions in project and programme activity.
- It establishes project and programme management systems, policies, methodologies and standards for the entire enterprise.
- It develops a pool of deep expertise in project management and programme delivery.
- It becomes an established capability of the enterprise.

Consider Figure 15.3, which illustrates a fairly typical organisation structure for a consumer products manufacturing company. It shows the complexity of an established organisation supporting a business whose core processes are regular, routine, well understood, well practised and highly developed over time.

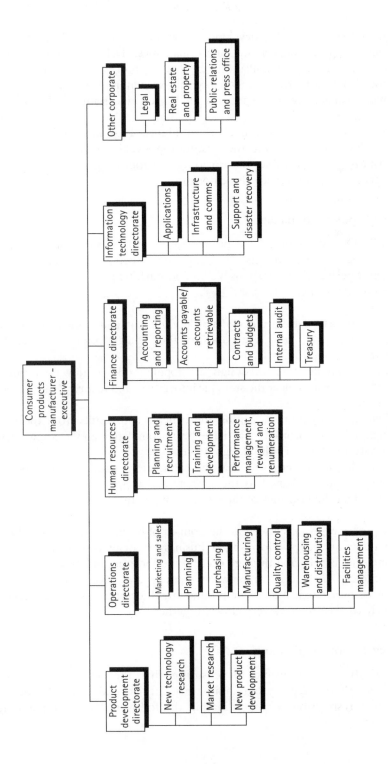

Figure 15.3 Organisation structure for a consumer products manufacturing company

Programmes require the development of new and unique ideas into new and unique products, services and capabilities. Delivering programmes involves undertaking unfamiliar and exploratory processes. It should be no surprise that major programme failures are so common, when the area of organisational activity that represents the highest risk, traditionally operates with the weakest organisational representation.

The modified organisation chart in Figure 15.4 illustrates (shaded) how a EPMO would fit into the existing top-level organisation structure. The EPMO is responsible for providing the following four programme management capabilities to the enterprise.

Strategic portfolio management

The EPMO is responsible for coordinating the processes that link the business strategy to the projects and programmes being undertaken in the business. Specifically, it is responsible for coordinating the following strategic portfolio management processes.

- Strategy articulation and review: development and translation of the business strategy and revalidation of the strategic priorities at regular intervals.
- Business architecture and design: developing models of how the business will transform to meet the strategic imperatives and mapping the journey there.
- Benefits realisation: measuring the benefits and results from the programmes and projects that have been completed and feeding these results into the portfolio design process.
- Portfolio design: ensuring that the enterprise portfolio of projects and programmes is aligned to the strategy and is appropriately prioritised according the priorities of the strategic imperatives.

These processes are often seen as the domain of business strategists and not programme managers. However, a business strategy (other than a do-nothing one) is delivered through execution of projects and business change programmes. The closeness between strategy and programme planning cannot be overstated. A strategic programme director and strategy director are likely to need to work very closely together.

Strategic resource planning

The EPMO is responsible for ensuring that the resources required to deliver the strategic programme are identified and sourced. Specifically, it is responsible for coordinating the following resource planning processes:

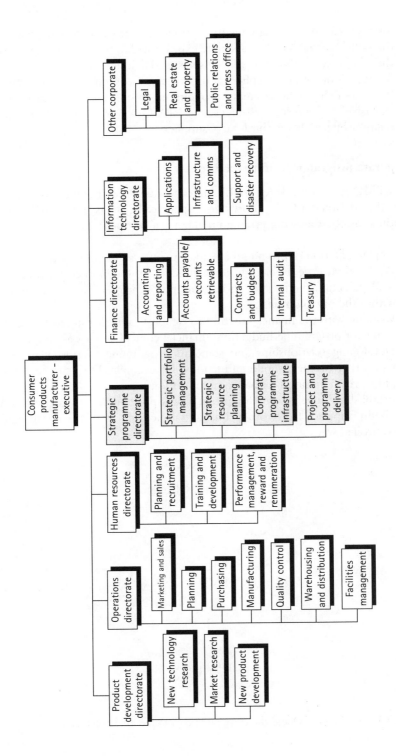

Figure 15.4 Revised organisation structure for a consumer products manufacturing company

- Strategic capability development: continuous review and development of the skills, knowledge and capability existing within the enterprise against the combined needs of everyday business and delivering the strategic plan.
- Identification of key suppliers and partners: recognising that the capability to deliver the strategic programme is unlikely to be provided exclusively by internal resources, the EPMO will identify and develop relationships with key third-party suppliers.

Corporate programme infrastructure

The EPMO is responsible for establishing the infrastructure required to support the delivery of the portfolio. Specifically, it is responsible for coordinating the following programme management processes.

- Implementation of programme management systems and tools.
- Working with the human resources function to establish essential career management structures for those working on projects and programmes within the organisation.
- Working with the finance function to establish standard support mechanisms for programme budgeting, financial control and accounting.
- Developing relationships and standard programme support processes with other business support functions: for example, IT, legal, facilities, public relations and internal communications.
- Establishing mechanisms for projects and programmes to request and obtain support from other business functions in a consistent and controlled way.

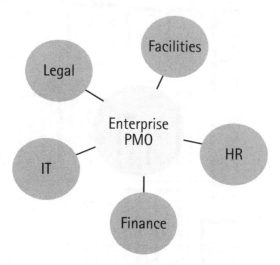

Figure 15.5 The EPMO and the corporate programme infrastructure

Project and programme delivery

The EPMO is responsible for establishing the project and programme management standards, methodologies, practices and pool of expertise required to support the delivery of the strategic portfolio. Specifically, it is responsible for coordinating the following programme delivery elements.

- Developing project and programme management methodologies for the organisation.
- Recruiting and developing deep project and programme management skills within the organisation.
- Establishing a career path for project and programme managers within the organisation, and a training and education programme to support career development.
- Deploying programme and project managers to delivery the strategic priorities for the business.
- Establishing quality assurance systems to ensure that the projects and programmes are being delivered effectively.

RATIONALE FOR ESTABLISHING AN EPMO

There are two fundamental questions to be addressed by organisations considering establishing an EPMO.

Why establish an EPMO?

How can the investment required be justified?

Why establish an EPMO?

There are a number of reasons organisations consider establishment of a EPMO.

- **Continuous investment in programmes and projects:** the continuous nature of change requires a permanent function focused on coordinating and delivering projects and programmes.
- **Major programme ahead:** the organisation is facing a major programme of work that will require significant coordination of resources across multiple organisational units.
- **History of failure:** the organisation has a history of having struggled to convert strategic good intentions into reality.
- **Changing balance of risk:** the balance of the business risk is moving away from business as usual towards the need for change.
- **Volume not value:** too many projects are occurring in the business and delivering insufficient value.

- **Competitive edge:** competitors are delivering change to their organisations faster and more effectively.

How can investment in an EPMO be justified?

The investment required to develop a programme management capability and an EPMO can be significant and will require justification. The justification for EPMOs comes from the four areas outlined in Table 15.1.

IMPLEMENTATION CONSIDERATIONS FOR AN EPMO

The major challenges in implementing EPMOs relate to establishing the PMO and gaining the acceptance of it by the groups in the business that will need to work closely with it.

Table 15.1 Reasons to justify creating an EPMO

Efficiency and cost saving	Strategic benefit realisation	Competitive advantage	Risk of inaction
Reduction of non-project activity allowing focus on programmes that create the most value Removal of duplicate programme management functions. It costs little more to establish one enterprise-wide set of programme management standards than it does for one programme or business area Economies of scale with respect to the procurement of project and programme services Fewer programme and project failures	Faster implementation of a strategic goal leading to earlier realisation of value Focus on the strategic priorities and elimination of valueless distractions Ability to respond and change when the strategic context or priorities change	Agility to implement strategic intentions and realise value faster than the competition Ability to be first to market with new ideas Ability to react to competitive pressures quickly	Current business cannot survive unless change is successfully implemented Future of the organisation is 'bet' on the successful implementation of a strategy

Specific challenges that will need to be overcome

These include:

- Managing the impact on existing disparate project and programme management functions within the business.
- Establishing the credibility and authority of the EPMO.
- Building the key relationships between the EPMO and the core business and support functions.
- Not allowing the forming EPMO to be consumed by fire-fighting existing programmes in trouble.
- Getting groups of people to work together who have avoided each other in the past.

Recommended strategies for establishing an EPMO

Trojan Horse

We have already acknowledged that pockets of excellence often exist within traditional PMO functions in the business. It is often very effective to work with existing areas of the business that are demonstrating good practice and extend their scope, reach and authority.

This is often an effective strategy where there is a risk of conflict with an existing function. It also ensures that knowledge, already within the business is captured and built upon rather than discarded.

When a major strategic programme is commencing, the PMO that is set up to support this initiative can be designed and groomed to evolve into an pan-organisational PMO over time.

Under promise and over deliver

Nothing is likely to destroy the credibility of a EPMO more than a fanfare announcement followed by a period of inactivity or setbacks. As we have seen the EPMO brings together many complex new capabilities, which take time to establish and work effectively. A phased introduction, with credible services, will be more effective than a grandiose design.

Leadership

The role of a EPMO must have 100 per cent support from an organisation's leadership. Once responsibility for the organisation's portfolio has been established with the PMO, leaders need to enforce and reinforce the working of the EPMO. Acceptance of maverick pet projects, hidden agendas and non-standard working practices will undermine the authority of the PMO.

CASE STUDY: ABN-AMRO

Background

ABN-AMRO is the seventh largest bank in Europe and fourteenth largest worldwide. It trades from over 3400 branches in over 60 countries, and is listed on several stock exchanges, including Amsterdam, London and New York. ABN-AMRO's business is structured into three very distinct Strategic Business Units (SBUs) (see Figure 15.6).

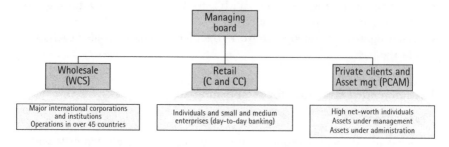

Figure 15.6 The structure of ABN-AMRO

ABN-AMRO recently reviewed the strategy for the bank. The revised strategy includes intentions to grow the business both by opening up new markets and by broadening the bank's offering to existing customers by capitalising on existing relationships within other SBUs. The strategy also addresses a need for the bank to operate more efficiently and to exploit opportunities for synergy between the SBUs.

ABN-AMRO found it needed to address one of the most common problems facing organisations about to embark on implementing a strategic programme: how to get business functions which traditionally operate as silos to work effectively together, while balancing demands with the need to keep control of the everyday business.

Challenges

There were a number of obstacles that, if not addressed, would have impaired ABN-AMRO's ability to execute this strategy effectively.

- Each SBU was largely autonomous, led by a team of dedicated Senior Executive Vice Presidents (SEVPs) whose performance and reward measures were aligned to those of their SBU. Consequently, there was little incentive for cross-SBU collaboration; in fact such behaviour was discouraged.
- Many in the business were supportive of the strategic intent but cynical about how collaboration would be achieved and would work in practice.

- Previous synergy initiatives had been sponsored outside the SBUs. There was therefore no accountability for success placed upon SBU leadership.
- There was a history of failed cross-SBU synergy initiatives. 75 per cent of early initiatives had failed to deliver against expectations, and this reinforced cynicism from within the SBUs.
- There was evidence that many early initiatives represented good ideas which were not properly researched in terms of value to the business versus cost. Hence there was a perception that the failure to deliver value was partly attributable to choosing to do the wrong things, compounded by a tendency to overestimate benefits while underestimating costs.
- Many of the common project and programme pitfalls regarding insufficient resources and inconsistent or ineffective project management were also being experienced.

Collaborating across business units is like kissing your sister ... mostly an unpleasant chore to be performed at the insistence of your parents, but hardly exciting and rich with possibilities!

ABN-AMRO Executive Presentation

There is nothing in next year's performance contracts about synergies.

Not another head office initiative getting in the way of real business.

We are trying to do this already, but it is those guys in ... who are constantly frustrating our efforts.

Just make sure this stays focused and delivers real benefits otherwise it will fail.

We need to be tough on selecting only those projects that will add real value.

The leadership will need to walk the talk on this one otherwise it won't happen – no matter how sensible it is.

We have to do this if we are to convince the analysts that our strategy has any value.

ABN-AMRO stakeholder interviews

How ABN-AMRO responded to these issues

ABN-AMRO recognised that it would be impossible to implement its strategic intentions without establishing a dedicated team with an organisation-wide remit, appropriate management and leadership, and an effective decision-making and governance model. It started a process of developing an enterprise programme management capability through the following four actions.

Establishing a dedicated task force

ABN-AMRO established a full-time task force to oversee all strategic programme activity, from business case development to benefit realisation. The task force was established not only to see one programme through, but with the intention of becoming 'the way the bank works'. It was made responsible for establishing enterprise-wide programme and project management procedures and controls, including the following:

- project identification, initiation and set-up
- documentation control
- benefits management
- executive dashboard production
- reporting to business leadership
- communication planning and execution
- risks, issues and dependencies tracking and management
- programme scope, change control and progress tracking
- performance tracking and planning.

The task force identified good practice around the bank, and existing project and programme management support systems that had the potential to be extended across the enterprise (in itself delivering synergies for the bank).

Establishing a programme organisation structure working across the business organisation structure

Programme support structures were established at all relevant levels of the business organisation (see Figure 15.7). The accountability for delivery of the strategy was made the sole focus of one main board director. This board director chaired an executive decision-making forum that made final decisions regarding all investment decisions.

A steering group/senior management team, known as the Spaghetti Council, was established. The remit of this was to coordinate initiatives across the distinct SBUs. The Spaghetti Council took responsibility for directing business case development, managing cross-SBU interdependen-

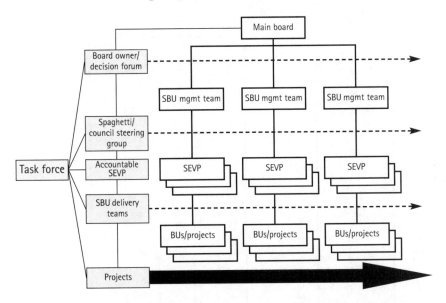

Figure 15.7 Revised ABN-AMRO structure with programme support structures

cies and reporting on costs and benefits. A key function of the Spaghetti Council was to solve issues relating to inter-SBU working by managing communications and 'opening doors'.

Each initiative was assigned a sponsoring SEVP, who was made accountable for the successful implementation of the initiative. This responsibility was reflected in the SEVP's contract and performance targets. The organisation model implemented was designed to ensure a line of report and visibility between projects being delivered and the senior bodies responsible for setting strategy and determining priorities.

Implementing a process for evaluating initiatives and managing the portfolio

ABN-AMRO recognised that it needed to ensure the initiatives chosen were the ones most likely and able to deliver value. A process was developed, utilising the newly established programme organisation, to evaluate and make decisions regarding investment priorities. Opportunities were reviewed along four dimensions:

- within scope
- materiality
- achievability
- level of interest.

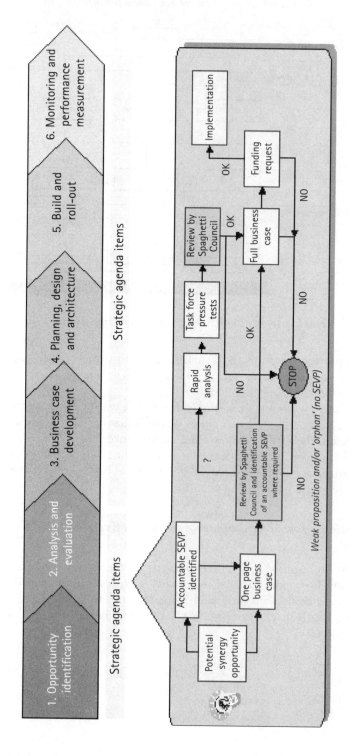

Figure 15.8 ABN-AMRO's initiative selection and portfolio management process

From a candidate list of 27 synergy opportunities and ideas, a three-tier priority list was generated.

Tier 1:   Strategic priorities
Tier 2:   Ones to watch
Tier 3:   Off strategy/out of scope.

Targeted quick wins first

ABN-AMRO recognised it had to prove to a cynical organisation that there was benefit to be had from collaboration and efforts to find synergies. The team deliberately prioritised some quick wins in the early initiatives in order to prove the concept and win hearts and minds within the organisation.

Outcomes

ABN-AMRO found that the organisation structures set up to support the programme started to bridge gaps between the SBUs, both in terms of programme effectiveness and also in broadening general understanding and communication across the bank.

The commitment of SBU leadership has slowly but consistently risen through demonstration of value from both the approach and the initiatives themselves.

The establishment of the enterprise programme management structures was itself a demonstration of the synergy strategy, and has helped make the strategy understandable and accessible to those the bank are relying on to deliver it.

Part III

Getting started

16 Introduction

In this section we have focused on how you could start to use some of the ideas we have introduced in this book in a practical way in your organisation. First, in Chapter 17 we introduce the enterprise programme management capability check, based on the enterprise programme management framework. The answers to the 60 questions will help you understand where to focus to enhance your organisation's capability.

In Chapter 18 we discuss issues relating to the different types of programmes organisations may be engaged in, and the priorities associated with this context.

In the final Chapter 19 we share some practical hints for delivering programmes successfully, based on the experience of the authors and their colleagues at Deloitte in managing large-scale programmes over many years.

17 Enterprise programme management capability check

The enterprise programme management capability check (PMCC) takes the form of a 60-point questionnaire which assess your organisation's capability around each area of the framework. By answering each of the 60 questions you can begin to gain an understanding of your organisation's programme management capability. It is often useful to get a number of people in your organisation to complete the questionnaire, to gain different perspectives of your situation.

The scale used for the questionnaire is a simple qualitative one: strongly agree/agree somewhat/disagree somewhat/strongly disagree, plus an option for 'I do not know'.

ENTERPRISE PROGRAMME MANAGEMENT CAPABILITY CHECK SECTION 1

The following statements and examples address the perceived level of programme management capability within your business. Please tick one response for each question.

Consider the way in which your organisation translates business strategy into manageable change initiatives:

		Strongly agree	Agree some-what	Disagree some-what	Strongly disagree	I do not know
1 Our organisation's vision is clearly and consistently defined and communicated.	*This might look like...* vision shared via our website or annual report.					
2 Members of the management team could give a number of examples of how our current situation is different from our desired state.	*This might look like...* 'We are currently No. 3 in our field, however our vision is to be No. 1 by 2005.'					
3 The leaders within our business clearly define our organisation's strategy and communicate this to others.	*This might look like...* our strategy is presented at all company-wide events.					
4 When undertaking major changes, we typically review our business in order to understand current and future needs.	*This might look like...* a report outlining technology and process needs.					
5 Our strategic planning process involves the translation of strategic objectives into change initiatives.	*This might look like...* a documented strategy impact analysis.					

245

Consider the way in which your organisation translates business strategy into manageable change initiatives:

		Strongly agree	Agree some-what	Disagree some-what	Strongly disagree	I do not know
6 Before any large-scale initiative can proceed, we insist upon detailed scoping to understand the key requirements, dependencies and outcomes.	*This might look like...* scope documents for each programme or project.					
7 Rather than operate multiple stand-alone projects, we frequently review initiatives to identify opportunities to group them.	*This might look like...* a monthly project review meeting attended by senior management.					
8 At any time, we have a high-level map of how each initiative relates to the others and will contribute to delivering our future vision and goals.	*This might look like...* a journey map depicting all initiatives and their impacts.					
9 The business benefits and the costs of the initiatives are identified, defined and agreed in clear and unequivocal terms.	*This might look like...* business cases are in place for all initiatives.					
10 Plans have been defined and agreed on how benefits will be achieved and measured within the business.	*This might look like...* benefit realisation plans are in place.					

Consider the way in which your organisation translates business strategy into manageable change initiatives:

		Strongly agree	Agree some-what	Disagree some-what	Strongly disagree	I do not know
11 When undertaking major change, we identify and build those capabilities required for success.	*This might look like...* an agreed capability development process.					
12 The programme is fully planned and relationships between projects are understood.	*This might look like...* detailed plans which include inter-dependencies.					
13 The group of initiatives or programmes under way is continuously monitored as a group as well as individually.	*This might look like...* performance management tools used.					
14 Mechanisms are successfully operating to monitor and report progress on the achievement of all business benefits resulting from the portfolio of initiatives.	*This might look like...* benefit realisation plans are documented and utilised.					
15 If our strategy or business context were to change, we would immediately review our current and planned initiatives to ensure fit.	*This might look like...* a monthly project review meeting attended by senior management.					

ENTERPRISE PROGRAMME MANAGEMENT CAPABILITY CHECK SECTION 2

The following statements and examples address your perceived level of programme management capability within your business. Please tick one response for each question.

Consider the way in which your organisation builds infrastructure to help programmes and projects succeed:

		Strongly agree	Agree some-what	Disagree some-what	Strongly disagree	I do not know
16 The roles and capabilities of our leadership are assessed regularly in order to understand their ability to lead change as well as business as usual.	*This might look like...* a leadership competency assessment.					
17 Our leaders regularly receive training and/or coaching in order to sharpen their ability to lead major change.	*This might look like...* a leadership development programme.					
18 The roles and responsibilities of those who lead the programmes are defined and agreed.	*This might look like...* each programme leader has a written role description.					
19 Before a strategic initiative commences, we always ensure that the appropriate stakeholders are involved in developing the goals and objectives.	*This might look like...* named stakeholders must sign off on key initiatives.					

Consider the way in which your organisation builds infrastructure to help programmes and projects succeed:

		Strongly agree	Agree some-what	Disagree some-what	Strongly disagree	I do not know
20 Creating an effective team environment is important to us and hence we create clarity around working patterns, training needs, goals and objectives.	*This might look like...* each initiative is supported by a team charter, induction pack and training plans.					
21 We routinely undertake status meetings within programmes in order to update all team members.	*This might look like...* fortnightly review meetings take place for each initiative.					
22 We have a team performance appraisal process in place.	*This might look like...* a documented team performance appraisal process is in place.					
23 In order to remove confusion regarding commitments, we publish programme meeting schedules to ensure that all key players understand their commitments.	*This might look like...* programme meeting schedules are published weekly.					
24 To ensure consistency of progress reporting, we create templates for team members.	*This might look like...* templates exist for meeting outputs and reporting formats.					

Consider the way in which your organisation builds infrastructure to help programmes and projects succeed:

		Strongly agree	Agree some-what	Disagree some-what	Strongly disagree	I do not know
25 Processes or mechanisms exist to support effective two-way communication between the various levels of the programme management structure.	*This might look like...* email, team briefings and the intranet are used for two-way communication.					
26 Before kicking off an initiative, we assess the office space and technology requirements of the team.	*This might look like...* team infrastructure needs are assessed by our Facilities personnel.					
27 A programme management office exists with defined and agreed terms of reference, tools and processes.	*This might look like...* an operational programme management office.					
28 Resource utilisation is planned on a programme-wide basis, with scope for sharing common resources.	*This might look like...* an agreed resource utilisation process is in place.					
29 Programme leaders build effective working relationships with HR advisors in order to ensure that all people-related programme needs are managed.	*This might look like...* HR advisors are involved in the people management aspects of the programme.					
30 The roles and responsibilities of all programme staff are defined	*This might look like...* each team member has a written role description. and agreed.					

ENTERPRISE PROGRAMME MANAGEMENT CAPABILITY CHECK SECTION 3

The following statements and examples address your perceived level of programme management capability within your business. Please tick one response for each question.

Consider the way in which your organisation manages the impact of change initiatives on the wider business:

		Strongly agree	Agree some-what	Disagree some-what	Strongly disagree	I do not know
31 Before undertaking a major change, we normally test the organisation's readiness and ability to change.	*This might look like...* a report outlining change issues to consider.					
32 We clearly understand the key impacts of our programmes on people within the business.	*This might look like...* an organisational impact analysis.					
33 Before undertaking a major change, we define a business case to justify investment in people change activities.	*This might look like...* a business case for change.					
34 At any one time, we have a good understanding of all initiatives that are under way and how they specifically impact our people.	*This might look like...* an inter-dependency map including the people impact.					
35 Our organisation has the ability to identify and shape the people and change activities required to support the pro-gramme or project.	*This might look like...* personnel have designated people and change responsibilities and skills.					

251

Consider the way in which your organisation manages the impact of change initiatives on the wider business:

		Strongly agree	Agree some-what	Disagree some-what	Strongly disagree	I do not know
36 Our people and change experts will develop a comprehensive plan to support the overall business change.	*This might look like...* an agreed and documented people and change plan.					
37 Those with expertise in people and change activities are actively sourced in order to leverage their expertise.	*This might look like...* external change experts are sourced if required.					
38 The specific interests and involvement of stakeholders within the business have been defined and acted upon.	*This might look like...* stakeholder plans are in place.					
39 When undertaking a major change, we focus on the individual/ personal change required as much as the organisational change required.	*This might look like...* individual transition plans are developed.					
40 We consider the communication requirements of the wider organisation and build these into a robust communications plan.	*This might look like...* an agreed and executed communications. plan					

EPM capability check

Consider the way in which your organisation manages the impact of change initiatives on the wider business:

		Strongly agree	Agree some-what	Disagree some-what	Strongly disagree	I do not know
41 We have a network of people through-out the business who we can call on to support or champion a new initiative.	*This might look like...* a defined and named group of supporters.					
42 Employee skills and competencies are new initiatives and changes to the way we operate.	*This might look like...* an established employee skills audit and development process.					
43 In order to understand the extent to which the organisation is actually changing in line with the programme, we continually monitor and interpret indicators of organisational change.	*This might look like...* an agreed and documented performance management process to track indicators of change.					
44 Owners are assigned to the people and change activities in order to ensure that these efforts continue to reflect business needs.	*This might look like...* a defined and named group of change owners.					
45 Throughout a programme or project, we endeavour to share earnings with the broader organisation in order to build a capability to change in the future.	*This might look like...* a learn and share process established to identify and transfer learnings.					

ENTERPRISE PROGRAMME MANAGEMENT CAPABILITY CHECK SECTION 4

The following statements and examples address your perceived level of programme management capability within your business. Please tick one response for each question.

Consider the way in which your organisation delivers major programmes or groups of initiatives

		Strongly agree	Agree some-what	Disagree some-what	Strongly disagree	I do not know
46 Each strategic initiative is supported by high-level programme planning.	*This might look like...* documented programme plans are in place.					
47 All project-level plans relating to a particular initiative are combined to create a master plan for that initiative.	*This might look like...* project plans are rolled up into a master plan.					
48 Programme leaders are able to kick-off or close projects as and when required.	*This might look like...* procedures are in place to initiate and close projects.					
49 Mechanisms are in place to ensure that any changes to the programme's original scope are assessed for impact prior to implementation.	*This might look like...* a scope and change control approach is agreed and in place.					
50 The programme generates effective management information enabling identification of variances and opportunities for improvement.	*This might look like...* an established financial management approach is used by all personnel.					

Consider the way in which your organisation delivers major programmes or groups of initiatives

		Strongly agree	Agree some- what	Disagree some- what	Strongly disagree	I do not know
51 Each programme and project has an effective risk and issue register.	*This might look like...* a risk and issue management approach is agreed and in place.					
52 Each programme subscribes to our performance management approach to enable regular and mean- ingful reporting.	*This might look like...* a performance management approach is agreed and in place.					
53 The quality perfor- mance of all parts of the programme is measured, monitored, reported and used as a basis for initiating ongoing improvements.	*This might look like...* a quality management approach is agreed and in place.					
54 In order to make the best use of our scarce resources, we follow an agreed resource management approach.	*This might look like...* an agreed resource management approach.					
55 Effective processes exist to share and access key information about plans, progress and learnings.	*This might look like...* a knowledge management approach is in place.					

PROGRAMME MANAGEMENT CAPABILITY CHECK
SECTION 5

The following statements and examples address your perceived level of programme management capability within your business. Please tick one response for each question.

Consider the way in which your organisation manages projects:

		Strongly agree	Agree some-what	Disagree some-what	Strongly disagree	I do not know
56 Every project within our organisation has a defined kick-off point and is initiated through use of our agreed procedures.	*This might look like...* project managers use consistent procedures to mobilise a project.					
57 Individual projects and work streams are planned in terms of activities, milestones and deliverables.	*This might look like...* projects have detailed plans that include activities and milestones.					
58 Each project is examined to understand its inter-dependencies with other initiatives.	*This might look like...* each project has a dependency register.					
59 Projects are monitored using our standard performance management tools.	*This might look like...* performance management tools are used to track progress.					
60 Each project has a natural end point at which our closing procedures are completed.	*This might look like...* project managers use consistent procedures to close down a project.					

256

YOUR COMMENTS

The following section provides an opportunity for you to write any comments or thoughts about your company's programme management capability. Please write your comments in the section below.

_____

_____

_____

_____

_____

_____

_____

_____

_____

End of questionnaire

18 Making sense of your current situation: knowing where to start

This book has focused on delivering an organisation's strategic objectives through a process of strategic portfolio management, programme delivery management and project management, and building a programme management capability. In reality it is very unlikely that in starting to take seriously the need to develop this capability, an organisation will currently have no projects or programmes ongoing. In fact, it is most likely that there are numerous projects and programmes currently at different states of development and implementation throughout an organisation. In this situation, it is often difficult to know where and how to start implementing some of the ideas described in this book.

The enterprise programme management capability check described in the last chapter is a useful tool for highlighting areas of weakness or deficiencies in the current approach, indicating where skills need to be enhanced and where process or structure is required around current programmes and projects. It is also useful to understand the status of current programme and project initiatives, and how they relate to each other and contribute to the delivery of the organisation's strategy or vision.

As part of the strategic portfolio management process, it is normal to assess current projects and programmes against criteria based on the organisation's vision and strategic objectives, in order to review their alignment. This may lead to decisions to stop or suspend some initiatives, or indeed start others. It is also important to assess the logic for managing projects within coordinated programmes with the associated processes, structures and controls.

In our experience, it is usually possible to characterise the current state of projects and programmes as one of four types, based on how clearly ongoing projects relate to the organisational vision and strategy, and how clear the approach to delivery is for these projects and programmes. (See Figure 18.1.) The differing types of programme have differing needs in terms of how their management should be undertaken. This analysis, along with the findings of the enterprise programme management capability check, help to define where to get started in enhancing an organisation's programme management effectiveness.

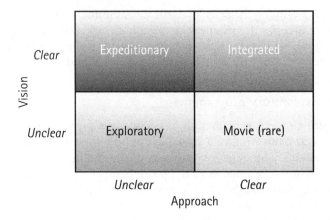

Figure 18.1 Categorisation of projects and programmes

Type 1: Integrated programmes

Integrated programmes are those where the organisation has a clear vision of what will be delivered and how this helps to deliver the organisation's vision and strategic objectives. In practice these are often technology-led, where the solution is clearly defined (for instance, an ERP package) and the approach and method of delivery is as clear and well defined. Usually this type of programme is made up of a number of streams of work or sub-projects, clearly structured to deliver an integrated solution.

Issues often found in the scope and structure of these projects include the failure to recognise the people and change implications of implementation. Therefore appropriate enabling projects addressing the change architecture issues are not scoped, planned and executed as part of the integrated programme. This often leads to solutions being delivered but the real value of business benefits not being realised.

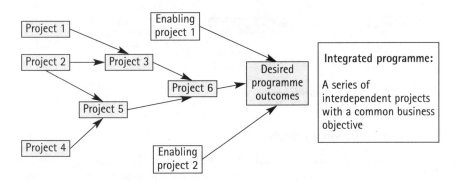

Figure 18.2 Integrated programme

Another common issue is that the programme architecture does not adequately identify the business or organisational accountability for delivery and implementation in the business. Again in these cases the solution may be delivered but the true benefits are not realised by the organisation.

Type 2: Exploratory programmes

In this situation, an organisation has numerous projects relating to many business issues, but without a clear view of how these will deliver an overall business vision or strategic objectives. Equally the interdependencies, relationships or multiple impacts of the projects on the business are not clearly understood. Surprisingly, this is one of the most common situations observed in organisations.

In this situation again, the Programme Management Capability Check and assessment of individual projects will be useful. The focus of initial activity must be on establishing whether the individual projects should be structured into programmes, and whether any of the projects should be stopped. This involves defining more clearly the strategic objectives and organisational vision, and assessing each project against criteria relating to their contribution to delivery of these objectives and their interdependence on other projects.

Clear business cases and benefits need to be identified for each project, and assessed against 'hurdle' criteria for inclusion in a programme of projects.

There may be some projects that can continue but are stand-alone and can run independent of inclusion in a programme. In these cases it is important that common project management processes and approaches are installed, and standards of management and control are maintained.

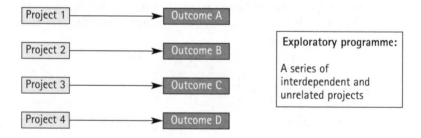

Figure 18.3 An exploratory programme

Type 3: Expeditionary programmes

These programmes are characterised by organisations having a clear vision of what they want to achieve, but lacking a clear road map and portfolio of projects and programmes to get there. There may well be a number of projects on the go to deliver a common organisational objective or vision, but little coordination between them.

The danger here is that unforeseen dependencies or impacts may affect the delivery of the overall objective, and resources may not be used efficiently across the projects. Opportunities for shared resources and processes may be identified.

In this situation, it is important to consider whether there is a sensible structure for a programmed approach that will help coordinate these projects, and an overall high-level plan that takes account of dependencies and multiple impacts of the projects on the organisation. There may also be opportunities to leverage consistent methods and processes across all the projects: for example, a shared programme office providing support services and maintaining common processes.

There is often the need to develop appropriate 'enabler' projects to support the people and organisational changes across all the projects within a programme.

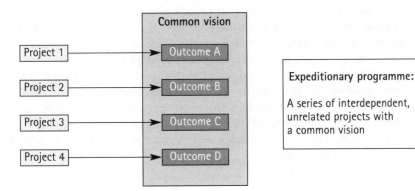

Figure 18.4 An expeditionary programme

Type 4: The movie

This type of programme is rare in business since it comes from a known approach (such as making a movie) where the outcome is not clear (the movie evolves).

REORGANISATION

Wherever an organisation is starting from, it is vital that the programmes are clearly related to delivering value aligned to the vision and strategic objectives, and that there is a clear approach or path by which this will be achieved. This means that an exploratory programme will evolve to an expeditionary programme, as the vision and objectives are clarified, and may then transit to an integrated programme. (See Figure 18.5.)

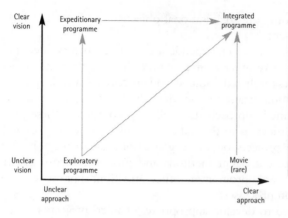

All projects and programmes should become part of an integrated programme clearly linked to delivering the organisation's vision and strategic objectives if value is to be created in the most efficient way from initiatives.

Figure 18.5 Programme transition

The conclusion reached is that an organisation is most likely to be successful in delivering real value through projects that are part of coordinated programmes clearly linked to its strategic objectives. The three programme management processes and two disciplines outlined in the book provide a best practice process for delivering value through business change, and a business capability to continue to implement and deliver change and value.

However, clearly understanding the status of your current projects and programmes and the quality of your programme management capability will provide an indication of the priorities, and the start point at which to develop this process in your organisation.

19 Practical steps for success

In the course of working with many clients across the globe, Deloitte is often asked to review existing programmes and to articulate the reasons they are not delivering the results that were anticipated. We have summarised our experience from a number of these situations to establish a set of practical suggestions that could help to drive success in programmes. In this section, we outline some practical considerations concerning strategic portfolio management, programme architecture and programme delivery management.

STRATEGIC PORTFOLIO MANAGEMENT

Build a tight linkage between the strategy articulation and the programme of change to implement it, rooted in a rigorous cost–benefit case

One of the most common issues relating to delivery of strategic programmes is creating and maintaining a clear link or 'line of sight' between an organisation's strategy and the programmes that are delivering it.

First, it is important to build time into the strategy development process, to understand the way the business will need to be configured in terms of technology, structures, processes and people to support the strategy. This helps to define the key changes and programmes that need to be delivered to implement a strategy.

Another commonly seen issue is that organisations are much better at starting new programmes and initiatives than they are at continuing to monitor and review programmes, and stopping activities that are not aligned to strategy. Stopping non-aligned activities is critical to focus effort on what is strategically important.

The best mechanism for linking programmes and the projects within them to strategy is through a rigorous business case, articulating clearly how the benefits delivered support the overall organisational strategy and business case associated with it.

Building a 'benefits' linkage between the strategic vision, the programmes and the projects is the best way to align all investments in the organisation. By tracking the benefits delivered by projects and programmes, progress towards delivering the vision can be measured.

Temper ambition with practical reality

It is very easy, in the hothouse atmosphere of strategy development, to become over-optimistic about what can be achieved within a particular time-frame. Thus targets are set at unrealistic levels, which could cause a destructive dynamic to occur between middle and senior management. Middle managers can see that the targets are over-ambitious, yet feel obliged to support the new strategy through fear of being seen as dissenters in a time of turmoil, which could potentially lead to job losses.

Managers tempering their short-term ambition and looking to the longer term can achieve long-term success. This can be achieved by structuring the programme to deliver smaller benefits in the first instance, to build support and belief in middle management, deliver benefits early into the business and create a cycle of success leading to greater success.

PROGRAMME ARCHITECTURE

Building the right balance of power

Many organisations are built along fairly traditional functional or business unit lines, with fairly strong barriers between organisational units. This is a reasonable organisational structure in a time of steady state, when the business only needs to focus on delivering financial results for the current quarter or fiscal year. However, most organisations are now faced with perpetual change driven by the forces outlined above. However, companies have not updated their organisation structures in response to the combined need simultaneously to deliver financial results and drive business change. This can lead to a number of potentially fatal issues for change programmes.

- The programme lacks sufficient support in the organisation to be high enough on the priority list of functional managers. This is why it is critical for the CEO to be involved in leadership and governance of programmes at the strategic portfolio management level.
- A linked issue is that often programme managers lack positional power when compared to functional managers in the organisation. This makes it extremely difficult to secure the right resources for the programme at the right time. One effective approach to address this involves seconding already well-respected resources from elsewhere with the organisation.

In most cases we suggest that major cross-organisational programmes are sponsored and led by a board director – this could be in addition to his or her normal line accountabilities. The executive team chaired by the CEO should act as the overall governing body for all programmes, resolving cross-organisational conflicts if they arise.

Aligning stakeholder expectations and objectives

Many modern programmes now create a need to build programme teams from many different organisations. For instance, the programme may be to build a joint venture company between two formerly fierce competitors. The programme may rely on the software from a particular company, require its preferred implementation partner to provide resources skilled in that software, another party to provide hardware and infrastructure, and may need to collaborate closely with the potential customers of the new venture.

Such an endeavour can very quickly become embroiled in the differing goals and objectives of all the parties involved. This is not least because all the parties may well have differing objectives, but also because not all those involved in the programme will be supporters of the programme.

It is imperative that when this situation arises, management takes a step back, prior to signing contracts, to review formally all the objectives of the parties involved, document them, and ensure that all parties sign up to the common objectives of the venture. Moreover, managers should do all they can to ensure that detractors from the venture, from any of the parties, do not participate in the venture in any form.

Structure and plan the decision-making process

In our experience, one of the most common issues and reasons for delays in programmes is the inability of the organisation to consider and make the necessary decisions to support and enable the progress of the programme.

There is often confusion over who needs to be involved in key decisions. Key decision points are often not planned, and people are unavailable to consider these at the appropriate time. There is confusion over those who need to be involved, and those who are accountable and responsible for key decisions. Decisions that could be made at a lower level are often passed to senior executives who have neither the time nor often the knowledge to make a correct decision.

It is critically important when designing the governance structures and planning programmes that clear accountabilities are defined, those responsible for decisions are identified, their roles are defined and the correct mechanisms are established. The regularity of key meetings (such as sponsors meetings) needs to match the likely pace of the programme.

It is also advisable to plan for decision-making. The programme plan can be viewed from a key decision-point perspective, and a plan and timetable of decisions can be established. This manages the expectation of key decision makers, and prepares them for their role at critical points in the programme. It is too late to try to sort this out once the organisation is facing time-critical and important decisions.

A flexible and dynamic programme structure

Many programmes continue over a long period of time: months and years. The nature of the programme will change during these extended periods. Different work streams and projects are required at different phases, and the emphasis on planning, executing and controlling will need to adapt, as will the nature of the interaction with the normal activities and functions of the business.

Those organisations that establish structure and clear accountabilities and roles often fail to adapt their programme organisations to reflect the changing nature of the activities and focus as programmes progress.

To generalise, structures usually need to focus on collaborative working and collective decision-making, in phases that are focused predominately on planning activities. When the main focus is design and development, a more clearly defined structure around distinct projects and work streams is required, with more formalised reporting and control mechanisms. As implementation or launch becomes the main focus, the structures then need to be much more integrated with the organisation's business structures, and processes such as risk and issues management become critical. At this stage, some of the normal management processes need to be managed through accelerated time cycles (for instance, daily rather then weekly programme review meetings).

In some cases where the programme is delivering a new organisational structure or launching a new business, the programme structure evolves to become the business structure post implementation.

PROGRAMME DELIVERY MANAGEMENT

Even if the strategic portfolio management and the programme architecture provide the right context and environment for programme delivery, there is plenty that can go wrong in delivering a large programme of change. The following are some tips that address some of the most commonly experienced problems.

Build the guiding star of the detailed business case

We have previously discussed the need to establish a clear and robust linkage, based on business benefits, between the business strategy, the business structure and the programme to effect the change. The first part of the programme planning process should be to take the resultant business case, and break it down to a lower level of detail.

The process should attribute benefits to be achieved to the functional department level, and devolve responsibility to the line managers. Moreover, the granularity of the timescales for measuring the benefits and costs should be narrowed down to appropriate measurement periods.

This will encourage business buy-in to the plan, ensure that middle management understands that senior management is very serious about achieving success in this programme, and generate a much greater level of certainty in the business case and in the plans that support it. This document should then form the 'guiding star' of the programme, ensuring that the rationale and reasoning behind the programme is robust and built on solid foundations. This document can very easily be updated to reflect changing circumstances in the marketplace that might justify fine-tuning the plan at a future point.

Build a two-level plan

It is probable that any transformational change activity will take place over quite a long time period. At the same time, the business context in which the programme is taking place is likely to be changing rapidly. Consequently, spending a great deal of effort resolving plans and business cases down to a monthly level, over say a three-year timeframe, is likely to be wasted effort.

We therefore suggest that a two-level planning approach is taken, where activities within the planning horizon (for instance, 6 to 12 months), are resolved to a low level of detail, and those outside this planning horizon are kept at a high-level cost—benefit case and major dependency level. This approach will necessitate a periodic (for instance, quarterly) planning exercise where previous assumptions are challenged, and future activities are resolved down to a lower level of detail before new projects are initiated. In this way, the programme and the business case can be updated on a periodic basis to ensure they stay firmly linked with the business strategy, and remain focused on delivering solutions that will benefit the business.

Drive minimum 'time to benefit' instead of minimum 'time to activity'

A common pitfall is for the programme manager to initiate too many projects or streams of activity at the same time. This generates a great deal of activity, with the illusion of significant amounts of progress. However, it is often the case that the resources required to deliver all of the projects that have been initiated far exceed the resources available within the business. It is then difficult to stop any of the projects that have been started, for fear of losing face, so the net result is that all projects are delayed, thus incurring costs earlier, and delivering benefits later, jeopardising the business case and damaging the image of the programme.

We recommend that senior management ensures that programme managers focus on delivering benefits early, by constraining the number of activities that are carried out concurrently.

Avoid over-optimism in estimating the effort and time required to effect procedural and organisational change

When embarking on change programmes, it is very easy to underestimate the amount of effort required to deliver a change to technology, people and process, and ensure that benefits are delivered. It is common, particularly in change programmes that involve significant information technology implementation, to focus too much on the tasks required to 'get the system in' and not enough on the activities required to deliver the benefits. Consequently, the business case can be built on shaky foundations, since the activities required to realise the benefits are only partially included in the plan.

We recommend that management thoroughly reviews the business case in the light of realistic estimate of costs and risk exposure. If the potential cost of the work or the exposure of the risks puts the business case in jeopardy, it is better to know this before expending most of the cost rather than after. It also gives the opportunity to review the scope of the projects, and constrain it to those areas of the business where benefits will be gained, thus reducing costs, and improving the overall business case.

Align the contractual structure with the management and responsibility structure

If the programme that is being embarked on involves building a new organisation as either part of an alliance or a joint venture, then it is likely that many parties will be involved in making it happen. Moreover, it is likely that the point of agreement that is made to go ahead with the endeavour will be characterised by the high emotion that surrounds high-profile deals. It is very easy in this circumstance to agree to elements of a deal or contract that misalign the contractual position of parties with the responsibility and accountability for making it happen.

The key to avoiding this is to ensure that a work breakdown structure to achieve the desired end goal is created, and mapped on to the organisation chart for the venture. From this a formal responsibility, accountability, consultation and information (RACI) chart can be created, which should form an integral part of the negotiations. In this way, management can be clear that costs, benefits and responsibility of the initiative are spelled out clearly, and negotiated openly in the discussions.

Managing suppliers

Most large programmes involve integrating the services, support and products of a number of third-party suppliers. Managing the inputs and contributions of consultants, vendors and contractors is fundamental to the success of programmes. Organisations often fail to get real value from their

Example RACI	Resource 1	Resource 2	Resource 3	Resource 4
Work item 1	R	C		C
Work item 2	A	R	C	
Work item 3	A	R		I
Work item 4	A	R		
Work item 5	A	C	R	I
Work item 6	R	C	C	A

Legend
R: Responsible
A: Accountablity/approve
C: Consultation
I: Informed

Figure 19.1 Simple RACI chart

third-party partners and do not manage their work as part of an integrated programme.

It is important to use these third parties in the appropriate way that best fits with the services they offer and the value they can provide. It is also important to coordinate effectively the input of different third parties in a seamless and integrated way. In general, the more specialist consultants should be used to help in planning, design, provide specialist advice, manage integration and build internal capability. Vendors (such as package software implementers) should be used to deliver specific solutions in their own product areas, and contractors used to supplement internal resources where a short-term requirement for internal resource with specific skill is required.

When setting supplier performance expectations, it is important to define broadly the performance criteria, and if possible, build these into the contracts. In addition to the obvious deliverables, performance objectives should be set around compliance to programme management standards and processes, working methods and behaviours (such as teaming expectations), accessibility of key supplier staff, and skill and competence requirements of the staff. Encouraging suppliers to work as part of the overall programme team is important, and often challenging if their contracts define only narrowly focused deliverables.

As well as the ongoing management processes, it is advisable to establish regular reviews with each supplier, to take a step back from day-to-day activities and review performance and relationships more broadly. These sessions should involve executives from the suppliers who have overall accountability for the service provided to the programme.

Finally, it is advisable for the programme manager to develop relationships at a senior level in the businesses of the key suppliers. This will provide a crucial point of escalation if and when the supplier teams on the ground are not resolving issues.

Confront and address conflict early

The initial planning stages of a programme, either to create a new venture or to bring the organisation to a new state, are very likely to lead to resistance being generated somewhere in the organisation. It is tempting to avoid this conflict in the early, planning stages of the programme in the hope that it will resolve itself over the coming weeks and months. However, a failure to address this conflict directly could be interpreted by middle management as a lack of resolve on the part of senior management.

The decisions on when to address and when to avoid conflict are often finely balanced. However, we would err on the side of counselling management to tackle sources of conflict directly, and where necessary make compromises or decisions to ensure that the path is cleared for the strategic change process to get under way in an atmosphere of certainty.

Secure the right resources on the right terms

The plan that was created in the planning phase may only have gone to the level of identifying the types of resources required, and the times they will be needed. The programme manager, and his or her project managers running each project, will then have to identify specific named resources to work on each project as it is initiated. If the balance of power has been established correctly ahead of time, it should be possible to work with functional and department heads to get the right resources assigned to the programme.

As far as possible, resources should be made available to work on the programme full-time. However, where this is not possible it is important that explicit contracts are made between the programme and the functional heads to ensure that the input required does not get subsumed by other initiatives or competing priorities.

Organise around outcomes

Many programmes, particularly those that include a significant information technology component, tend to organise themselves around activities to be carried out (analyse, design, build, test and so on). However, particularly with programmes that cover multiple projects and multiple releases, this structure does not give sufficient focus on the outcomes of achieving the benefits. Balanced against this are the economies of scale of grouping together the technical skills of analysis, design and so on.

The programme manager needs to build a focus on the deliverables to ensure that someone has the responsibility for delivering each major component of the programme, along with responsibility for delivering the expected benefits and outcomes. In this situation he or she has two main choices. The first is potentially to lose the economies of scale by breaking up the technical teams and assigning them solely to projects. The second is to implement a matrix structure within the programme, which appoints a project manager to provide focus for the deliverable, and negotiates the right resources from the technical team leaders.

Monitor and control effectively

It is perhaps obvious to say that the programme should be monitored and controlled effectively by the installation of:

- progress reporting
- issues tracking
- risk management
- earned value analysis.

However, in our experience this is not done formally very often, and where some of these policies are in place, they are often inadequate.

It is important, however, that processes and templates for reporting are simple and easy to complete and that these processes create the minimum of bureaucracy, and provide quality useful information to all those involved in programmes.

Be prepared to be flexible in the face of changing circumstances

The business world is changing very rapidly, and the actions of competitors or new entrants into the marketplace may well have a significant impact on the strategy of a business over the life of a transition programme.

Management should recognise this reality and be prepared to change tack, by revisiting the objectives of some of the projects during their life, and perhaps cancelling some projects if they will no longer deliver results aligned to the business strategy. This approach will take courage and may cause some difficulties, but is a preferable course to spending money and expending valuable management time on projects that no longer add value.

Ensure that the business benefits of each project are achieved before closing each project

When each project in the programme is closed, a formal assessment should be carried out to ensure that the benefits of the project have been achieved, and establish what actions need to be taken.

271

Ensure that adequate time and resources are allocated to learning lessons from all projects so that the subsequent projects in the programme can be improved

When running programmes at a fast pace, perhaps running concurrent projects across multiple geographies, it is important to build time into the process to ensure that any lessons, skills, tools or techniques are shared amongst geographically diverse project teams. This will enable subsequent projects to deliver their results faster, better and cheaper than the trailblazing project.

Regular review and learning sessions, if action oriented, can also enhance performance during a programme or project lifecycle.

Glossary

Action log	A record of the tasks that need to be completed, by whom, and by when.
Agile organisation	An organisation that is able to direct effort and capability where and when they are most needed in order to deliver change and respond quickly to its environment.
Audience	Those individuals and groups of people who need to be informed and communicated with during a programme of change.
Balanced scorecard	A set of performance measures covering a range of areas that reflect a broad and balanced view of business or organisational performance.
Baseline	The combination of a scope, timescales and budgets usually agreed at the start of a programme or project.
Benefits realisation plan	A plan of activities that links the delivery of programme and project deliverables and objectives to the delivery of real and measurable business benefits over time.
Business case modelling	Building the financial justification for an initiative, and identifying detailed costs and benefits, including investment requirements, cashflow requirements and payback schedules. It usually uses a financial measure such as return on investment or internal rate of return.
Capability assessment	An analysis of an organisation's ability to perform a certain activity or set of activities. Capabilities are usually built up from a combination of processes, systems, structures, and people's skills and knowledge.
Cause and effect diagrams	A method used to identify the root cause of a particular problem, and to understand

the relationships between different factors in organisations.

Change agent network
A local network of people in an organisation who are used to influence a change programme and its implementation. These agents normally receive change management training and have a specific role in supporting the change process.

Change architecture
The scope of the activities required to support the effective implementation of changes to an organisation. Focused primarily on people change, these may include the specific blend of HR policy changes, structures and roles, communication mechanisms, training and development, recruitment, redeployment, redundancy and rewards.

Change control
The orderly process of managing, investigating and authorising/rejecting a request for a change on a project or programme. Changes can be related to scope, schedule, resources or the agreed supporting management processes.

Change impact assessment
An activity to consider the roles, processes and systems impacted by the project or programme, to gauge the magnitude of the overall change that will be brought about by the project.

Change overload diagnostic
A tool to address the risk of the enterprise being unable to cope with the degree of change required, and the management of change necessary in relation to business as usual.

Change readiness assessment
This activity assesses the organisation and its willingness to change, and identifies the challenges and risks.

Comparative risk and reward analysis
A useful diagrammatic technique to plot and group the programmes and projects based on their level of risk and reward type.

Content management
Usually refers to the storage, organisation, management and accessibility of digital data, information and multimedia content.

Contingency management
Planning for unexpected circumstances that could lead to extended time or costs

	on programmes. This normally involves the allocation of resources to a reserve, and their subsequent distribution and use to deal with these unexpected events.
Core competencies	The critical abilities of an organisation that allow it fulfil its purpose.
Cost and benefit component analysis	Tool based on Monte Carlo cost model, enabling the identification of key risk components, and facilitating meaningful scenario analysis and budgeting activities.
Criteria weighting model	A mechanism for applying different levels of importance to the criteria used in selection exercises.
Critical path analysis (CPA)	Understanding the sequence and relationship between activities that define the timescales and logical order of a plan. This allows high-impact risks and issues that impact this critical path to be assessed and managed.
Cumulative cost curves	A graphical representation of the costs accumulated over time on a programme or project.
Customer relationship management (CRM)	The processes, systems, people and their organisation for the management of all interactions with an organisation's customers.
Decision tree analysis (DTA)	A method for depicting choices as a route through layers of decisions. Decisions points are shown as nodes, and choices made as lines between nodes.
Deliverable	An agreed output from a piece of work, project or programme. Could be physical product, a document, a business change or a decision.
Design authority (DA)	An individual or more often a group who are responsible for the coherence and applicability of the product design. This group is responsible for ensuring that the design of the solution meets the needs and objectives of the organisation and acts as a key quality assurance and control function. It is normally responsible for any technical specifications required to define the product or output.
Discounted cash flow (DCF)	Financial model to understand the value of

future cashflows taking account of inflation or the real cost of money.

Earned value analysis (EVA) A tracking mechanism for both cost and schedule performance that can be used predictively to determine likely total over-runs.

Enterprise programme management office (EPMO) An organisational function that supports the enterprise programme management process across the organisation, from portfolio management at a leadership level through to developing the appropriate systems, processes and capabilities to deliver programmes consistently and efficiently throughout the organisation.

Enterprise resource planning (ERP) system A information system that supports key organisational functions and processes, and is usually integrated across areas such as HR, finance, operations, customer management and supplier management.

Executive dashboard A graphical depiction mostly used by senior executives on their desktop computers to gain a high-level oversight of the performance of a business, or progress of a programme. These should provide summary information and draw attention by exception to key performance or progress issues.

Expected monetary value (EMV) Model to enables risk exposure to be assessed financially.

Fish-bone A type of cause and effect diagram for breaking down different aspects of a problem or issue.

Gantt chart Graphical representation of project activities and their independencies related to a timescale.

Gap analysis A comparison between the status quo and the blueprint for the future, to determine what needs to be done to make the transition to the desired position.

Gatekeeper An individual who controls access to another, and acts to open or close communications with that individual or sometimes to a team or group.

Groupthink A situation when a team becomes so integrated that it develops a common view,

	new ideas are not generated and existing ideas are never challenged.
Insourcing	The practice of an internal function, such as IT, acting more like a external service provider. As a profit centre it offers services to the other departments based on service level agreements.
Internal rate of return (IRR)	Financial modelling method to take account of the cost of using capital which could be used to earn a return elsewhere. The method takes account of the opportunity cost of capital.
Ishikawa	A type of cause and effect diagram.
Key performance indicator (KPI)	An agreed appropriate measure to show how well something is performing.
KISS principle	Keep it simple and straightforward.
Knowledge capital	The value that is retained in the combined knowledge of an organisation.
Knowledge management	The effective storage, management, dissemination and development of the data, information and knowledge resources of an organisation.
Knowledge transfer	Transferring knowledge from one medium or person to another.
Leadership responsibility assignment matrix	A tool for defining the roles of senior executives in matrix organisational or programme organisational environments. The matrix maps areas of responsibility against the level of involvement required by individuals. Sometimes this is defined by RACI analysis: responsible, accountable, consulted or informed.
Lifecycle model	Projects or programmes can be described as following a lifecycle model based on phases. These phases can vary but often include initiation, design, detailed design and implementation. Some projects with specifically defined phases have 'gateways' or review stages between phases.
Logical architecture application mapping	Developing a diagrammatical representation of the information system applications that support an organisation's activities, and the relationships between them.

Management information systems (MIS)	Systems in place to provide aggregated information to management for the primary purposes of control and decision making.
Milestones	Points in the programme or project plan defined by time. Usually they are events such as end of phase review, key sponsors' meeting or end of testing.
Monte Carlo cost model	A method of assessing and quantifying risk based on operations research simulation techniques.
Net present value (NPV)	A measure developed by a financial modelling method to calculate the true value of an investment taking into account inflation and other depreciating factors.
Pilot stage	Stage of a project when a completed solution is tested in real-life working conditions with a limited group or on a small scale before being fully implemented.
Portfolio impact assessment	An analysis to be performed to identify whether the proposed project will affect or is dependent on any projects and programmes underway.
Portfolio management	Translating strategy or organisational objectives into a portfolio of programmes and projects, prioritising, sequencing and continuously monitoring and reviewing the portfolio.
Portfolio plan	The time-based map showing the sequencing of the programme and projects within the portfolio.
Portfolio planning	The process of creating a portfolio road map or plan.
Portfolio prioritisation diagnostic	A tool for evaluating and prioritising projects into a portfolio.
PRINCE2	A standard and widely used project management methodology.
Programme architecture	The establishment of support structures and mechanisms that allow effective programme leadership and provide the programme team with the environment, skills, tools and support they need in order to operate effectively.

Programme delivery management	The management and consistent application of specific processes, tools and methods in order to enable the coordinated delivery of projects within the programme, in a consistent and efficient way.
Programme management office (PMO)	A function to support the delivery of specific programmes. It normally provides all programme management process, systems and administrative support to the programme manager. Functions include planning, monitoring, risk and issue management, reporting and financial control.
Programme management system (PMS)	Those applications that enable the delivery of interrelated projects with common goals. They are often thought of as multi-user project management systems with enhanced resource management, and this is where many current solutions originated.
Project audit	The process of reviewing the status of a project and the effectiveness of the management processes and approach.
Project brief	The project objectives, scope and proposed plan, outlining key deliverables, milestones and resources required. This is usually prepared in the initiation phase of a project.
Project exception reports	Reports generated on a needs basis to highlight significant risks, performance or progress issues.
Project initiation document (PID)	A document that outlines the scope of the work to be undertaken within the confines of a project, the expected timescales, resourcing requirements and capital expenditure, the deliverables as well as the baseline plan.
Project management	The application of knowledge, skills, tools and techniques to project activities to meet project requirements, where a project is a temporary endeavour that is undertaken to create a unique product or service.
Release management	In technology-related programmes, release management involves the coordination of activities that contribute to a release of software (cross-project management) and the

coordination of products that contribute to a release (architecture, integration and packaging).

Responsibility assignment matrix
A documented view of clearly defined accountabilities and interfaces between different parties.

Return on investment (ROI)
A quantitative measure of what the expected return will be as a percentage of the original capital investment.

Risk management maturity diagnostic
A tool to identify the current maturity of the risk management capability in the organisation. Areas covered include mind-set, process, people, information, tools, structure and decision-making capability.

Risk response planning
Determining whether the response to a risk is to accept, mitigate or avoid, and developing the appropriate actions and plans in response to the risk assessment.

Road map
A high-level plan showing the sequence of programmes and projects that will be implemented over time.

Selective sourcing
Sourcing where suppliers are engaged based on their unique specialist expertise.

Service level agreement (SLA)
An agreement made between two parties that specifies a level of service to be provided and the commercial arrangements for the provision of that service. This normally involves defining key measurements of the service quality.

Smart-start kick-off meeting
Workshops designed to introduce and mobilise a team quickly. Key items include working patterns, goals and objectives, context and background as well as team-building activities.

Solution design document (SDD)
A technical document that details the design for the proposed solution.

Sponsor
The owner of a project or programme, with responsibility for the delivery of the benefits of the programme.

Stakeholder
All those individuals and groups who have an interest and influence in the outcome of a programme or a project.

Stakeholder management
The process of identifying and engaging appropriately with all those identified as

	having an interest and/or influence on a programme.
Strategic portfolio management	The continual process of creating, managing and evaluating a portfolio of strategic initiatives focused on delivering strategy, organisational objectives and benefits.
Strategy translation	Taking the articulation of a strategy and turning it into a number of programmes, projects and activities that when executed will deliver the strategy.
Statement of work document	A document that outlines the scope of the work to be undertaken within the confines of a project, the expected timescales, resourcing requirements, capital expenditure and deliverables.
Super user	Someone who will use a solution extensively. He or she is often involved in depth so he/she can help design new solutions, pass on knowledge to other users and test solutions prior to complete implementation.
Team charter	A document that details the agreed approach to working in a team. Usually this defines ways of working, behaviours, processes and procedures, guidelines and rules relating to the human aspects of working together.
Team induction pack	A set of documents to be provided for those joining a programme to facilitate their integration into the programme.
Technical design authority (TDA)	A design authority with a systems or technical focus.
Transformational alignment matrix (TAM)	A tool that maps activities to the core objectives and targets of the overall business.

References and further reading

CCTA (1994) *Achieving Benefits from Business Change*, HMSO, London.

Cranfield School of Management (CSM) (undated) *Benefits Management: Best Practice Guidelines*, CSM, UK.

Deloitte (Consulting) Ltd (2002), *Benefit Realization Strategy*, Deloitte (Consulting) Ltd.

Murphy, Arthur (2002) *Project Risk Management: Reducing Benefits*, paper to Project World Seminar, Birmingham, 2002.

Office of Government Commerce (OGC) (2002) *Managing Successful Projects with Prince2*, OGC, London.

OGC (2002) *Business Benefits Through Project Management* (www.ogc.gov.uk), OGC, London.

OGC (2003) *Managing Successful Programmes*, OGC, London.

Parker, Marilyn M. and Benson, Robert J. (1988) *Information Economics*, Prentice Hall, London.

PMI (2000) *A Guide to the Project Management Body of Knowledge*, 2000 edn, Project Management Institute, USA.

Standish Group (1994) *The Chaos Report* (www.standishgroup.com/sample_research/chaos_1994_1.php), Standish Group, West Yarmouth, MA.

Thiry, Michel (2002) *Delivering Benefits through Programme and Value Management*, paper to Project World Seminar, Birmingham, 2002.

White, Dr Phil (2002) *Benefits Management through the Project Lifecycle*, paper to Project World Seminar, Birmingham, 2002.

Worsley, Christopher (2002) *Project Justification*, paper to Project World Seminar, Birmingham, 2002.

Index